New Liberalism

John A. Hobson was a prominent member of a small band of British radicals who argued around the turn of the century that the consistent application of liberal ideas required the reorganization of capitalist societies along socialist lines. Allett here suggests that their march toward socialism was marked by a caution not overly to damage the liberal heritage of their forefathers and yet to provide a philosophical foundation for the creation of the welfare state, justified on the basis of right and efficiency.

The author emphasizes Hobson's doctrine of imperialism and the related theory of under-consumption for which he is best known, while arguing that the lesser known of Hobson's doctrines – which the author describes as the 'organic theory of surplus value' – is essential to a full appreciation of the coherence of Hobson's thought.

Allett compares the analyses of Hobson, Adam Smith, J.S. Mill, the Webbs, T.H. Green, Bosanquet, Marx, Lenin, Keynes, and Hobson's comrade-in-arms L.T. Hobhouse and puts in perspective the dismissive critiques of those contemporary scholars who claim that Hobson's work is value-laden, simplistic, and contradictory.

This study presents an integral analysis of the life, times, and thought of a profound and original thinker, whose legacy to social democratic thought has yet to be fully appreciated.

John Allett is assistant professor in Political Studies at Trent University.

JOHN ALLETT

New Liberalism
The Political Economy
of J.A. Hobson

UNIVERSITY OF TORONTO PRESS
Toronto Buffalo London

© University of Toronto Press 1981
Toronto Buffalo London
Reprinted in paperback 2014

ISBN 978-0-8020-5558-3 (cloth)
ISBN 978-1-4426-5140-1 (paper)

Canadian Cataloguing in Publication Data

Allett, John, 1947-
 New liberalism

 Bibliography: p.
 Includes index.
 ISBN 978-0-8020-5558-3 (bound) ISBN 978-1-4426-5140-1 (pbk.)
 1. Hobson, J.A. (John Atkinson), 1858-1940.
 I. Title.
 HB103.H62A44   330.15′5   C81-094652-1

The photograph of J.A. Hobson on the cover is from an original
in the files of Geoge Allen & Unwin.

To my Mother, Father, and Gail

Preface

Comments passed by modern scholars on the works of John Atkinson Hobson often attest, even if only *en passant*, to the significance of his contribution to the philosophy of social democracy. J.K. Galbraith, for example, has written that Hobson was 'the most original of English ... social reformers,' a view shared by British historians like Robert Skidelsky and Peter Clarke, the latter finding Hobson to be a profound if somewhat incautious thinker. Similarly, Michael Freeden has recently declared that, despite the better established reputations of T.H. Green and L.T. Hobhouse, Hobson was 'by far the most original and penetrating of the new liberal theorists at the turn of the century' and deserves 'far greater credit as an outstanding social thinker.'[1] Nevertheless, comments such as these have not resulted, to date, in the publication of any specialized study of the corpus of Hobson's work.

Hobson was a prolific writer of books and articles, the best known of which, no doubt, are *Imperialism: A Study*, which received praise from Lenin, and, to a much lesser extent, *The Physiology of Industry*, which was commended by Keynes. This remarkable juxtaposition of influences, in itself, should have secured Hobson from neglect, but it would seem that praise from high, as it were, obscured the view to Hobson below.

The theme of both these books is the economic theory of underconsumption. This theme is certainly a recurring one in Hobson's works, but in this study it is not taken as the central motif of his thought. Instead, it is argued that a lesser known doctrine, which I have labelled 'the theory of organic surplus value' is the key to Hobson's philosophy. Although other scholars have drawn attention to this aspect of Hobson's thought, most notably Alan

---

1 Galbraith, *The Age of Uncertainty* (1977), 147; Skidelsky, *Oswald Mosley* (1975), 55; Clarke, *Liberals and Social Democrats* (1978), passim; and Freeden, *The New Liberalism* (1978), 253

Lee and Michael Freeden, this is the first work fully to explore the *organic* nature of Hobson's concept of surplus value, and to utilize it in integrating both his economic and political thought. What emerges is a surprisingly coherent philosophy – surprising in the light of Hobson's reputation for inconsistency – which seeks to show that socialism is a prerequisite for the consistent application of liberal principles. This is the doctrine of New Liberalism in a nutshell.

Chapter 1 attempts to locate Hobson in his time and place; the rest of the book is thematic rather than chronological. In the thematic sections a conscious effort has been made to quote extensively from the wide range of Hobson's works, partly because much of his work is now long out of print and it is hoped that the resuscitation of these lost scripts will prove of interest to the reader, and partly because the relative lack of historical development in Hobson's thoughts allows a free range in choosing the most apposite passages for quotation.

It is, of course, the burden of this study to show that Hobson is not deserving of the neglect he has received in the past. For the most part this task has been undertaken by indicating the seminal contributions he made to economic and political thought, but it also has been necessary, on occasion, to attempt to reduce some standard, dismissive criticisms of Hobson's thought to what might be termed justifiable proportions.

Although Hobson was keen to stress that all production was the result of joint efforts, the one exception he seemed to make was his own works. Rarely did he acknowledge any intellectual indebtedness. Not wishing to share in this inconsistency, I am very pleased to acknowledge the help and encouragement I received from my friends and colleagues, Jim Moran, Sten Kjellberg, Sally Zerker, Virginia McDonald, John Saul, Helmut Grost, David J. Bell, and Donald Smiley. Special thanks are due to Professor J.T. McLeod for leading me to, and R.I.K. Davidson for leading me through, publication. I also would like to note my appreciation of the efforts of Beryl Logan who typed the original manuscript. Finally, I would like to thank Norman Higson, Head Archivist at Hull University, S.K. Ellison, House of Lords Record Office, and C.E. Barralet, the South Place Ethical Society, for helping make my research visits to England both pleasant and productive.

This book has been published with the help of a grant from the Social Science Federation of Canada, using funds provided by the Social Sciences and Humanities Research Council of Canada, and from the Publications Fund of University of Toronto Press.

J.A.

Contents

'Were all the works of orthodox Economists from Adam Smith down to the latest representatives ... thrown overboard once and for all, and a fresh start made from the works of ... Mr. Hobson, ... the world ... would be the better for it.'

J.B. Crozier, *The Wheel of Wealth, being a Reconstruction of the Science and Art of Political Economy on the Lines of Modern Evolution* (1906), 511-12

NEW LIBERALISM
THE POLITICAL ECONOMY OF J.A. HOBSON

1

The Life and Times of
J.A. Hobson

Mr. Hobson is tall, spare and of delicate health, and one of those ardent spirits
enthusiastic for work even beyond his strength, as if the sword was wearing out
the scabbard. *Harper's Weekly* (c1900)

John Atkinson Hobson was born on 6 July 1858 in Derby, England. Seven
years earlier, Britain had celebrated its industrial supremacy in the world by
holding the Great Exhibition of 1851. For the moment, the social classes in
England were experiencing a respite from the conflicts of the 1840s. The
manufacturers had gained a victory over the landlords with the repeal of the
Corn Laws in 1846, whilst the last Chartist demonstration, held in 1848, had
been, all told, a quiet affair.

For the most part Hobson's childhood experiences shared in this mid-
Victorian calm. 'Born and bred in the middle stratum of the middle class of a
middle-sized industrial town of the Midlands,' he was, in his own words,
favourably situated 'for a complacent acceptance of the existing social order.'[1]
Hobson's father, William Hobson, was a prominent figure in civic affairs. He
was founder, editor, and joint proprietor of the *Derbyshire and North Staf-
fordshire Advertiser*; a founder member of the local branch of the Liberal
Unionist Association; and twice elected mayor of Derby, in 1883 and 1885.
Of Hobson's mother, Josephine Hobson (née Atkinson), little is known
except that she bore three sons and one daughter.

---

1 *Confessions of an Economic Heretic* (1938), 15. To avoid unnecessary repetition, Hobson's
 books are referred to by title only, and where possible the title has been shortened in all
 subsequent references. The date of publication is given at the first citation in each
 chapter.

Hobson's elder brother, Ernest William (1856-1933) was to become Sadleirian Professor of Pure Mathematics at Cambridge University. His essay on 'spherical harmonics' written for the Royal Society in 1896 has the reputation of being 'a classic in its field,' and his major work, *Theory of Functions of a Real Variable* (1907), did much to convert Cambridge mathematicians to 'modern theories of measure and integration.'[2] Ernest Hobson is also remembered as a tutor to J.M. Keynes, when the latter was an undergraduate at King's College. J.A. Hobson, incidentally, shared none of his elder brother's love for mathematics; indeed, he viewed the application of mathematical techniques to economics to be a dangerous intrusion and warned, along with Oliver Wendall Holmes, that mathematics bred 'a despotic way of thinking.'[3]

Hobson's younger brother, Henry Mortimer, took over the running of the *Advertiser* when William Hobson died in 1897; and his sister, Mary Josephine, married Charles Milner Atkinson, a barrister and editor of some of the writings of Jeremy Bentham.[4]

William Hobson's occupation placed his family on the borders of the upper stratum of Derby 'society.' Hobson was later to recall that during his boyhood it was the 'push and sagacity' of members of this top echelon that impressed him most, rather than the 'ragged, shoeless condition' of the poor who inhabited Derby's 'Back Lane,' although the latter did generate an 'incipient feeling that "all was not right" in this best of all possible worlds.'[5]

But if Hobson was given to occasional doubts as to whether the poor deserved their fate, he was, nevertheless, convinced at that time that nothing could be done about it. Thus he relates in a telling comment on the times that as a boy he had

no idea ... that politics had anything to do with industry or standards of living. Nor was this merely a failure to understand a really intricate relation. At that time the two-party system was engaged half-consciously in keeping out of politics all deep and drastic issues of 'the condition of the people' ... Gladstone kept Liberalism upon issues of franchise, education, public economy and foreign policy, hardly touching any of the graver economic issues, except where they impinged on his Irish policy. This *laisser-*

---

2 G.H. Hardy, 'Hobson, Ernest William (1856-1933),' *The Dictionary of National Biography, 1931-40*, 433-4

3 *The Social Problem* (1901), 60

4 A. Lee, 'The Social and Economic Thought of J.A. Hobson,' Ph.D. thesis, London University (1970), 24

5 *Confessions*, 18

faire attitude of the Liberalism of the sixties and seventies was the accepted basis of my earliest political education. The gulf between politics and workaday life was fixed and complete.[6]

Hobson's formal education did little to unsettle his complacency. Between 1868 and 1876 he attended Derby Public School. The headmaster of this school was, according to Hobson, a 'snob of the crudest order' who, in his anxiety to secure local patronage, designed a curriculum which concentrated on 'dead languages' – the Classics – and history, which was 'almost entirely English, stopped dead before modern politics began to emerge and consisted only of the dramatic activities of kings and the ruling classes.' None the less, Hobson proved to be a good student, even winning in his fifth year a prize for 'divinity' which was bestowed upon him by the Prince of Wales.[7]

Interestingly, Hobson records that in his final year of school he found himself, despite this honour, 'a religious heretic.' 'The doctrines of the atonement and of everlasting punishment for unrepentant sinners' failed to satisfy his 'elementary sense of reason and of justice.'[8] This religious criticism, decrying the overvaluation of earthly conduct in matters of salvation, can no doubt be related to Hobson's subsequent criticism of protestantism's preoccupation with the worldly concerns of thrift and industriousness as religious virtues. At the centre of Hobson's later economic writings was the warning that thrift might be a public vice. As will be seen, this was a warning good Victorians found difficult to accept.[9]

In 1876, Hobson 'went up' to Lincoln College, Oxford, on an open scholarship, to continue his study of classical literature. Oxford does not appear to have had any startling effect on Hobson's outlook, although looking back Hobson suggested that imbibing 'the atmosphere of an Oxford in which Jowett, T.H. Green and Mark Pattison were leading figures,' combined with his study of the ancient Greek and Latin civilizations, contributed 'not a little towards the rationalism and humanism' which later on he 'strove to apply to economics.'[10] But this was also an Oxford at which John Ruskin taught, and

6 Ibid., 18-19
7 Ibid., 21, 22
8 Ibid., 20
9 Hobson elaborated the relationship between protestantism and capitalism in his book, *God and Mammon* (1931). It is also interesting to note that Keynes travelled a similar path to Hobson, moving from religious to economic heresy, but Keynes' attack on the virtue of thrift was more assertive. See R. Skidelsky, ed., *The End of the Keynesian Era* (1977), chap. 1.
10 *Confessions*, 26

given the profound effect, as shown below, that his ethical critique of classical economics was later to have on Hobson it is remarkable that Hobson only
once attended his lectures. Hobson recalled that this lecture presented a
'scathing indictment of the triumph of mechanics,' yet he never returned to
hear Ruskin again.[11] Obviously, not only was he not 'disturbed' by Oxford,
but he was also not particularly looking for the unorthodox.

Hobson left Oxford in 1880, having attained a lower second-class honours
degree – a relative failure, which came as a 'painful shock' to his 'intellectual
self-assurance.'[12] – and a blue for high jumping. To those who knew Hobson
later in his life this record of athletic prowess was a surprise, since he was
often sickly, and his life seemed, as one of his friends commented, to hang
by a thread.[13] He returned to Derby and for a while helped his father with
editing the *Advertiser*. But within the year he managed to secure a position as
a schoolmaster, teaching classics at a school in Faversham. Later he transferred to a school in Exeter, where he remained until 1887.

It was in Exeter that Hobson met, and in 1885, married Florence Edgar,
the eldest daughter of a wealthy lawyer from New Jersey. They were to have
two children: a son Harold, and a daughter Mabel. Harold Hobson became
an engineer and general manager of the Central Electricity Board;[14] Mabel
married Edward Scott, the son of C.P. Scott, the 'legendary' owner/editor of
the *Manchester Guardian*.[15] In addition to her family duties, Florence Hobson was also to take a keen interest in social matters, especially those relating
to the status of women, upon which she wrote some articles; she also wrote
several plays, books of poetry, a collection of short stories, and the occasional fiery letter 'to the editor.' All told, she appears to have been a woman
of considerable spirit and self-confidence, although, like her husband, she
was often not in good health, having contracted tuberculosis.

In 1887, Hobson left his teaching post in Exeter and moved to London to
work as a University Extension Lecturer in Literature and Economics.[16] His
migration to London was, as R.H. Tawney commented, 'a turning point in

---

11 'The Ethical Movement and Natural Man,' *Hibbert Journal*, vol. 20 (1921), 672
12 *Confessions*, 26
13 H. Nevinson, *Fire of Life* (1935), 214
14 G.D.H. Cole, 'J.A. Hobson 1858-1940,' *Economic Journal*, vol. 50 (1940), 351-2.
   Glimpses of Florence Hobson's biography can be found in her essay, 'In Search of
   Relations,' *Shifting Scenes* (1906), 141-58
15 David Ayerst, The Manchester Guardian: *Biography of a Newspaper* (1971), 431
16 It is not clear why Hobson was accepted to teach economics. The only formal education
   he had received in this subject was one course offered at the pre-university level by the
   Cambridge University Extension Movement. *Confessions*, 23

his career.'[17] It brought Hobson face to face with the problems of poverty and unemployment and into contact with various radical groups seeking to investigate and offer solutions to these problems.

In 1887, England was barely recovering from four years of industrial depression. This recovery, however, was short-lived; it was succeeded by six more years of slump. London, the world's richest city, exhibited that supreme paradox of industrialized nations: poverty in the midst of plenty. Nearly one-third of its population was estimated to be living under conditions of abject poverty, irregular employment, and overcrowding.[18] These poor were to receive increasing publicity throughout the 1880s. The investigations made by Charles Booth into the conditions, types, and degrees of poverty in London's East End made a particularly deep impression on Hobson. 'Modern life has no more tragical figure,' he wrote, 'than the gaunt, hungry labourer wandering about the crowded centres of industry and wealth, begging in vain for permission to share in that industry, and to contribute to that wealth; asking in return not the comforts and luxuries of civilized life, but the rough food and shelter for himself and family, which would be practically secured to him in the rudest form of savage society.' For the poor, a toilet was a square of paper in the corner of a room; the room was a temporary shelter, for the city poor were 'a wandering tribe'; food was purchased in minute quantities, sometimes as many as ten distinct purchases of tea being made within a week; most of the food received was adulterated; consumptive diseases were common; deaths from starvation were 'vastly more numerous than in any other country,' and many of London's poor died dependent on public charity.[19]

But the depression was not only ugly; no less significant, it was also immensely perplexing. Traditional liberal doctrine seemed ill-equipped to explain the persistence of unemployment on such a scale and across so many trades in an economy that was assumed to be self-correcting. Nor did its explanation of poverty, as an individual fault or failure, seem to encompass the magnitude of the problems uncovered by Booth and his fellow investigators.

Fortunately, although London was a place in which there was great material impoverishment, it also provided an environment rich in ideas. Fabians, Social Democrats, Christian Socialists, Single-Tax Reformers – all had their organizations in London. And Hobson did the rounds. Overall, he was not

17 'Hobson, John Atkinson (1858-1940),' *Dictionary of National Biography, 1931-40*, 435-6
18 *Problems of Poverty* (1891; 2nd. ed., 1895), 9. The estimate was Charles Booth's.
19 Ibid., chap. 1, esp. 17

impressed. He considered the Christian Socialists 'too sentimental,' and the Social Democrats 'too inflamatory.'[20] In particular he found the manner and argument of H.M. Hyndman, the leader of the Social Democratic Federation, to be 'those of an oily mouthed, half-educated, self-conceited Dissenting Minister.'[21] And although Hobson was impressed with the ideas and impact of Henry George, he considered the 'Single Tax' and 'Land Nationalization' movements that sprang up to foster George's cause to be too narrow a base for social reform.[22] He also refused to join the Fabian Society, even though he quickly became a good friend of two of its founding members, Graham Wallas (whom he had first met at Oxford) and William Clarke. (Both of these friends were later to waiver in their allegiance to the Fabian Society.) At various times Hobson accused the Fabians of opportunism, élitism, and of failing to 'assail capitalism at its weakest points.'[23]

The man who helped supply Hobson with some of the answers to his questions about poverty and unemployment was neither a Fabian nor a Marxist nor even a Londoner, but a businessman and mountaineer, A.F. Mummery, whom Hobson had first met while he was living in Exeter.[24] Hobson and Mummery collaborated to produce *The Physiology of Industry*, published in 1889. This book contained the essence of an argument that Hobson was to spend the next half-century elaborating, namely that unemployment was the consequence of oversaving (underconsumption). Along the way Hobson's ideas gained sway among a younger generation of radicals including G.D.H. Cole, Harold Laski, H.N. Brailsford, and C. Delisle Burns; surprisingly, among Hobson's immediate contempories and friends, Wallas, Hobhouse, the Webbs and Beveridge, his theory of underconsumption never took firm root.

20 *Confessions*, 29
21 Lee, 'The Social and Economic Thought of J.A. Hobson,' 40
22 Cf. *Confessions*, 27-8, and Hobson's essay on Henry George in the *Fortnightly Review* (Dec. 1897).
23 *Confessions*, 29. This latter comment probably refers to the fact that the Fabians did not give serious consideration to Hobson's theory of underconsumption. See A.M. McBriar, *Fabian Socialism and English Politics, 1884-1914* (1966), 48. The Fabian attack on the principle of interest, on the other hand, was an assailing of capitalism which Hobson, as is shown below, considered extreme, and this might have made him wary of the Fabians when he first attended their meetings. Hobson's severest statement regarding Fabian élitism is found in his article, 'Ruskin and Democracy', *Contemporary Review* (Jan. 1902).
24 Mummery died in 1895, as the result of a climbing accident in the Himalayas. See *Confessions*, 30.

J.A. Hobson 9

Prior to meeting Mummery, Hobson had already discovered that certain elements of classical economics, especially its notion of a wage-fund 'stuck' in his 'gizzard,'[25] but an appreciation of Mummery written in 1908 makes it clear that Mummery was the main heretical force:

He was first made known to me by common friends as a hard-headed businessman who had, in the course of his experience, developed certain heretical notions about saving and spending, which he sought to get discussed. For a year or two we threshed the matter out ... until, by persistent force and ingenuity of argument, he overbore all my preliminary objections. We then went together into the close work of developing what seemed to us a new and necessary statement of the relations between Production and Consumption in the modern industrial system, involving a diagnosis of under-consumption or over-saving, as the main cause of trade depressions. ... As a thinker he was, ... above all else, original. ... For, ... in boldness of speculation, he surpassed Ricardo among the economists, approaching at times the compactness of Spinoza's philosophic systematisation. At any rate, it was a bracing experience to follow him.[26]

In *The Physiology of Industry*, Mummery and Hobson presented a frontal attack on the liberal notion of the 'natural harmony of interests' in a competitive economy and, in particular, attempted to demote thrift from its place of honour among the economic virtues. The classical economists had argued that supply creates its own demand (via incomes earned in production); consequently, a deficiency in effective demand was considered an impossibility. This proposition had come to be known as Say's Law of Markets.[27] From this they concluded that the main limit to a nation's prosperity was the amount of capital its citizens were able to save and invest (it was assumed that these two acts occurred simultaneously). In short, the key to the wealth of nations was thrift.

25 Ibid., 25
26 'An Appreciation' in A.F. Mummery, *My Climbs in the Alps and Caucasus* (2nd ed., 1908), 9-10, 13. It is also worth noting that the authorship of *The Physiology of Industry* breaks alphabetical conventions by putting Mummery's name before Hobson's, suggesting the former as the senior partner.
27 Hobson defined a classical economist as one who accepted the validity of Say's Law and adhered to an 'individualist notion of production.' Both these concepts will be explained in detail later. According to this definition, classical political economy was dominant throughout Hobson's lifetime, and included the works of Adam Smith, Ricardo, J.S. Mill, the Marginalists (e.g., J.B. Clark and S. Jevons), and 'neo-classicists' like A. Marshall and A.C. Pigou.

Mummery and Hobson, on the other hand, insisted that it was the level of consumption that determined the extent to which factors of production could be usefully employed. Too much saving/investment, therefore, would not bring prosperity but depression, since the level of productive power would exceed the level of effective demand and this would bring prices tumbling down below costs of production. In effect, Mummery and Hobson were asking economists to make an enormous leap in their conceptualization of economics, putting consumption in the place of thrift and godliness (given the close association of protestantism and capitalism).

In the 1930s Keynes was to write that *The Physiology of Industry* marked an 'epoch in economic thought,'[28] but at the time it was the subject of hostile reviews by professional economists who seemed especially peeved at being told by two amateurs (a label Hobson was to wear thereafter) that the teachings of classical economics were a hindrance to understanding the problem of unemployment. These economists could accept that there might be certain impediments to the workings of Say's Law, giving rise to temporary disequilibria in the economy, but they refused to countenance the idea that bouts of unemployment were endemic to capitalism. Especially damaging in this regard was the review by F.Y. Edgeworth. Edgeworth's account of Mummery's and Hobson's book was very demeaning. He wrote, for example, that 'the attempt to unsettle consecrated tenets is not very hopeful, unless the public, whose attention is solicited, have some security against waste of their time and trouble. It may fairly be required of very paradoxical writers that they should either evince undoubted genius or extraordinarily wide learning.'[29]

Needless to say, Edgeworth found none of these qualities in the authors of *The Physiology of Industry*. But Edgeworth did not stop at reviewing Hobson's book; apparently he also used his influence as Professor of Economics at King's College, London, to see to it that Hobson was not permitted to lec-

28 *The General Theory of Employment, Interest and Money* (1936), 365. Keynes was not always so impressed by Hobson's contributions. In a review of one of Hobson's later works, *Gold, Prices and Wages* (1913), Keynes wrote: 'One comes to a new book by Mr. Hobson with mixed feelings, in the hope of stimulating ideas ... but expectant also of much sophistry, misunderstanding, and perverse thought. This book is ... made much worse than a really stupid book could be, by exactly those characteristics of cleverness and intermittent reasonableness which have borne good fruit in the past.' *Economic Journal* (Sept. 1913), 393-8; cited in Alvin Hansen, *Full Recovery or Stagnation* (1938), 15. Hansen's addendum also might be noted: 'This characterization by Mr. Keynes himself is not altogether inapplicable, some may perhaps say, to his own book.' [*The General Theory*].

29 Cited in T.W. Hutchison, *A Review of Economic Doctrines, 1870-1929* (1953), 118

ture on economics for the London University Extension Board. Hobson was confined to lecturing on Literature. And a few months later, when Edgeworth succeeded to the Chair of Political Economy at Oxford, Hobson again found himself barred from lecturing on economic theory, this time from the Oxford University Extension Movement.[30] On top of this, the Charity Organisation Society withdrew its invitation to Hobson to give a series of lectures on economics. And a little later his application to join the prestigious Political Economy Club was turned down.[31] Mummery's and Hobson's work was thus judged destructive of both truth and morals. The publication of *The Physiology of Industry* marked Hobson as an heretic and he was never invited, and he never asked, to return to academia.[32]

Overall, Hobson was remarkably sanguine about the consequences of his exclusion from the institutions of higher learning. He admitted that 'the quiet atmosphere of an academic life' might have enabled him to develop 'in a more orderly way' his 'humanist theory,' but then he attributed his awareness of the 'common human element' in social life precisely to the fact that he was not isolated in an 'ivory tower.'[33] He was also of the opinion that the institutionalization of higher learning brought pressures on scholars to become overspecialized, which further helped divorce them from the 'actual concrete experiences of life.'[34] Certainly Hobson's own keen interest in the sociology of knowledge[35] and his lack of faith in the educational system as an instrument for spreading reason and free thought was unusual for a liberal of his time and must be attributed in part to the rough handling he received in these early years from those professors who lambasted him in the name of economic science.

30 Edgeworth's efforts to insulate Oxford from Hobson's teachings seems to have been very successful. G.D.H. Cole, for example, recalled that his own attempt, sometime later, to teach Hobsonian economics at Oxford, made him feel like 'an economic leper.' Cf. *The Means to Full Employment* (1943), 48-9, and *Socialist Economics* (1959), 43, 49.
31 *Confessions*, 30-1, 84
32 Given his friendship with Graham Wallas and L.T. Hobhouse and his association with the Webbs, it is surprising that Hobson was never invited to join the faculty of the London School of Economics. There is undoubtedly a certain peevishness in his comment that 'Jonathan Hutchinson' (a mistaken reference to Henry Hutchinson), who provided the original funding for the LSE, would have turned in his grave had he foreseen 'that his money would go into paying Professor Foxwell for teaching why not to socialise banking. ... [and] Mr. Ackworth why not to nationalise railways' (ibid., 80). Foxwell had also given *The Physiology of Industry* a bad review. Hobson does mention that he received 'one or two invitations to posts in America' (ibid., 83)
33 Ibid., 83-4
34 Ibid., 86
35 Hobson's main work in this area is *Free Thought in the Social Sciences* (1926).

For the next few years, Hobson continued to lecture on literature and did some occasional journalism. He also wrote two books, *Problems of Poverty* (1891) and *Evolution of Modern Capitalism* (1894), in which he once more broached the subject of underconsumption, but this time in a much more circuitous fashion. In the former work, Hobson criticized many of the alternate proposals his contemporaries were making for dealing with the unemployment problem. For example, he dismissed emigration as impractical. The 'age of loose promiscuous pauper emigration' had gone, not least because the colonies were no longer willing to take 'large bodies of the lowest and least competent workers.'[36]

Those reformers who devoted themselves to improving the moral standards of the unemployed work force were taking too narrow a view of the problem. Not only was it far from clear, in Hobson's opinion, to what extent the 'vices' of the poor, drink, gambling, etc., contributed to their unemployment, or how much blame could be attached to the poor for such habits, but this approach also simply failed to tackle the problem of creating more jobs.[37] Consequently, even if such a campaign were successful, it would only increase the number of workers looking for too few jobs. The clearest evidence that it was the number of jobs available and not the moral standards of the unemployed that was the real issue was the fact that during times of industrial prosperity the rate of unemployment declined: 'That in 1890 the mass of unemployed was almost absorbed, disposes once and for all of the allegation that the unemployed in times of depression consist of idlers who do not choose to work.'[38]

Public works programs seemed more promising as a remedy for unemployment; but even here, Hobson pointed out, there were many difficulties. There was some merit to the conventional liberal argument that state assistance might sap the 'growth of self-reliance in the lower ranks of the working classes,' although the low priority Hobson gave this argument was not typical of liberals of this time. Further, if the public works undertaken were not socially useful, then such schemes would likely find the sense of 'degradation and disgrace attaching to the workhouse' extended to them and this would keep away 'the more honest and deserving' among the unemployed. On the other hand, if the state did subsidize programs that directly competed with private industry, then this might exacerbate unemployment by forcing some private firms into bankruptcy.[39]

36 *Problems of Poverty*, 137
37 Ibid., 171-82
38 Ibid., 16
39 Ibid., 140, 143

Hobson's general conclusion was that none of the various schemes for remedying unemployment was of any real assistance unless it increased the net amount of employment, and the only sure way of accomplishing that was by 'raising the standard of consumption for the community,' and especially the working classes.[40] Thus, in *Problems of Poverty* Hobson attempted to show that all roads led back to his underconsumption thesis, although this time he stopped short of actually taking his readers down that road.

Hobson's next book, *The Evolution of Modern Capitalism*, was only slightly less circumspect. It contained a fairly lengthy chapter on 'Machinery and Industrial Depression' in which Hobson expressed his disturbing ideas on underconsumption, but as J.M. Clark has pointed out, this time these ideas were 'not generalised as laws and labelled as attacks on accepted theory,' but remained immersed in history.[41] For those who wished to draw disquieting conclusions, the material was at hand and many radical thinkers came to regard the work as a classic. But for those who preferred not to delve, the book could still be considered a very lucid and studious account of industrialization, and it was adopted as a standard text in many colleges in Britain and the United States. Hobson noted that the *Evolution of Modern Capitalism* almost won for him 'a place of academic respectability.'[42]

It is also worth noting that in preparation for writing his first three works Hobson had made early use of the first volume of Marx's *Capital* (first translated into English in 1887), especially those sections dealing with industrial technology. At this time, however, Hobson did not appreciate Marx's account of poverty and unemployment in capitalist societies and was to criticize him specifically and persistently for limiting his analysis to the exploitation of the wage-earner. Nevertheless, Hobson seems gradually to have softened in his attitude towards Marx and in a lecture delivered in the early 1930s he made a belated acknowledgment of Marx's contribution to the analysis of cyclical unemployment:

When I was treading this path [of economic heresy], I was not aware that Karl Marx had preceded me, by an analysis which showed how impossible it was for capitalism to dispose of its productivity under a wage system which kept the purchasing power of the masses at a subsistence level ... Though I have never been a full blooded Marxist, I desire to acknowledge the great services he rendered by tracing trade depressions and unemployment to vices inherent in the profiteering system.[43]

40 Ibid., 147
41 'John A. Hobson, Heretic and Pioneer,' *Journal of Social Philosophy* (July 1940), 358
42 *Confessions*, 37
43 Lecture, No Title, Hobson Papers, Hull University, Item 24 (k), 12-13

No such softening, however, is evident in his criticism of historical materialism. Even though he was eventually to accept, perhaps under the influence of G.D.H. Cole, that Marxists were not blind to the impact of non-economic factors on social events, none the less he always considered their doctrine to be simplistic. Thus around the same time he was praising Marx for his analysis of trade depressions, Hobson also wrote an assessment of historical materialism which suggests that he viewed the doctrine as one grand illustration of the 'post hoc ergo propter hoc' fallacy:

what plausibility attaches to [the doctrine of historical materialism] rests upon an extension of the meaning of the term economic to cover the whole field of biological activities. If you premise that all forms of the physical and psychical activities of man consume energy that must be replaced by food, since food-getting is an economic process[,] you may claim positive proof of the economic determination of history. But all you have really proved is that food is a necessity to human life, and that all other activities and institutions must be consistent with the activities and institutions of food-getting. You do not prove, either that food-getting is the only necessary activity, or that its urgency is such as to mould all other activities to its need. For biological survival and growth there are other activities related to sex, care of offspring ... group protection, etc., which lie outside any accepted meaning of the term economic. ... [These activities] have their separate origins in the inherited structure and character of man. Thus only by stretching 'economic' so as to make it coterminous with biological can an appearance of validity be given to 'the economic determination of history.' Even so, this school of determinists would have to reckon with ... [many] sociologists ... who ... find an evolution of mind which in its higher levels is liberated from the survival economy.[44]

Hobson, then, had little regard for a theory of history that at best seemed severely reductionist and at worst appeared to keep men forever the instrument of 'base' economic determinants.

Perhaps emboldened by the popular success of *The Evolution of Modern Capitalism*, Hobson's next work, *The Problem of the Unemployed* (1896), presented an overt and systematic attack on the fallacious reasoning of the classical economists, very much in line with the earlier argument of *The Physiology of Industry*, except that Hobson added a new dimension centred

44 *Wealth and Life* (1929), 78. See also *Le Sens de la responsabilité* (1938), 16.

on the maldistribution of incomes in capitalist society as a major cause of industrial crises. Hobson was later to reflect that this addition to his analysis was 'a dangerous advance in the application of the [theory] of oversaving' as far as orthodox economists were concerned and guaranteed his banishment to the underworld of economics.[45]

However, as the result of an untoward event, Hobson found himself relatively immune from any personal repercussions that the publication of *The Problem of the Unemployed* might have occasioned. Within a few months of the book's publication, Hobson's father died and Hobson inherited just sufficient wealth to enable him to give up lecturing as a career. Thus it was the security afforded by inherited wealth that enabled Hobson to sustain his attack on unearned income as the source of industrial malady: the irony of the situation left Hobson somewhat perplexed.[46]

The decade between 1897 and 1910 was Hobson's most creative period. It was during this time that Hobson, in the words of P.F. Clarke, 'hunted down the individualistic fallacy' of classical liberalism, not only in economics, but 'in all its guises' and substituted in its place an organic view of society which he believed preserved what was best in old liberalism whilst ridding it of its faults.[47] The stimulation for much of Hobson's best writing during this period came from his close association with a brilliant group of radicals known collectively as New Liberals. Along with L.T. Hobhouse, Hobson quickly ascended to the intellectual leadership of this group (the membership of which is described later in this chapter).

New Liberalism differed from the old in three vital aspects.[48] First, in Hobson's words, 'it envisaged more clearly the need for important economic reforms, aiming to give a positive significance to the "equality" which figured in the democratic triad of liberty, equality, and fraternity.'[49] Classical liberalism was faulty because it had compromised too quickly with the interests of the rising bourgeoisie and in doing so had sacrificed equality for liberty (i.e., the freedom to compete and accumulate). This compromise had

45 Lecture, No Title, 12
46 *Confessions*, 72-4
47 'Introduction' to *The Crisis of Liberalism* (1909; new ed., 1974), xix. This broadening of Hobson's critique is best evidenced in *The Social Problem*. Clarke also notes, quite correctly, that 'all the important elements of Hobson's thought are present by the turn of the century.'
48 The following description reflects Hobson's priorities. Each point is discussed in much greater detail in subsequent chapters. Here the primary concern is to indicate some of the formative influences on Hobson's thinking. For a less selective assessment of New Liberalism, see Freeden, *The New Liberalism*, passim.
49 *Confessions*, 52

virtually abandoned the lower classes to a life where liberalism was little else than a parade of false promises and unrealizable ideals. The aim of New Liberalism was to give expression to the 'socialism in liberalism,'[50] by incorporating 'economic equality of opportunities in its full sense as equal access to nature, capital, education and enterprise, as an integral factor of popular self-government.'[51] In this way the New Liberals hoped to extirpate the roots of social inequality which had made a mockery of liberal ideals. A good dose of socialism was required in order to make liberalism consistent.

The socialism of the New Liberals, however, was of a special kind. It has its origins in the Ricardian analysis of rent and especially in the suggestion, as J.S. Mill put it, that where rent had swelled 'from the growth of towns,' or some other social cause, it was 'no violation of the principles on which private property is grounded, if the state should appropriate this increase of wealth.'[52] In other words, landlords were not to be allowed to grow rich on 'unearned income' which was social in its origin. Mill was the first regularly to use 'unearned income' in this sense as a synonym for rent. A major part of Hobson's contribution to New Liberalism was his attempt to deepen Mill's insights into 'social value' and extend this analysis to the industrial realm, thereby providing a comprehensive critique of orthodox liberalism's ongoing effort to legitimize economic inequalities on the basis of an erroneous 'individualistic notion of production.'[53]

The second major flaw of classical liberalism, according to the New Liberals, was its monadic account of social relations. It tended to view society as an agglomeration of individuals, where every citizen was armed either with a set of natural rights, which it was assumed to be in the general interest to protect, or with a personality, no less fixed by nature, that sought to maximize private utility, which, again, it was assumed to be in the general interest to facilitate. In both cases the individual's interests appeared to be largely determined prior to his entering into or becoming conscious of his social relations

---

50 This is the title of an article Hobson wrote for the *Nation* in 1907 and reprinted in *The Crisis of Liberalism*, 133-8.

51 'Thoughts on Our Present Discontents,' *Political Quarterly*, Jan. (1938), 54

52 *Principles of Political Economy* (1848), book V, chap. II, sec. 5

53 It might be noted that Hobson nowhere indicates the origin of his ideas on surplus value. He expresses no indebtedness to Mill in this regard or, as McBriar points out, to the Fabians, who, for a while, worked in this same area of thought building on the analysis of Jevons, Francis Walker, and other neo-classical economists. McBriar also notes that, although the Fabians congratulated themselves on their formulation of the doctrine of economic rent, it did not seem to play a pivotal role in their reformist schemes. This is in marked contrast with Hobson. See A.M. McBriar, *Fabian Socialism and English Politics* (1962), chap. II.

with other individuals. It followed that 'society' was accorded only an instrumental value: it was a means to promote the general stock of private satisfactions.[54]

Classical liberalism was therefore blind to the fact, as the New Liberals saw it, that social relations had a transformative effect on individual character. This had two important ramifications on New Liberal thinking. First, it opened up the possibility that the sum of individual or particular satisfactions might not add up to the social good. What a man desired as an individual considered apart from society might vary substantively from what he desired when considering his position as a member of society. And if individual and social personality could be distinguished in this way – how sharply they could be distinguished was a matter of some dispute among New Liberals – then society could no longer be viewed simply as an arrangement for maximizing private utility. This meant that the sympathies, desires, and benefits of social or co-operative life had to be consciously protected, for individuals *qua* individuals, could not necessarily be relied upon to promote the social good. The converse of this was that New Liberals were also doubtful as to whether social problems were amenable to solution on an individualistic basis. Only collective solutions seemed appropriate. Consequently, the New Liberals also came to regard the state, not as a negative force in men's lives, but as an organ for directly promoting the social interest. In sum, 'society' was beginning to take on a distinct identity for New Liberals, which called into question the orthodox liberal contention that society was best understood simply as an aggregate of individuals.[55]

Hobson's own analysis of the individualistic assumptions of classical political economy was especially indebted to the writings of John Ruskin. Hobson considered Ruskin 'the greatest social teacher'[56] of the nineteenth century and although he vigorously rejected Ruskin's 'medieval-paternalism,' there remains an appreciable element of truth in E.T. Grether's quip that Hobson was the Elisha of Ruskin the prophet.[57] Ruskin provided Hobson with a concept of 'social welfare' that was in marked contrast with the approach of orthodox liberal economists. Ruskin did this by redefining the concept of wealth. Instead of equating wealth with exchange value, and the quantity of

---

54 See K. Minogue, *The Liberal Mind* (1968), chap. II.

55 In this light it is not surprising that New Liberals showed an active interest in the setting-up of the British Sociological Society in 1903, as a forum to further their cause of studying society as an 'evolving unitary system.' Cf. *Confessions*, 75-6. A good account of the Sociological Society is given in Stefan Collini, *Liberalism and Sociology* (1979), 198-208.

56 *John Ruskin, Social Reformer* (1898), v

57 'John Ruskin – John Hobson' in *Essays in Honour of Jessica B. Peixotto* (1935), 145

utilities, Ruskin assigned value according to an article's 'intrinsic worth,' i.e., its 'life-sustaining properties.' 'There is,' he said, 'no wealth but life.'[58] He thus substituted an ethical value for the 'commercial standard of money,' and concentrated on the quality of life, rather than on the quantity of possessions. On this basis he effectively transformed the meaning of utility, so as to establish what Hobson termed a theory of social economics.

For Hobson, Ruskin's economics confounded the monadic assumptions of the orthodox economists in two important respects. First, it called into question the validity of their chosen monad – 'economic man.' Ruskin's appeal, according to Hobson, was made 'not to a mere cluster of self-seeking instincts, but to the whole nature of man,' and this insistence on the 'organic unity' of man broke down the 'barrier separating industrial processes from other serviceable human activities.'[59] Ruskin's social economics recognized that 'even the purely marketable wares ... really involve the play of other human forces which cannot reasonably be excluded, and which cooperate organically to modify, or even reverse, the operation of the narrower economic motives.'[60]

Secondly, Ruskin called into question the liberal economists' right to attach the term 'political' to their economic studies, since the 'good of the polis [was] neither the conscious good nor the directing influence' of their 'economic man.' Put differently, Ruskin accused the liberal economists of having no distinct notion of social utility – a failure that resulted from their inability to appreciate the impact of social relations on individual character. Hobson expressed Ruskin's concern as follows:

[One] great reform in Mr. Ruskin's method has reference to the term 'Political'. Although the first great English treatise on Political Economy bore the title '*Wealth of Nations*', the science in the hands of Adam Smith's successors had never taken a true 'social' or 'national' standard even for the computation of commercial wealth. The *laissez faire* assumption that each individual, in seeking to get the most for himself, must take that course by which he would contribute most to the general well-being, *implied a complete failure to comprehend the organic structure of society*. A nation was conceived of as a mere aggregate of its constituent members: the good of the whole as the added good of all the parts. ... Economic laws

58 *John Ruskin*, 83, 78
59 Ibid., 76, 74
60 'Ruskin as a Political Economist,' in J.H. Whitehouse, *Ruskin the Prophet* (1920), 86

J.A. Hobson 19

were merely generalisations of the discreet action of individual businessmen ... 'writ large' and called political ...
In passing from Mercantile Economy to Mr. Ruskin's science and art of
Social Economics, we do not abandon the self-seeking motives ... [but] we
enlarge the scope and expand the nature ... [of] the 'self' which is seeking
satisfaction ... by imposing sacrifices of the narrower self in favour of a wider
self *which grows as we identify our good with that of others.*[61]

What Ruskin impressed upon Hobson, then, was the concept of 'total-
ity' – the 'organic integrity and unity of all human activities and the organic
nature of the cooperation of the social units.'[62] Hobson saw this as a key to
explaining why orthodox liberalism seemed so inadequate for the tasks of
social reform. Its narrow utilitarian assumptions prevented it from seeing the
'social problem' as a whole.
Lastly, and closely related to the previous argument, the New Liberals
criticized the classical liberals for fixing man's rational capacities at a level
that equated reason with mere reasoning and calculation – a concept, of
course, that was consistent with Smith's description of a market economy in
which each individual was assumed to have sufficient reason to calculate his
own self-interest, but where there apparently existed no fund of reason
sufficient to exercise central control over the system.[63] Such a contention
served to bolster the liberals' faith in the necessity of *laissez-faire*.
Interestingly, it was Darwin's theory of evolution that encouraged the
New Liberals to support their demand for state intervention with an argument that man's capacity for reason had evolved to a point where he could
now assert deliberate and conscious control over his environment. Not that
this was an obvious conclusion to be drawn from Darwin's works. Herbert
Spencer, for example, who was generally considered to be one of the leading
social theorists of his time, had managed to read into Darwin's study of the
natural world a justification for ruthless competition in human societies and
support for the policy of *laissez-faire* based on the law of natural selection.
Moreover, Spencer insisted that the social organism had no social sensorium
and hence no general will. Consciousness was to be found only in the 'cells'
of the organism – an idea that was fully in accord with the liberal economists'
view of the location of reason in the system.[64]

61 *John Ruskin*, 79-80, 85-6 (emphasis added)
62 Ibid., 89
63 *Rationalism and Humanism* (1933), 15ff
64 Ernest Barker, *Political Thought in England 1848-1914* (1915, rev. ed., 1947), 97-101

One fairly obvious reply to Spencer's reading of Darwin was to point out that the social realm and the natural realm were qualitatively different, so that laws discovered in the latter did not necessarily have any applicability in human affairs. This, in essence, was the stand taken by T.H. Huxley in his famous Romanes Lectures, delivered in 1893. Huxley juxtaposed the survival of the fittest with the survival of the ethically best, and claimed that it was the latter process which distinguished human societies.[65]

Although the New Liberals sympathized with Huxley's rejection of the struggle for survival as the principle of social development and made use of some of his specific arguments against Spencer's adaptation of Darwin's theory, none the less for the most part they rejected Huxley's dualism, that is, his sharp antithesis of nature and man. This was especially true in Hobson's case. Hobson praised the works of Spencer precisely on the point that they extended evolutionary thought to the social sciences and made man 'henceforth a part of nature.'[66] On the other hand, he expressed grave misgivings about the kind of position that had been advocated by Huxley:

If we regard [ethical ideals] ... as pure products of rational consciousness, of a moral and intellectual nature supervening upon our animal inheritance, it is easy for the materialist, the economist, the realist in politics, to dismiss them as illusions or shadowy epiphenomena. But if we recognize that the stuff out of which these ideals, even the loftiest and most spiritual, have been generated is not of ultimately diverse nature from the animal desires and the selfish cravings with which these ideals seem to conflict, the charge of unreality collapses.[67]

Various attempts were made within the New Liberal school of thought to utilize Darwin's notion of evolution, whilst at the same time avoiding Spencer's conclusions and Huxley's dualism, and of these the one that had the most influence, particularly on Hobson, was the theory of 'orthogenic evolution' proposed by Leonard T. Hobhouse. Hobhouse agreed with Huxley that it was necessary to avoid any abstract application of natural laws to the social realm and that 'consciousness' should be singled out as the primary difference between men and animals. But Huxley was incorrect to oppose 'mind' and 'nature.' Mind, too, was a part of the natural evolutionary

65 Ibid., 115-18
66 'Herbert Spencer, 'South Place Magazine, vol. 9 (1904), 51; cited in Freeden, The New Liberalism, 74
67 Problems of a New World (1921), 132. See also 'Character and Society,' in P. Parker, ed., Character and Life (1912), 103, and John Ruskin, 104-5.

process. It might be incongruous to suggest that there could be an 'ethics of evolution,' for nature had no ethics, but in pressing this point against Spencer, Huxley had missed the opportunity to discuss the possibility of an 'evolution of ethics.' This was the task Hobhouse set himself in 1904, in *Democracy and Reaction*, and developed in a number of dense, detailed works, the most notable being *Morals in Evolution* (1906), held by some to mark an epoch in the study of sociology, and *Social Development* (1924). In these works Hobhouse carefully traced man's natural evolution towards self-consciousness and argued that with the emergence of self-consciousness human evolution became increasingly purposive. Man was able to help make his own history and thereby abridge the natural laws binding lower forms of life. The gist of Hobhouse's argument is to be found in the following statement from *Democracy and Reaction* (pp. 103, 105, 106-8):

Mind is to be treated primarily as a factor in evolution, and mind becomes a factor in evolution in so far as it determines the behaviour of the individual, and thereby the life and development of the species. ... Throughout the animal world the main lines of behaviour are laid down by ... instinct ... In the human world this is changed. Each child is born not only with its own inherited ... impulses, but into a society with rules of life inherited in a different sense, handed on by tradition. ... As the mind comes to itself and learns to measure its capacities and use its powers there is a gradual purging of [traditional] codes. There is an attempt to ... go back from the rules which men repeat and hand on, to the principle which underlies and justifies them, and the great religious and ethical systems are born. ... In these and other ways ... there arises by degrees the ideal of collective humanity, self-determining in its progress, as the supreme object of human activity, and the final standard by which the laws of conduct should be judged. ... Orthogenic evolution then is conceived as a process in which the control of the conditions of life gradually passes to ... intelligence.

Hobhouse's studies provided New Liberals with material and a framework for arguing that state intervention marked a higher stage in the progress of society than did *laissez-faire*. It was a mark of man's self-determination, his capacity to regulate his environment and place economic laws under ethics.

This is not, of course, to suggest that the New Liberals became full-blooded collectivists. On the contrary, with certain interesting differences in degree, all New Liberals were anxious to preserve what they considered to be the progressive elements of the 'individualistic society' which they believed was now, none the less, entering its period of general decline. 'If the Radical policy of social reconstruction is to be effective,' Hobson wrote in 1907, reflecting on past liberal shibboleths, then it had to take seriously the objections to collectivism which 'beset the wavering mind of [the] 'centre' Liberals':

The right limits of state and municipal collectivism must be laid down; the questions, how far brains, how far 'labour' are the makers of wealth, how far freedom of private profitable enterprise is essential to secure the work of 'brains'; whether efficiency of labour can be got out of public enterprise; whether the tyranny of bureaucracy would become unendurable; whether the tendency of such socialism will be to dwarf individuality and to make for a dead level of humanity; whether the general result of impaired productive motives will lead to so create a diminution of wealth as no improvement in distribution can compensate – these ... questions ... demand thorough and impartial consideration.[68]

The fact that these objections could be met meant Liberals should 'press forward with energy and confidence along the path of social reconstruction'; but the fact that these questions also demanded 'thorough and impartial consideration' was no less a warning to 'hard-cast' revolutionary socialists not to dismiss the 'doubts and fears' of traditional liberals out of hand.[69] New Liberals were to advance towards socialism as if looking through a rear-view mirror.

Aside from a small but influential parliamentary group, which included Herbert Samuel, J.M. Robertson, and Charles Trevelyan, most of the New Liberals were connected with one another through their association with various publications, like the *Nation* under the editorship of H.W. Massingham, and the *Manchester Guardian*, when it was run by C.P. Scott, and through various discussion groups and ethical societies.

One of the first New Liberal associations was the Rainbow Circle, formed in 1894. The Circle had its origins in a series of informal discussions attended by Hobson, William Clarke, Herbert Burrows, Richard Stapley, Ramsay MacDonald, and J.R. MacDonald. These discussions, however, were apparently of a 'desultory character' and in August 1894 it was decided that the Circle should meet on a regular basis, recruit new members so as to raise the membership to around twenty, and focus its efforts on providing 'a rational

68 *The Crisis of Liberalism*, 137-8
69 Ibid., 137

and comprehensive view of political and social progress ... which could be ultimately formulated in a programme of action' and a 'rallying point for social reformers.' With this program of action in mind the Circle proposed to examine three main issues: '(1) the reasons why the old Philosophic Radicalism and the Manchester School of Economics can no longer furnish a ground of action in the political sphere; (2) the transition from this school of thought to the so-called "New Radicalism" or Collectivist politics of today; (3) the bases, ethical, economic and political, of the newer politics, together with the practical applications and influences arising therefrom in the actual problems before us at the present time.'[70]

This program proved sufficiently attractive to recruit Herbert Samuel, Charles Trevelyan, J.M. Robertson, Graham Wallas, Sidney Olivier, T.F. Husband, the Rev. A.L. Lilley and others to the ranks of the Circle. Several of its members already had been acquainted with one another through the Russell Club at Oxford University, which was strongly influenced by the ideas of T.H. Green, and there is evidence that Green's philosophy remained a guiding light for a number of the Circle's participants.[71] The fact, however, that the Rainbow Circle took its name from the Rainbow Tavern in Fleet Street, where it first held its monthly meetings, is also a fair indication that its program was going to differ somewhat from Green's emphasis on temperance as a key instrument of social reform. In fact, the diversity of ideas expressed at its meetings was a matter of some pride to the Circle. Hobson was later to reflect that the Circle discussions were of 'immense value in widening and deepening' his outlook.[72]

In February 1895 the Circle decided to issue its own monthly publication, the *Progressive Review*, in recognition that 'existing monthlies are either mere open platforms or have distinct leanings of a reactionary kind.' Unabashedly, the Circle claimed that its *Review* should do for the progressive movement what the *Edinburgh Review* had done for the Whigs and the *Fortnightly Review* for the Positivists. The Circle was to take care that their journal did not 'fall into the hands of a particular sector of the progressive party,' a task that was entrusted to Hobson and Clarke as joint editors (Clarke holding the senior position) and Ramsay MacDonald, who was appointed secretary.[73] In this they were largely successful, and contributions were published from a wide range of social reformers. In Hobson's opinion the publication of

70 Samuel Papers, File A/10, Circular, Aug. 1894
71 H.V. Emy, *Liberals, Radicals, and Social Politics, 1892-1914* (1973), 104
72 *Confessions*, 52
73 Samuel Papers, File A/10, Letter 27 Feb. 1895

the *Progressive Review*, in September 1896, marked the beginnings of New Liberalism as a distinct creed, although great ingenuity was shown by some of the contributors in linking new tenets with traditional liberal beliefs. Clear evidence of this is found, for example, in an article Hobson wrote on 'Collectivism in Industry' where the case for public ownership was argued as an extention of principles laid down by Adam Smith in Book V of the *Wealth of Nations*.[74] Overall, even though the *Progressive Review* remained aloof from party ties, it did retain the hope, as David Marquand has commented, that the Liberal party was still susceptible to 'prodding.'[75]

But although successful in helping spearhead the progressive movement in the 1890s, the *Progressive Review* was a sorry failure in almost every other regard. Its circulation never exceeded 700 copies, and it quickly ran into financial difficulties. More seriously, there were acrimonious disputes between Clarke and Ramsay MacDonald over what constituted the duties of an editor and a secretary, and mutual suspicions (largely founded) that each was denouncing the other behind the closed doors of the directors' office. It was MacDonald's refusal to resign his position as secretary for 'the good of the journal' that eventually forced Samuel and Stapley to pull the rug from under his feet, and close it down.[76] More ominous but less dramatic was a second dispute brewing in the offices of the *Progressive Review* at this time, between Clarke, Hobson, and Samuel over the issue of imperialism. Clarke believed that the *Review* housed a 'pestilent mischievous clique' led by Samuel which was seeking to use its pages to promote 'a lot of imperialist bosh.'[77] Hobson sided with him on this issue, and only the closing of the journal stopped the matter from coming to a head.

Despite these difficulties the Rainbow Circle continued to function for several decades. And it is worth stressing that the Circle's attempt to reformulate liberal doctrine so that it might provide a 'rallying point for social reformers' was undertaken before the emergence of the Labour party had come to be considered a threat to the Liberal party's electoral fortunes. Certainly by the mid-1890s a fairly well defined working-class movement was afoot. Hard-pressed unskilled labourers were for the first time beginning to form unions alongside the better established unions of the skilled artisans,

---

74 Reprinted in *The Crisis of Liberalism*, 114–32
75 *Ramsay MacDonald* (1977), 56
76 The details of this row can be traced in the letters between Samuel, Stapley, MacDonald, and Clarke contained in the Samuel Papers, File A/10. Along with Stapley and Samuel, Hobson was a director of the *Progressive Review*, but he does not seem to have played an active part in this dispute, excusing himself on the grounds of ill-health.
77 Cited in B. Porter, *Critics of Empire*, 165

now newly disgruntled about the destruction of their crafts by the increasing mechanization of the workplace. Moreover, among both these groups socialism had some appeal. But the Independent Labour Party (ILP) was not established until 1893, and the Labour Representation Committee (LRC), backed by the trade unions, was not formed until 1900. Thus, as Henry Pelling has argued, in the 1890s 'it was in fact only a tiny minority of the so-called "working class" which had as yet responded to the [socialist] cause.'[78] In this light, it is reasonable to suggest that New Liberalism was not a rear-guard action but a genuine progressive movement within the evolution of liberal doctrine.

Given that the New Liberal approach to social questions was basically humanist, it is not surprising that London's several ethical societies also provided a useful forum for the expression of New Liberal ideas. On first coming to London, Hobson had joined the London Ethical Society, which was led by Bernard Bosanquet, J.H. Muirhead, and several other academics who had close associations with Oxford University and were sympathetic to the teachings of T.H. Green. Hobson remained with the London Ethical Society for five years. He considered it 'excellent in its assertion of free discussion,'[79] an opinion he continued to hold even when its sister organization, the Charity Organisation Society, sanctioned him for the thoughts he and Mummery had expressed in the *Physiology of Industry*. But gradually Hobson came to believe that the London Ethical Society's 'stress on individual moral character as the basis of social progress' was so strong as to make it 'an enemy of that political-economic democracy' which he was beginning to regard 'as the chief instrument of social progress and justice.'[80]

In 1895 Hobson transferred his membership to the South Place Ethical Society, which had been founded in 1793 by the Rev. Elhanan Winchester as a centre for religious dissent, the area of dissent being gradually enlarged, especially under the leadership of William Fox (1817-52), Stanton Coit (1888-91), and Moncure Conway, who was resident minister when Hobson joined. The society had traditionally placed emphasis on the virtue of fellowship and this made it more receptive to Hobson's collectivist approach to social issues.

Hobson was first introduced to the society by his friend Wallas. He had occasionally lectured before its members in the early 1890s,[81] and did so

---

78 *A Short History of the Labour Party* (1961), 3

79 *Confessions*, 56; also Lord Snell, *Men, Movements, and Myself* (1936), 160f

80 *Confessions*, 56

81 The first lecture by Hobson noted in the *South Place Magazine* is 'The Academic Spirit in Education,' dated 3 April 1892. The lecture was later published as an article in the *Contemporary Review*, vol. 63 (Feb.), 1893

more regularly after 1897, when the society decided to appoint a rota of lecturers to lead its meetings, rather than a full-time minister. In 1900 his appointment was made permanent,[82] a position he initially shared with J.M. Robertson and Herbert Burrows, later to be joined by C.Delisle Burns, Joseph McCabe, and S.K. Ratcliffe. In the first six months of his appointment he lectured on such diverse topics as the works of George Eliot and George Meredith, 'The Inevitable in Politics,' 'The Tyranny of Books,' John Ruskin as a revolutionary, imperialism, hypocrisy, and the 'Break-up of China.' Hobson was to lecture on a similar range of subjects, health permitting, every fourth Sunday morning, for the next thirty-five years. The society also provided him with study groups to examine his books – rather like Bible classes – and gave Mrs Hobson access to a theatre for the production of her plays, or 'amusing little farces' as they were described in the society's magazine. Finally, the society provided Hobson with his first editorship of a relatively successful and influential journal, the *Ethical World*. Included among its contributors were James Bryce, William Clarke, S.G. Hobson, H.M. Hyndman, and George Bernard Shaw. Hobson's own contributions were later collected together to form the basis of his book, *The Social Problem* (1901), which, along with Hobhouse's *Democracy and Reaction* (1904), represents the best statement of New Liberal doctrine.

Hobson, however, did not stay at his editorial post more than a few months, because in July 1899, C.P. Scott, editor of the *Manchester Guardian*, asked Hobson to go to South Africa to report on the problems that had been brewing between the British and the Boers ever since gold was discovered in the Transvaal in 1886.[83] Hobson's name had been suggested to Scott by his chief leader-writer, L.T. Hobhouse, who had been much impressed by an article Hobson had written for the *Contemporary Review* in which he expressed the gist of his economic theory of imperialism.[84]

The South African War of 1899 was not the first occasion Liberals had been at loggerheads over imperial policy. Uganda had provided a flash-point in the early 1890s resulting in serious divisions within Gladstone's cabinet. But events in South Africa, starting with the Jameson Raid in 1896, mark-

---

82 South Place Ethical Society, Annual Report 1900-1, 5

83 Ayerst, The Manchester Guardian, 274

84 *Confessions*, 60. The article in question was 'Free Trade and Foreign Policy.' However, it was actually published in August 1898, not 1899 as Hobson states. It is also worth noting that as a matter of strict chronology it is incorrect to suggest, as does Fieldhouse, for example, that Hobson's interest in imperialism 'arose immediately out of [his] visit to South Africa.' See D.K. Fieldhouse, 'Imperialism: A Historiographical Revision,' in K. Boulding and T. Mukerjee, eds., *Economic Imperialism* (1972), 97

edly escalated the level of rancour within the party.[85] Although it had been out of office since 1895, imperialist policy in South Africa had remained to some extent a Liberal affair. Its main practitioners were Liberals, including of course, Cecil Rhodes; and a sizeable proportion of the Liberal party, and especially the parliamentary party, including such notables as Rosebery, Asquith, Haldane, and Grey, continued to support the 'imperial idea.' Ranged against this Liberal imperialist faction was the 'Little Englander' group whose stronghold was the National Liberal Federation. Lloyd George, John Morley, and later, Campbell-Bannerman (who was elected party leader in 1899), were to gain prominence in this group, as was Hobson.

Hobson was in South Africa for several months of 1899 during which time he interviewed most of the leading figures involved in the controversy over the Transvaal, including President Kruger, Olive Schreiner, James Hertzog, and General Smuts on the Boer side, and Milner and Rhodes for the British.[86] The reports that Hobson sent back to the *Guardian* were generally 'pro-Boer' in that they discounted rumours about Boer atrocities vis-à-vis the British. On the other hand, he attacked both the British and the Boer for their ill-treatment of the native Bantu, Zulu, and Matabele. According to Kropotkin, these reports constituted 'one of the most striking documents on the history of serfdom.'[87] The war itself was viewed by Hobson as a capitalist plot organized by investors in South African mines. Two years later Hobson was to incorporate the South African case into a general theory of economic imperialism, published under the title *Imperialism: A Study* (1902). In this work he linked imperialism with his theory of underconsumption, by arguing that the former was the result of increased pressures on capitalists to find an outlet for their surplus profits. *Imperialism* soon acquired the status of a classic. John Strachey, for example, looking back over nearly forty years of debate on the question of imperialism claimed that Hobson's study marked 'the highest point of development ever reached by liberal thought in Britain,'[88] although, as is well known, the book's influence, thanks to Lenin, extended far beyond liberal circles.

85 Hobson's perspective on these events is given in a chapter he contributed to H.J. Ogden's book, *The War against the Dutch Republics* (1901), entitled 'Before and after the Jameson Raid.'

86 *Confessions*, 61

87 From a letter to Hobson, Hobson Papers. See also *The Crisis of Liberalism*, 244 where he attacks the racist policies of the new South African Union, warning that they 'sow a crop of dark and dangerous problems for the future.'

88 *What Are We to Do?* (1938), 87

When Hobson returned to England he found that his reporting had made him notorious among radicals. He was guest of honour at numerous 'Welcome Home' dinners, the most prestigious being that given at the National Liberal Club in December 1899. Chaired by Sir Robert Reid and Lloyd George, it included among its 'stewards' Harold Spender, J.L. Hammond, F.W. Hirst, and E. Belfort Bax. However, outside radical circles Hobson's reception was far less cordial; many times he faced hostile audiences. As his friend H.N. Brailsford has commented, this period in Hobson's life gives some indication of his civic 'courage and his moral stature,' for in facing the 'Jingo' he did not do 'what the typical Liberal publicist does at such times – plead for moderation [and] seek a middle-course'; instead, he delivered 'a frontal attack on Imperialism in all its aspects.'[89]

Hobson's abuse at the hands of the masses also had an interesting effect on his thinking. He began to devote attention to the deep wells of irrationalism in the 'public mind' and the mechanisms which enabled a person to avoid rational conclusions whenever some preconception or prejudice was about to be contradicted. This made him sympathetic to the work of Graham Wallas, although it is worth noting that Hobson's own first work in this area, *The Psychology of Jingoism* (1901), predates Wallas' better-known and more ambitious study, *Human Nature in Politics* (1908), by several years. Disturbing as this discovery of the 'irrationalism of the masses' must have been to Hobson, it is none the less accurate to continue to describe him, as did Brailsford, as a 'rationalist to the core,'[90] for Hobson largely attributed the perversity of the masses to bad institutions and class manipulation; he intended no slight on the common man as such.[91]

Hobson considered the Boer War both 'a turning point' in his career and an 'illumination' to his understanding of the 'real relations between economics and politics.' He found that his engagement in 'controversial causes and movements' helped consolidate his thinking on social issues, although he also admitted that, as yet, he had not 'gathered into clear perspective the nature of the interaction between economics, politics, and ethics.'[92] He

89 *The Life-Work of J.A. Hobson*, L.T. Hobhouse Memorial Trust Lecture, no. 17 (1948), 21
90 Ibid., 6
91 In this light, and also taking into account Hobson's comment in the same work that the most striking feature of popular reaction to the Boer War was the credulity displayed by the 'educated classes' (21), the following assessment by R. Price appears much too harsh: 'Hobson's book, *The Psychology of Jingoism* was a moralistic comment coloured by a failure to observe society at any deeper level than that of events like 'Mafeking Night' ... It merely revealed Hobson's low opinion of the 'brutal' and 'credulous' working class.' *An Imperial War and the British Working Class* (1972), 175-6
92 *Confessions*, 59, 63

seems to mean by this that he was still prone to viewing events in terms of a simplistic 'economic conspiracy theory,' although here Hobson is being, perhaps, too severe in his self-criticism, especially with reference to *Imperialism*, as will be shown later.

It also might be argued that with the close of the Boer War the New Liberals were intellectually fairly well prepared for the rest of the history of their times. Certainly in Hobson's case the Great War and the Depression of the 1930s seemed to hold much the same lessons as the Boer War and the Depression of the 1880s – only more so. It merely took New Liberals longer to salvage their rationalist faith after the end of the First World War, and few of them, of course, lived to see the end of the 'hungry thirties.'

Imperialism continued to preoccupy Hobson's attention when, in 1905, he travelled to Canada to gather material for a series of articles that had been commissioned by the *Daily Chronicle*.[93] This time he concentrated on the 'second arm' of imperialism, namely protectionism. The issue of protectionism had re-emerged as a major public debate after Joseph Chamberlain's famous Birmingham speech on 15 May 1903, in which he called for a strengthening of the policy of imperial preference. Chamberlain was at this time Colonial Secretary in Balfour's Conservative Government, and his speech split the cabinet. Liberals, on the other hand, were quick to rally to the defence of free trade and this new campaign did much to overcome the disunity in the party resulting from the Boer War. Indeed Hobson's writing for the *Daily Chronicle* was one sign of this, for the *Daily Chronicle* had been anti-Boer for almost the whole period of the war.

Canada, in Hobson's opinion, was an appropriate place to examine the merits of Chamberlain's arguments since the Fielding tariff of 1897, which granted tariff reductions to Britain, marked the shaky beginnings of the policy of imperial preference, whilst Canada's attempt to build a tariff wall between herself and the United States was a good example of a protectionist policy.

The Canadian example illustrated the futility of both these policies. After an exhaustive examination of Canada's trade figures, Hobson concluded that the tariff preference given to Britain had done little to stem the relative decline in trade between the two countries. Further, the pressures placed on the Laurier government by Canadian manufacturers to repeal these trade preferences suggested that Chamberlain had seriously underestimated the desire within the colonies to establish strong domestic industries. This was of higher priority than that of establishing favourable trading links with Britain.[94]

93 These articles formed the basis of Hobson's book, *Canada To-day* (1906).
94 *Confessions*, 65; *Canada To-day*, 70

Similarly, Hobson argued that Canada's attempt to protect herself from American domination by establishing trade barriers was a failure. Canada's dependence on the American market was increasing. Moreover, a number of large American manufacturers had managed to slip under the tariff wall by setting up subsidiaries in Canada. Some of the politicians Hobson interviewed, like R.P. Roblin, the premier of Manitoba, were attempting to present this policy as a victory. Hobson, however, was not convinced and alluded to the threat American branch plants presented to Canadian economic, political, and cultural independence.[95] The result, he suggested, would be the eventual economic integration of the two economies based on the interests of strongly organized American business trusts.

From Canada Hobson travelled south on a lecture tour of the East and Midwest of the United States. Hobson had first visited the United States in 1888. Writing in 1938, he reflected that his American experiences were invaluable in the development of his economic thought:

I saw a business system which had grown up under free competition and equality of opportunity passing into trusts and other combines ... [and gained] a clearer understanding of the defects of political democracy divorced from the terms of economic equality that are essential to its equitable working. ... America ... taught me more of the ethics and politics of the economic system in its modern capitalistic shape and development than any experience available in England.[96]

In short, America provided Hobson with a model of advanced capitalism. His visits to the United States also brought him into personal contact with several of its leading intellectuals, including E.A. Ross, Richard T. Ely, John Graham Brooks, and Henry D. Lloyd.[97] Although Hobson makes no mention of ever meeting Thorstein Veblen, they did correspond, and Hobson was especially impressed with Veblen's writings. He made several attempts to get Veblen's work better known in Britain, including writing a book on Veblen in 1936. The fact that Hobson kept abreast of the situation in America and had personal contacts there no doubt contributed to the 'considerable influence' he had on American social thought.[98]

Soon after Hobson had returned to England domestic issues once more came to the fore. In January 1906 the Liberal party was elected to office with

95 *Canada To-day*, 25-6, 53, 54-5
96 *Confessions*, 67-8
97 Ibid., 68-9
98 Joseph Dorfman, *The Economic Mind in American Civilisation* (1959), vol. IV, 174

a huge parliamentary majority which, while predominantly composed of lawyers, small businessmen, officers, and others of the liberal centre, did contain a radical section including ten of the twenty-five members of the Rainbow Circle.[99] No less encouraging for New Liberals was the fact that Lloyd George had received a position on the government front bench as President of the Board of Trade. Lloyd George's pro-Boer stand in the South African conflict had already identified him as a sympathizer with radical causes. Likewise, Winston Churchill's appointment as Under-Secretary to the Colonial Office pleased liberal radicals. A few months after his appointment Churchill gave a public lecture in Glasgow where he spoke of his desire 'to see the State embark upon various novel and adventurous experiments' in social reform and of his conviction that 'the present Parliament' would envince a 'pretty steady determination' to carry out such reforms.[100] There were many like Hobson, with whom Churchill's ideas at this time showed a notable similarly, who shared in this anticipation of an early introduction of a wide range of social legislation.

This was also a pleasing time for Hobson at a more personal level. In March 1907 he joined the staff of the *Nation* newly inaugurated under the editorship of H.W. Massingham, which included among its regular journalists H.N. Brailsford, C.F.G. Masterman, H.W. Nevinson, J.L. Hammond, and L.T. Hobhouse. It was an association Hobson found entirely congenial and it lasted for well over a decade. Brailsford's description of Hobson's participation at the *Nation*'s weekly staff meeting is worth noting. It reveals an aspect of Hobson's style that is not very evident in his written works:

Rather older than most of us round the table, Hobson looked the student he was, sparely and slightly built, rather tall and in his later years very frail. ... When he spoke ... it was usually to give a new turn to the discussion, often a rather startling and original turn. He generally spoke as he wrote, soberly weighing his words, but he would express himself at times with a blunt violence that was not wholly humorous. Under the balanced, objective manner of his books ... there burned strong and deep feelings. What I recall most vividly of his part in our talks was the brilliance of his wit. We always knew when something good was coming. He raised his right eyebrow, and paused to indulge in a peculiar stammer, which one rarely noticed at other times, while he was giving his epigram the neatest possible verbal shape. He had a formidible gift for irony and satire.[101]

99 Emy, *Liberals, Radicals and Social Politics*, 105
100 Reprinted in *Liberalism and the Social Problem* (1909), 67-84
101 *The Life-Work of J.A. Hobson*, 4

Nevinson's reminiscence of Hobson is in much the same vein.[102] These references to his mordant sense of humour would have pleased Hobson, for he placed a high value on humour as an aid to reason in detecting the inconsistent elements in an argument. Misjudgement, self-righteousness, and intolerance were seen by Hobson as the natural accompaniment of an 'eclipse of humour' and signified, as he claimed in the case of jingoism, a state of 'mental collapse.'[103]

Initially the writers on the *Nation*, Hobson perhaps less so than the others, were cautious in their assessment of the new administration, especially with regard to its commitment to social reform. Campbell-Bannerman, the Prime Minister, was well liked for his stand on free trade when this hallowed liberal principle was attacked by Joseph Chamberlain in 1903, and it was Campbell-Bannerman who was in part responsible for establishing, also in 1903, electoral accommodations between the LRC and Liberal candidates. But a willingness to seek an electoral pact with Labour did not, in itself, signify a commitment to social reform. Here it was much more difficult to anticipate the government's position. After all, it was the Old Liberalism – free trade and support for nonconformists (newly outraged by Balfour's 1902 Education Act) – that had enabled Campbell-Bannerman to rally his party and win the election, not the New Liberalism of social reform. For a while, then, the *Nation* adopted a wait-and-see position.

By the end of 1907 the conclusion seems to have been reached that the government's reform program was not sufficiently ambitious. Two important by-election defeats at the hands of socialists in Colne Valley and Jarrow that summer helped hurry this conclusion.[104] Moreover, the government's timid response to having over half its major bills rejected by the House of Lords raised fresh doubts about its commitment even to those few social measures it had proposed. Name-calling and passing resolutions was no way to muzzle 'Mr. Balfour's poodle.'[105] Thus, by October 1907, Hobson was expressing

102 Nevinson, *Fire of Life*, 214. The best of Hobson's satirical writings for the *Nation* were published pseudonymously in book form under the title *1920: Dips into the Near Future*, 1918 [by 'Lucian']. See also his *The Recording Angel* (1932) for other examples of satire.

103 *The Psychology of Jingoism*, part I, chap. v, 'The Eclipse of Humour'

104 Henry Pelling, *Popular Politics and Society in Late Victorian England* (1968), chap. 8

105 The two major pieces of social legislation rejected by the House of Lords were the education and licensing bills, both aimed at appeasing traditional Liberal allies. The Trades Disputes Act, however, which repealed the Taff Vale judgement, was passed in 1906. The House of Lords, for the moment, was clearly wary of making itself an issue which would help further the alliance between the Liberal and Labour parties, an alliance which in other respects was quickly disintegrating.

concern that the Liberal party was 'doomed to the same sort of impotence as had already befallen Liberalism in most of the Continental countries.' The situation was not hopeless, since an 'advanced guard' was still pushing for reforms, but the bulk of the party lacked 'passion and principle,' their resolve for social reconstruction being weakened either by fears of high taxation and encroachments upon private enterprise or by their being held captive by certain 'spectres and phrases.' This was, Hobson concluded, 'the last chance for English Liberalism.'[106]

In April 1908 Campbell-Bannerman retired from politics and Herbert Asquith succeeded him as Prime Minister. New Liberal hopes were revived. Not that Asquith was a favourite with radicals – his sympathies for imperialist policies were well known. But Asquith's budget of 1907 had favourably impressed the *Nation* and indeed had called forth a series of articles and editorials on Hobsonian economics, designed to buttress the tentative distinction the budget had made between earned and unearned income and to encourage its use of progressive taxation as an instrument of social reform. No doubt even more encouraging to New Liberals were Lloyd George's promotion to Chancellor of the Exchequer and Churchill's ascent to the Board of Trade. A month before his promotion Churchill had written a long letter to the *Nation* in which he supported the journal's position of 'a sober but unflinching Radicalism' and assured its readers that he was 'acutely conscious that political freedom, however precious, is utterly incomplete without a measure at least of social and economic independence.'[107]

Within a year the new Liberal administration had laid much of the foundation of Britain's welfare state, and by the close of 1909 Hobson felt able to write that the government's financial claims to unearned income, combined with its legislation on old age pensions, wage boards, labour exchanges, and small holdings, suggested a 'coherency of purpose, an organic plan of social progress, which implies a new consciousness of Liberal statecraft.'[108]

But the crisis of liberalism was not yet passed. On 30 November 1909, the House of Lords rejected Lloyd George's Peoples' budget which was to pay for the Liberals' 'war against poverty' – and eight dreadnoughts. The budget raised the income tax, super tax, and death duties, and, to the even greater distress of the Lords, it placed a 20 per cent tax on the 'unearned increment' of land whenever it was sold, and a small yearly tax on undeveloped land. This was the first time the Lords had vetoed a finance bill in over 250 years.

---

106 *The Crisis of Liberalism*, 135
107 Reprinted in K. Morgan, *The Age of Lloyd George* (1971) 144-8
108 *The Crisis of Liberalism*, xii (preface dated December 1909)

Needless to say, liberals were incenced, yet at the same time they were also confident, for the battleground had been drawn very much to their liking. As Hobson wrote in the *Nation*:

The House of Lords debate showed us some eighty judge and bottle lords, directors and shareholders of breweries and distilleries, gathered round their chairman to defend their right to batten on the degradation of the people. Several hundred rent-receivers gathered there confederate, to dodge their contributions to the upkeep of the State. ... What a lifting of the veil! These heroes of romances were all out for cash. ... How completely the invaluable asset of romance has been squandered by these weeks of common selfishness may, we think, be tested by the instinctive grin which would appear on the face of the dullest citizen who was invited by Lord Salisbury to accept his description of the House of Lords 'as an independent body ... doing its utmost to interpret and consider the wishes and views of the country.[109]

It was in the fracas that followed the rejection of the Peoples' budget that Hobson's attitude toward the Liberal government began to sour. He sensed a failure of nerve in the Liberal party which prevented it from tackling the forces of reaction head-on. For Hobson this was a matter of momentous consequences. He did not believe that the confrontation with the Lords was an isolated event, but viewed it as the first move by the propertied classes and their political agents to repudiate democratic government now that the popular will had become more radical in its demands. 'The House of Lords,' he wrote, 'only forms the first line of trenches.'[110] The unconstitutionality of the House of Lords' veto of the budget marked the first critical move towards extra-parliamentary action, which was to dog the Liberal government from 1910 onwards and, for some historians, also marked the point at which 'The Strange Death of Liberal England' began.[111]

Interestingly, when Hobson listed the row of trenches to be found behind the House of Lords in the service of reaction, he omitted to mention the army.[112] Yet it was the so-called Curragh Camp mutiny in 1914 that was to

109 'Our Lost Romance,' reprinted in *A Modern Outlook* (1910), 299, 301
110 *The Crisis of Liberalism*, x
111 This is the title of a controversial study by G. Dangerfield, first published in 1935. The best-known opposing view is Trevor Wilson, *The Downfall of the Liberal Party, 1914-1935* (1966). The lack of importance attached by Wilson to the pre-war years is conveyed in the title of his book.
112 See *The Crisis of Liberalism*, x-xi

provide Hobson with the occasion for what is perhaps his most scathing indictment of the forces of reaction, *Traffic in Treason*.

When Asquith placed the issue of the House of Lords before the people in the general elections of January and December 1910, he was, on both occasions, returned with majorities which left him captive of the Irish MPs, if he wished to retain office. The price of their support, of course, was Irish Home Rule. With the passing of the Parliament Act of 1911 restricting the powers of the House of Lords to a right of delay only, the 'first line of trenches' had been breached. The Army, in Hobson's opinion, proved to be the second.

In 1914, the same year the Liberal Home Rule bill supposedly was to become law, after being delayed for two years by the House of Lords, Bonar Law, the Leader of the Conservative-Unionist Party, was implicated in an attempt to get British officers stationed in Ireland to disobey orders, issued by the Liberal government, to curb street demonstrations then being planned by Ulster Unionists. Although Bonar Law's part in this 'mutiny' was clouded by intrigue, such action fitted well with his ominous warning that 'there are things stronger than Parliamentary majorities.' Hobson, anyway, was of no doubt as to his complicity. In *Traffic in Treason* Hobson warned of the portents of this event:

The affair of the Curragh ... presented a clear vision of a great political party drifting rapidly away from its traditional moorings and embarking on an open sea of unconstitutionalism. ... [The] qualified approval of recourse to arms by English Conservative statesmen, indicates a political state of mind ... fraught with ... far-reaching implications. ... That issue, to put the matter plainly, is the question whether it is not possible and desirable for Conservatives to abandon the pretence of submission to the popular will and to fall back upon their control of organised physical force for the protection of [their] rights and privileges. The instinct of rightful rulership has never disappeared from the master-class. ... [The Constitution] was sacred only so long as it would serve their interests. If it will no longer do this, they will have no use for it. It is good only for the scrap-heap. ... What wonder that Conservatism should turn with eager eyes to ... the Army.[113]

The Conservatives' rebellion showed the essential correctness of the New Liberal policy of parliamentary radicalism. This was the lesson Hobson held

113 *Traffic in Treason* (1914) 5, 6, 17, 15. Details of the Curragh mutiny are given in G. Dangerfield, *The Strange Death of Liberal England*, part III, chap. 1.

out to those segments of the working class and those members of the suffragette movement, who were at this time also turning away from parliamentary methods in favour of 'direct action.' Hobson was sympathetic to their predicament and a supporter of their cause. He lectured the National Liberal Club on the fall in real wages that had taken place since 1905 and how the 'spirit of class hostility' had grown 'more conscious' since the workers felt their poverty not only absolutely but also relatively 'in the open face of opportunities which lie beyond their reach.'[114] Likewise, he wrote a number of articles for the *Nation* where he urged that 'feminism moves along sane lines of progress,' and in *Traffic in Treason* his comment on the government's part in inciting suffragette violence was sufficiently sympathetic for Sylvia Pankhurst to draw her readers' attention to it in *The Suffragette Movement*.[115] Nevertheless, Hobson was convinced that ultimately the parliamentary method was more effective than any street demonstration or general strike. Illegal actions played into the hands of the reactionary classes, whereas parliamentary action had the great advantage of delegitimizing the latter's strategies:

[These] uprisings of Socialism, Trade Unionism and Feminism do not in themselves ... explain why the Conservative Party should be abandoning constitutional government in favour of a physical force policy. For illegal disorder can be put down without abrogation of the Constitution. It is because they have now learned, to their surprise and consternation, that under the shelter of the Constitution attacks can be made upon the privileges and the 'rights' of property, that they are preparing to resort to force.[116]

The Liberal government's vacillation in the face of such 'treason' stretched Hobson's allegiance to the Liberal party to the breaking point.

Unless the organized working people of the country in the Labour Party, and their trade unions, can be brought in to stiffen, and if necessary *to direct*, Liberalism, there is little hope of victory. The impotence of the

---

114 'Industrial Unrest,' an address delivered to the National Liberal Club, 15 Jan. 1912
115 The articles are collected in *A Modern Outlook*. It might be added that, whilst most of the opinions expressed in these articles are indeed quite 'modern,' Hobson is unable to resist fully the 'biology is destiny' thesis, especially when discussing the relationship between female liberation and the latest findings of eugenicists. Pankhurst's book (1931) mentions Hobson's support on p. 548.
116 *Traffic in Treason*, 13

existing Liberal Party to face the true requirements of the situation should be manifest.[117]

The break, however, did not come until the middle of the First World War. Curiously, the issues which finally convinced Hobson to leave the Liberal party were essentially ones that offended the old liberal verities rather than the new. The rumour of war had reinforced Hobson's commitment to Cobdenite principles of non-intervention[118] and in the few hectic days between Austria's declaration of war on Serbia and Britain's declaration of war on Germany, he organized along with Graham Wallas, Gilbert Murray, Bertrand Russell, and others, the British Neutrality Committee to campaign against Britain's involvement. Hobson's opposition to the war continued even after the invasion of Belgium, although many of his friends, including Hobhouse, Murray, and the Hammonds, now gave their support to the Liberal government in its prosecution of the war.[119] Hobson attempted to explain his position in a letter he wrote to C.P. Scott on the day Germany declared war on France:

If there is war tomorrow ... our Neutrality Committee will drop that name, and lie low as a watching Conciliation Committee, waiting some opportunity to press for peace. Grey's speech appears to have converted some even of our friends to regard the war as justified. What Grey said about the French defenceless north coast makes it clear we had a real obligation to defend that coast. But that would have been met by accepting Germany's undertaking not to cross the Straits of Dover. When we refused that bargain for neutrality, and insisted further on the preservation of neutrality of Belgium, we virtually made *that* the *casus belli*. This I personally regard as indefensible, though Germany's brutal behaviour to Belgium merits every reprobation.[120]

Clearly Hobson held the Liberal government responsible for turning the war into a general war.

117 Ibid., 62-3 (italics added)
118 See, for example, his pamphlet, *The German Panic* (1913).
119 An excellent account of this split among New Liberals, utilizing a distinction between Cobdenites and Gladstonians, is given in P.F. Clarke, *Liberals and Social Democrats* (1978), chap. 6
120 Reprinted in Trevor Wilson, ed., *The Political Diaries of C.P. Scott 1911-1928* (1970), 94-5

Aside from opposing the government's declaration of war, Hobson was also perturbed by its handling of the war, especially on the domestic front. The government's whittling away at civil liberties, its extension of executive powers, its concessions to war profiteers, and its suspension of the party system and free trade culminated in Hobson's resigning from the Liberal party in the summer of 1916.[121] This was the same year Sir John Simon resigned from Asquith's (Coalition) cabinet in protest over the introduction of the conscription bill. Simon charged that the government was introducing one of the most hateful institutions of Prussian militarism.[122] This was a sentiment Hobson shared. In *Democracy after the War*, a work written shortly after his resignation, Hobson fulminated at length on the growth of militarism and warned that it was striking roots sufficiently deep to outlast the war. The final straw, however, seems to have been the government's agreement, at the Paris conferences of March and June 1916, to join its allies in imposing, or so it appeared to Hobson, a new protectionist order upon the world.[123] In this light Hobson's book *The New Protectionism*, which he hurriedly wrote in 1916 to warn the nation of this impending danger, also may be read as his statement of resignation.[124]

Hobson's departure from the Liberal party was also assisted by the fact that the outbreak of war brought him into closer contact with many of those members of the labour movement who, like him, supported the idea of an early negotiated peace and were concerned about the bad effect the war was having on the conduct of domestic politics. Hobson met these socialists primarily through his association with the Union of Democratic Control (for Foreign Policy). This organization, of which Hobson later became chairman, was originally founded by E.D. Morel and others in 1914, although its doctrinal roots stretched back to the mid-nineteenth century and the philosophies of Richard Cobden and John Bright. The UDC blamed the war on secret diplomacy and sinister business interests, and centred its campaign for a successful peace settlement on five cardinal points: that there should be no transfer of territory without a plebiscite, and no treaty without parliamentary

---

121 Hobson's list of the transgressions of the Liberal (Coalition) government is given in his pamphlet *Forced Labour* (1917).

122 See Chris Cook, *A Short History of the Liberal Party 1900-1976* (1976), 67.

123 *Confessions*, 126

124 The McKenna budget of 1915 already had abandoned free trade for purposes of prosecuting the war. The fact that Hobson did not resign at this time suggests he was trying to distinguish between policies taken by the government for the war effort from those that seemed to foretell a very unliberal future. It was upon the latter issues that he resigned.

sanction; that balance-of-power politics should be replaced by the arbitration of an 'international council'; that there should be a reduction in armaments; and that there should be universal free trade.[125] This last principle was a late addition to the UDC's charter and was introduced largely on Hobson's initiative. Hobson also took a special interest in the proposal for an international council, and like several other members of the UDC he became involved with various League of Nation societies springing up at this time.[126]

It was to the UDC that the Labour party turned when it began to have doubts about the war, a move that was facilitated by the fact that aside from recruiting notable individuals like Bertrand Russell, Norman Angell, and Israel Zangwill, the UDC also sought affiliations among working-class organizations.[127] It was in this way that Hobson discovered he was able to work well alongside delegates from trade unions, co-operative societies, and the ILP (which had opposed the war from the beginning). The UDC thus helped provide him with a springboard from which he was later to join the Labour party.

Much the same service was provided by the 1917 Club – the last of the Lib-Lab organizations – set up after the March revolution in Russia. Kerensky's call for peace 'without annexations or indemnities' heightened demands for a negotiated peace among British liberal and socialist opponents to the war, and the 1917 Club took it upon itself to promote the Russian cause.[128] Most of its members were associated with the rising Labour party and it was these contacts that proved of lasting value to Hobson, since in other respects, as Brailsford has commented, the Russian revolution, which meant 'so much' to Hobson's younger contemporaries, meant 'much less to him.'[129]

At the end of the war Hobson decided to pit himself officially against the Liberal party – both its Coalition and Asquithian variants – by standing as an independent candidate in the December 1918 election. This election was the famous 'coupon election' in which certain Liberal and Conservative candidates were given official endorsement by the Coalition government of Lloyd George and Bonar Law. This was also the first election to be fought on the basis of universal manhood suffrage, although the constituency Hobson chose was fairly well insulated from the levelling effects of the Representation of Peoples Act of February 1918. He stood for a joint-university seat,

125 A.J.P. Taylor, *The Trouble Makers* (1967), 123-4
126 *Confessions*, 106ff
127 Taylor, *The Trouble Makers*, 123. See also Catherine A. Cline, *Recruits to Labour 1914-1931* (1963), chap. I, 'The Break with the Liberal Party.'
128 Cline, *Recruits to Labour*, 17-18
129 *The Life-Work of J.A. Hobson*, 7

whose electorate comprised of the graduates at the universities of Birmingham, Bristol, Leeds, Durham, Liverpool, Manchester, and Sheffield. Two members were to be elected from this constituency and the election was conducted on the basis of a system of proportional representation (single transferable vote). In a four-man fight, Hobson came second on the first ballot, receiving 366 of the total 1,944 votes cast. However, this was not sufficient to secure him election, and on the second ballot, when the votes for the candidate who came last were redistributed according to the voters' second preference, Hobson dropped to third place, behind H.A.L. Fisher, a Coalition Liberal, and Sir William Conway, a Coalition Conservative.[130] These results were reflected throughout the country. The Coalition government of Lloyd George and Bonar Law was returned with a greater majority than even that received by the Liberals in 1906. Hobson could not have chosen a worse time to fight his first (and only) election.

Although opposition to the Great War had helped bring Hobson into an alliance with a large section of the Labour party, it was his disillusionment with the peace that eventually convinced him to take out party membership in 1924. In particular, he was critical of the terms of armistice that Lloyd George had agreed to at Versailles, which he believed made the recovery of Europe a virtual impossibility.[131] As for Lloyd George himself, Hobson now described him as a 'non-principled man,' a 'powerhouse of flickering ideals and evanescent enthusiasms,' for whom politics was 'a game of short range expedients.'[132] Hobson was equally disturbed by the government's failure to make war profiteers pay for the costs of reconstruction at home by way of an imposition of a capital levy.[133] The Labour party seemed much more sympathetic to this kind of appraisal of the post-war situation.

When Hobson actually joined the Labour party, he did so under auspicious circumstances, having at the same time personally advised Ramsay MacDonald to risk forming the first Labour government out of the shambles of an election which had provided neither the Liberals nor the Conservatives with a clear majority of seats.[134] Despite Hobson's long acquaintance with MacDonald and the strong philosophic influence he had exercised over the

---

130 Details taken from F.W.S. Craig, ed., *British Parliamentary Election Results 1918-1949* (1969).
131 See, for example, Hobson's pamphlets, *The Obstacles to Economic Recovery in Europe* (1920) and *The Economics of Reparation* (1921).
132 *Problems of a New World* (1921), 120-1
133 This policy was advocated by Hobson in his book, *Taxation and the New State* (1919).
134 Chris Cook, *The Age of Alignment* (1975), 191

latter around the turn of the century,[135] their relationship was not especially close, although, during the early days of the Rainbow Circle, Hobson was considered a sufficient friend to be named by Margaret Gladstone, MacDonald's fiancée, as someone her father could contact in order to vouch for Ramsay's good character.[136] Certainly during the period of the second Labour government of 1929, Hobson was very critical of MacDonald's economic orthodoxy, claiming that the government's collapse was the result of the 'failure of most of its leaders ... to realize the dangers of a financial situation which lay outside their understanding of politics and economics.'[137] And on a personal note, Hobson also refused a peerage offered to him by MacDonald in 1931.[138]

On the other hand, Hobson was on very friendly terms with H.N. Brailsford, with whom he had worked on the *Nation* and the UDC, and it was possibly Brailsford who, as a leading figure in the ILP, encouraged Hobson to associate with this radical faction of the Labour party. What was especially gratifying to Hobson was not only that he was quickly seconded onto the ILP Advisory Committee on International Relations, but that as the signs of a postwar industrial depression became clearer so the ILP began to take serious interest in his theory of underconsumption. The war had seemed to bear out Hobson's conclusion that the economy could be made to run at full employment provided that measures were taken to sustain consumption demand. Now that in peacetime the level of employment was once more falling, it seemed wise to re-examine Hobson's contention that income redistribution would sustain the rate of consumption as effectively as making war, but without the horrendous consequences.

Hobson's theory of underconsumption was in fact incorporated into the official doctrine of the ILP during the late 1920s. But Hobson first had to compete for attention with C.H. Douglas, another noted underconsumptionist, and founder of the Social Credit movement. A special committee, of which Hobson was a member, was set up in 1921 by the Labour party executive to consider Douglas' proposals. Its report, published in 1922, was not favourable.[139] In addition to participating on this committee, during 1922

135 Cf. Bernard Barker, ed., *Ramsay MacDonald's Political Writings* (1972), 'Introduction,' 37-8
136 Marquand, *Ramsay MacDonald*, 48
137 *Confessions*, 121
138 Lee, 'The Social and Economic Thought of J.A. Hobson,' 179
139 See C.B. Macpherson, *Democracy in Alberta: Social Credit* (1962), 123-4, for a brief description of the political circumstances surrounding this exchange. A useful overview of Douglas' economic doctrines is given in John L. Finlay, *Social Credit* (1972), chap. 5.

Hobson also exchanged views with Douglas in the pages of the *Socialist Review*, an organ of the ILP. Again, Hobson was judged the winner. However, it is reasonable to suppose that Hobson's advantage over Douglas, as far as the ILP was concerned, was not simply a matter of clarity of analysis, but also reflected the fact that it was easier to fit Hobson's theory into the tradition of socialist ideas as to the struggle between workers and capitalists. With certain qualifications, Hobson attributed the lack of effective demand to the exploitation of the worker by the capitalist classes, whereas Douglas was satisfied with the contribution of both worker and industrialist, blaming only the financier for defects in the system. The problem, according to Douglas, was not the maldistribution of income, but its total deficiency, a situation aggravated by the tight money policies of bankers who refused to remedy this deficiency by pumping credit into the economy – hence the need for government or 'social' credit. This blurring of class divisions, however, was not appreciated by the ILP.

In 1924 Hobson was appointed chairman to the Living Wage Committee which had been set up by the National Administrative Council of the ILP to propose a strategy aimed at providing a 'living income for every worker' and an 'end to mass unemployment.' Reporting in 1926 in *The Living Wage*, Hobson, along with his fellow committee members, H.N. Brailsford, A. Creech Jones, and E.F. Wise, recommended that a Labour government should take measures to establish a national minimum wage adequate to meet the needs of a civilized life, and combine this with a scheme for providing family allowances. Further, the committee endorsed the Labour party's policy of nationalizing the mines, railways, and electricity, and added to this list the banks in the hope that the control of credit would help stabilize prices which might otherwise go spiralling upwards once minimum wage legislation was introduced. The committee also recommended that an industrial commission should be set up with powers to reorganize any industry which failed to meet minimum wage requirements. Finally, the committee maintained that its various proposals were knitted together in a logical whole by the need to raise the purchasing power of the mass of the population and urged, in words that bore further testimony to Hobson's influence, that 'the Labour Movement must base itself upon this fact of underconsumption.'[140]

When the report of the Living Wage Committee was incorporated into the ILP's manifesto, *Socialism in Our Time*, and officially endorsed at the 1926 Annual Conference of the ILP, Hobson's influence within the Labour party was at its zenith. Brailsford, for example, believed that 'around this time

140 *The Living Wage* (1926), 9

Hobson was the most respected intellectual influence in the Labour Movement,'[141] an evaluation shared by other contemporary observers of Labour
history, like John Stratchey and Barbara Wootton.[142]

The Labour party leadership, however, refused to adopt the ILP's program.
MacDonald thought it was too radical and would prove to be like 'millstones'
around the parliamentary party's neck.[143] Herbert Morrison and Philip
Snowden expressed similar views, and Beatrice Webb said of the 'living
wage' proposal in particular, that it was 'a combination of conceit and
ignorance.'[144] It was not so much the content of the 'living wage' proposals
that upset MacDonald, for he had long been sympathetic towards Hobson's
views on underconsumption, but the attempt by the left wing of the ILP to
use the document to attack the principle of evolutionary socialism. Brailsford
wrote in the *New Leader* that the object of a 'living wage' campaign was to
'challenge the deadening idea that Socialism can only be established by slow
gradualism over generations of time.'[145] Clifford Allen, who also had been a
member of the Living Wage Committee during its early months, in turn,
spelled out the political corollary as he saw it: 'We shall henceforth reject the
notion that it is the function of democracy to initiate ... Rather it is the business of democracy to check the use of power, after schemes have been sub-
mitted to Parliament.'[146] In short, the ILP should not have to await a popular
mandate in order to act. In this way Hobson's associates on the Living Wage
Committee pushed to have the program accepted as ready for immediate
implementation.

It would seem that Hobson was somewhat disconcerted by this power
struggle within the Labour party and in a private letter to MacDonald he
attempted to distance himself from Brailsford's political tactics:

I was asked as an economist, not as a politician, to join the small committee which drew it up [the 'living wage' report] and am not concerned with
the use which may be made of it in the Labour Party ... In the committee
at an early stage I found some disposition to utilise the minimum wage in
a way that seemed to me dangerous. Its present form is not I think at all
open to such criticism. How far all its proposals are financially practicable I

141 *The Life-Work of J.A. Hobson*, 13
142 Cf. Strachey, *The Nature of Capitalist Crisis* (1935), 43; Wootton, *Plan or No Plan*
     (1934), 124.
143 Cited in Marquand, *Ramsay MacDonald*, 454
144 Cited in R. Skidelsky, *Oswald Mosley* (1975), 151
145 Cited in Marquand, *Ramsay MacDonald*, 453
146 Cited in Robert Dowse, *Left in the Centre* (1966), 133

do not feel sure, but in this country it is necessary to formulate fairly drastic proposals in order to get *anything* done.[147]

Moreover, the 'living wage' report also angered the trade unions. Although Hobson and his fellow committee members had been very careful in their report to argue that the state's regulation of minimum wage levels was not intended to undermine the authority of the trade unions, many unionists were fearful of the committee's conclusion that 'if the rule that wages are the concern of the Trade Unions exclusively, is rigidly followed, it is difficult to feel confident that any general improvement in the level of wages can be secured. It is still more difficult to look forward to the removal of the gross inequalities which obtain at present in the various trades.'[148] As one scholar has noted, the trade unions at this time were 'utterly opposed to state interference in collective bargaining.'[149] It was not surprising therefore, that the 1927 Labour party conference officially endorsed MacDonald's rejection of the ILP program. This was the beginning of an open rift between the ILP and the Labour party, and in 1932 the ILP disaffiliated and thereafter went into irreversible decline.

By 1932 Hobson was well over seventy years old, and he was quickly outliving his friends. Hobhouse had died in 1929. 1932 was especially dismal. At the beginning of the year C.P. Scott died and in the spring Ted Scott, Hobson's son-in-law, was drowned in a tragic boating accident. Four months later Graham Wallas was dead. Hobson's old haunts, his clubs, and his journals were also fast disappearing. The *Nation* group, under Massingham, had disbanded in 1923, with Hobson and his colleagues walking out over what they considered to be the shoddy treatment given their editor by the proprietors.[150] The 1917 Club closed its doors in 1931, when, in a moment noted by Taylor as symbolizing crest-fallen idealism, 'Hobson, withdrawing in protest against the confusion of the accounts, fell heavily downstairs.'[151] The Rainbow Circle had failed to survive the 1920s.

In the last decade of his life Hobson was not politically active. However, he continued to lecture at the South Place Ethical Society and to write books; indeed, what is perhaps his finest piece of synthetic writing, *Wealth and Life*, was written at the beginning of this period. He also rose to defend, once more, his theory of underconsumption, this time from the criticisms of Evan Durbin, a lecturer at the LSE and a rising light in the Labour party along with

147 7 Oct. 1926. Quoted in Marquand, *Ramsay MacDonald*, 455
148 *The Living Wage*, 5
149 Skidelsky, *Oswald Mosley*, 153
150 Cf. Nevinson, *The Fire of Life*, 397ff
151 Taylor, *The Trouble Makers*, 132

his friend Hugh Gaitskell.[152] Hobson also contributed the occasional article
to the *Political Quarterly*, having played a small part in helping launch the
journal in 1929, and to the *New Statesman*, in which he showed great concern with the emergence of fascism in Europe. In a sense, Hobson detected
in the origins of fascism testimony to the failure of his own ideas to gain
sway. He viewed fascism primarily as an authoritarian response to underconsumption crises, in which the capitalist was willing to abide by a 'costly subservience to the totalitarian state,' in order to defend his property and profits
from an even more costly assault by the working class.[153] This, combined
with what fascism revealed as to the 'irrationality and brutality of "civilised"
peoples,' might have left Hobson very pessimistic about the value of his
life-work. However, this was not entirely the case, for in the western demo-
cracies, he saw signs of a 'grudging acquiescence from large ... numbers of
the ... possessing classes' in policies designed to redistribute incomes and to
'equalise the general level of economic welfare.' Hobson attributed this
acquiescence not only to the longer tradition of democracy in Britain and the
United States, for example, as compared with Germany and Italy, but also to
the fact that in the former countries the ruling classes' 'early confidence in
their rights to property' had been effectively shaken by the New Liberals'
appeal to 'reason and justice.'[154] Roosevelt's New Deal was one sign of
this,[155] the publication and response to J.M. Keynes' *General Theory of
Employment, Interest and Money* was another, although in neither case did
Hobson consider the prescription radical enough. Despite this reservation,
however, there was good reason for Hobson to have felt pleased that after
nearly half a century of writing and campaigning, his thinking was still having
an impact. Keynes paid him lengthy tribute in *The General Theory* and,
according to Brailsford, at least one member of Roosevelt's 'Brains Trust,'
which drafted the New Deal, was known to be a Hobsonian.[156]

152 See Hobson and Durbin, 'Underconsumption: An Exposition and a Reply,' *Economica*,
      XIII (1933), 402-27.
153 'Thoughts on Our Present Discontents,' 50. See also the analysis of fascism in *Demo-
      cracy and a Changing Civilisation* (1934) chap. III.
154 'Thoughts on Our Present Discontents,' 47, 53, 54
155 See 'Roosevelt's Triumph,' *Contemporary Review* (Dec. 1936), vol. 150, esp. 653. For
      Hobson's comment on Keynes, see *Property and Improperty* (1937) 56, n. 1, where he
      writes with regard to Keynes' comments on the 'socialisation of investment,' that 'the
      question remains open whether this delicate task can be performed, so long as the
      "ownership of the instruments of production" remain in private hands.'
156 Brailsford, *The Life-Work of J.A. Hobson*, 12. This is possibly a reference to Rexford
      G. Tugwell. For Tugwell's own account of his advocacy of Hobson's ideas on under-
      consumption, see his book *The Democratic Roosevelt* (1969), 254.

Hobson died on 1 April 1940 at his home in Hampstead, London. He was 81 years old. According to an obituary in the *New Statesman*, he died without ever fully appreciating 'how great his own influence was.'[157]

---

157 C. Delisle Burns, 'J.A. Hobson,' *New Statesman*, 6 April 1940

2

Economics and Ethics:
A Human Valuation

1 THE OLD POLITICAL ECONOMY

Science knows no hard facts, absolute laws, or dry reasoning. Everywhere human
selection and arrangements come in. *Rationalism and Humanism*, 29

For Hobson economics was properly a branch of ethics. Consequently he was
both fascinated and appalled by the development of economics as a separate
science. It was a lesson in how men became entrapped within systems of
their own making, by conceiving them 'as mechanical processes, abstracted
and divorced from the wills of men.'[1] This chapter examines Hobson's
analysis of the development of classical economics, and the basis upon which
he sought to challenge its conclusions and substitute for them the ideals of a
'humanist economics.'

Throughout the eighteenth and nineteenth centuries liberal economists
were preoccupied with discovering, refining, and humbling man before the
laws of economics. This humbling was justified on two grounds. First, it was
suggested by Adam Smith and others that man's faculty of reason was too
small to enable him to regulate society on his own terms; therefore it was
better for all concerned that each individual concentrate on his affairs, using
his small dose of reason to calculate his maximum self-interest, and leave
the regulation of society to economic law, activated as 'if by a hidden hand'
behind the backs of men and beyond their control. Smith, of course, had
been optimistic about the benevolence of such a 'law-abiding' economy.
However, as capitalism developed so economics became a more dismal field

1 *Free Thought in the Social Sciences* (1926), 26

of study. It was discovered, in Hobson's words, that Smith's 'simple system' of natural liberty was not so simple as it sounded, and throughout the latter half of the nineteenth century classical economics was exposed to a steady fire of criticism designed to show that it was 'based upon a denial of "real" economic liberty to the vast majority of the population.'[2]

Hobson suggested that classical economics rallied from this assault only by squeezing out 'many of the human qualifications' Smith had attached to his study of economics. In seeking a second line of defence for the laws of economics, Smith's successors had become ever more strident and assertive: economic laws were now transformed into 'iron laws' of wages, population, etc. In large part this was accomplished by drawing tight analogies between the study of economics and the study of natural phenomena. The economist, so it was argued, like the physicist, dealt only in facts. And although an economist might sympathize with the poor, it had to be appreciated that these feelings or values – whether Christian, humanist, or otherwise inspired – had nothing to do with the facts. It was as pointless for man to resist economic laws, as it was for them to complain, say, about the laws of gravity.

Thus by the mid-nineteenth century classical economists felt sufficiently confident in their role as the impartial observers of economic laws to label the radical humanist critique of capitalism mere utopian foolishness. Reflecting on this course of events, Hobson was convinced that:

The real failure of the earlier humanitarian or ethical criticism of the economic system by nineteenth century thinkers was chiefly due to the conviction of businessmen and their economists, that it was as irrelevant to blame the economic system for its admitted barbarities and wastes as it was to blame nature for its greater apparent wastefulness in all her other inorganic and organic processes. It was mere foolishness to suggest that any other economy than that which operated *ought* to have operated.[3]

In contemplating a renewal of the ethical critique of capitalism, Hobson had to re-evaluate the scientific status of classical economics. What is especially interesting about Hobson's approach to this matter is that he managed to reject the goal of a 'value-free' social science, which had dominated the thinking of many scholars around the turn of the century, making strange bed-fellows of liberal and Marxian economists.[4]

2 Ibid., 75
3 *Wealth and Life* (1929), 122
4 Cf. *Free Thought*, 28-9.

In so far as the classical economists' deference to economic laws was a consequence of their depreciation of the role of reason in human conduct, Hobson accused them of misunderstanding their subject matter and taking too static a view of human nature. The classical economists had allowed 'reason' only an instrumental role in human conduct – the calculation of means – whereas Hobson believed that human conduct, if viewed from an evolutionary perspective, revealed that reason had a much more substantive, commanding, and moral role to play:

While ... we may still hold that certain important factors in the operation of the economic system ... are for any immediate purposes to be regarded as fixed and operable by relatively fixed laws, an ever increasing part is played by the intellectual and moral powers of man subject to his changeful purposes, and acting upon 'nature' so as to alter the economic significance of many of those characters that are most fixed. Thus the barriers set against the social control of economic processes by human intelligence and will are continually being weakened.[5]

This interpretation of social progress (for which Hobson found confirmation in the works of L.T. Hobhouse) stood as a challenge to the classical economists' goal of a 'value free' or 'positive' science of economics. By placing the purposefulness of human conduct at the centre of social inquiry, Hobson believed that he had found a way to break down the tight distinction between 'is and ought,' 'fact and value,' upon which the classical economists relied:

Human conduct differs from every other known sort of organic conduct in that the operative units entertain, and are immediately influenced in their activities by advance images of 'the desirable' termed ideals. The drive or urge towards these ideals is an 'ought.' Seeing that these ideals and this feeling of ought ... are more and more potent factors in the economic conduct of today, the disposition to deny the term 'normative' to economic science, or to draw tight limits to its application, is an obstructive procedure which hampers the progress of a social science.[6]

The 'ought' is not something separable and distinct from the 'is'; on the contrary, an 'ought' is everywhere the highest aspect or relation of an 'is.' If a 'fact' has a moral import (as, in strictness, every fact of human signi-

5 *Wealth and Life*, 125
6 Ibid., 125-6

ficance must have ...), that moral import is part of the nature of the fact, and the fact cannot be fully known as a fact without taking it into consideration. We may, of course, institute an inquiry which ignores the 'ought' ... it may often be convenient to pursue this course; but do not let us deceive ourselves into believing that we are investigating all the facts and excluding something which is not fact. This is only another instance of the protean fallacy of individualism, which feigns the existence of separate individuals by abstracting and neglecting the social relations which belong to them and make them what they are. To abstract from any fact those relations of cause and consequence which give it moral significance is to make it less of a fact than it is. ... Ethics do not 'intrude' into economic facts; the same facts are ethical and economic.[7]

The points made here are essential for understanding Hobson's humanist approach to economic matters. To separate facts from values is to grant the former a coercive authority that is not warranted. Contrariwise, the fusion of facts and values serves as a reminder of the human authorship of the social world. As Bernard Porter has pointed out, it was this assertion of the primacy of moral values over impersonal economic ones that provided the basis for Hobson's intellectualist faith.[8] It brought economics within the scope of policy, since man's evolving rationality, his increasing capacity for self-direction, and the attainment of conscious ideals undermined the universality and immutability of the laws of classical economics. In Hobson's estimation, 'social experience' was 'continually presenting "novelties" not wholly explicable by any laws derived from earlier experience in the same field.' These 'novelties' were the 'growing points in human history,' and thus 'of necessity baffle[d] law and prediction.'[9] Classical political economy was able to universalize its laws only by constructing a closed system and pretending history was no more; it then felt justified in ignoring or depreciating broad speculative questions about what ought or might be. A humanist methodology, according to Hobson, would be very different. It would be informed by a 'social ideal constructed to accord with human facts and

7 *The Social Problem* (1901), 66-9
8 *Critics of Empire* (1968), 172
9 *Wealth and Life*, 95. It is important not to misunderstand Hobson here. This was not a plea for 'indeterminism' in social conduct. On the contrary, in his pamphlet, *Rationalism and Humanism* (1933), Hobson made it clear that he considered 'hazard or chance' a very inadequate basis for the 'freedom of the will.' Freedom was to be found in 'self determination,' which required full knowledge of the facts and circumstances. Indeterminism would wreck this freedom.

human possibilities, but transcending existing facts';[10] thus the methodology would incorporate the principle of social change, as befitted its subject matter. Laws of human conduct would be viewed as being historically specific, not universal. No longer would economists be able to give their laws eternal validation under cover of a 'great bluff' about 'human nature being what it is ... etc. etc.'[11]

Hobson also believed that it was the lack of a guiding principle of human valuation in classical economics that caused it to become dangerously overspecialized. Hobson did not doubt that specialization, in itself, was a convenient and fruitful procedure, but the 'abandonment of central intellectual control' meant that there was 'no proper correlation of specialisms,' no 'sound principle of cooperation' underlying and dominating the divisions of studies, so as to maintain 'the supremacy of the unity and harmony of the whole process.'[12] Consequently, economics became insulated from the disturbing influence of other studies of social life. It was not surprising, therefore, that on economic matters economists could easily delude themselves into believing that their word was law. Moreover, Hobson contended that this specialization added to the economists' insensitivity to moral appeals, because it turned their science into an instrument of self-alienation:

The reaction of over-specialism upon the student is closely analogous to its effects upon the industrial worker; by peering incessantly into one little group of facts, he blunts his intelligence and injures the focus of his mental eyesight. His abandonment of the wider survey of knowledge ... destroys his intellectual judgment. Every bit of new knowledge needs to be assayed by submission to the touchstone of the Universal before its value can be ascertained. ... The over-specialist has let slip the standard of knowledge, and is at the mercy of all sorts of private superstitions and illusions. ... Man is the measure of all things, and the specialist who has made himself less than a man can measure nothing.[13]

Hobson's final attempt to undermine the economists' confidence in the impartiality of his science was to show that, even though the economist might claim to be disinterested in the moral import of the facts he studied, this did not make economics 'value-free'; it merely left those values unexamined. Thus, in reply to the 'devotee of an inductive social science,' who would

10 *The Social Problem*, 66
11 *Problems of a New World* (1921), 258
12 *The Crisis of Liberalism* (1909), 265-6
13 *The Social Problem*, 233-4

claim that to impart '*a priori* ethics or teleology' into a description of economics is 'illicit,' Hobson suggested that:

> This strict ruling out of *à priorism* is quite untenable. The first and simplest step in every 'inductive science' is directed *à priori*; no collection and ordering of crude facts is possible without importing from outside some principles of collection and order which embody the objects or ends of the process of investigation in a hypothetical way. ... [This] 'end' [is] hidden, doubtless, as a conscious motive for the detailed student buried in his tiny group of facts, but none the less ... [it permeates] the whole process with 'teleology'. ... There is no independence of inductive method; induction always rests on the support of principles derived *à priori*.[14]

To assert that economic science was value-free was the same thing as to advocate a policy of 'moral emasculation.'[15]

In conclusion, it is important to stress that Hobson did not consider his ethical critique of the classical economists' faith in economic law to be 'anti-science.' Rather, he saw his stress on human values as a corrective to the 'crude realism' of the older economics, which dealt only with facts that were 'hard and dead';[16] his aim was to bring a 'fuller realism' to scientific study, by emphasizing that '*so far as the selection, valuation and utilisation of "realities" go, Man is the maker of the Universe.*'[17] Science was to be vitalized by an appreciation of the emergent powers of man to shape his own ends.

2 WELFARE ECONOMICS:
THE APPLICATION OF A HUMAN SCIENTIFIC CALCULUS

Ruskin was speaking not in terms of sentiment but of science when he said, 'There is no wealth but life.' *Rationalisation and Unemployment*, 107

It has been shown that Hobson's questioning of the premises and method of classical economics was based on his view of man as a purposeful actor in the world, continuously remaking that world and changing the potential of his own life accordingly. Thus, whereas he envisaged 'an actively changing human nature, with its changing activities,'[18] the 'laws of industry, as con-

14 Ibid., 65
15 Ibid., 67
16 *The Crisis of Liberalism*, 275
17 Ibid., 273 (emphasis added)
18 *Wealth and Life*, xxiv

ceived and formulated by the makers of Classical Political Economy,' were fixed upon a 'conception of a great mechanical system ... abstracted and divorced from the wills of men.'[19] In fine, classical economics was the domain of reified concepts.

It would seem almost a natural corollary from this for Hobson to go on to formulate his standard of human valuation in terms of the self realization of the subject, an idea that had been made familiar to liberals through the works of T.H. Green. But in fact he found this conception vague and suggested that Green and others 'inevitably' slipped into the 'language of utility' whenever they were 'confronted with a practical issue of conduct.'[20] What Hobson appears to have meant by this is that ultimately reliance had to be placed on some calculus of costs and benefits in order to evaluate proposals for social reform. Hobson, therefore, chose to retain the concept of utility, while at the same time revising orthodox Benthamite utilitarianism, so as better to fit it for the task of providing a 'human valuation' of social conduct.

Hobson considered Benthamism (which provided the underpinnings of classical economics from Ricardo onwards) inadequate in this regard, for a variety of reasons. First, he judged its 'hard-shell' rationalism untenable in the light of the discoveries of 'modern psychology.' The urge to act was not immediately determined by the quest for pleasure, as had been supposed, but was largely instinctive. Pleasure could no longer be taken as a person's 'necessary motive, still less his accepted standard of conduct.' It had to be understood as an 'added incentive' rather than as an 'original urge.'[21] Hobson suggested, for example – and as will be shown, the example was crucial to his own theory – that an act of self-sacrifice should be viewed as an instinctive urge in its own right, to be evaluated on the basis of its service to the good of the species. There was little merit to the utilitarian argument that such acts were merely exceptional ways of pursuing pleasure and avoiding pain (e.g., the pain of being called a coward or a weakling). To suggest this, in Hobson's opinion, was simply to 'beg the question by identifying the 'pleasant' with the 'preferable.'[22] Hobson did not elaborate but it seems clear that he was suggesting that Benthamism provided no 'criteria of falsification,' to borrow Karl Popper's famous phrase. In other words, Bentham was prevented by his very logic from recognizing exceptions to his rule.

Although Hobson demoted pleasure from the sovereign position Bentham had ascribed to it, thereby allowing other motivations into his calculus, he

19 *Free Thought*, 26
20 *The Social Problem*, 64; see also 5
21 *Free Thought*, 167-8
22 Ibid., 167-8

nevertheless refused to disassociate action from pleasure altogether. Thus, in commenting on Veblen's more radical critique of this aspect of utilitarianism, Hobson cautioned that 'the denial of such conscious satisfaction as a motive must lead to the doctrine of behaviourism,' and this he found objectionable.[23] Despite his objections to Bentham's presentation of hedonism as an empirical or descriptive proposition, Hobson clearly believed that pleasure had its place as part of an ethical ideal.

Closely related to this argument was Hobson's criticism of the Benthamite calculus for its 'separatist approach' to questions of human welfare, that is, its assumption that the general happiness was merely the composite or aggregate of each individual's happiness. There is a vital distinction, according to Hobson, between an individual's interest, when that individual is considered apart from his fellows, and his interest as a member of society. It follows that the good of 'the whole' may be quite different from the good of the sum of its separate parts. There had been, of course, a collectivist aspect also to Bentham's doctrine. In making a distinction between the motive and the consequences of individual action, Bentham had allowed that various forms of sanction could be used by legislators to ensure that these actions did not create more displeasure for others than the pleasure attained by the individual carrying out the action. Yet, that 'collective' none the less was viewed as being composed of individuals motivated solely by the principle of self-preference. And since the legislators, who were to redirect the activities of the rest of society so as to promote the greatest happiness, were also individuals of this type, Bentham was left with the problem of determining why these legislators should feel obliged to promote the general happiness rather than rule in their own self-interest.[24] In Hobson's opinion the answer to this quandary would not be discovered until it was admitted that men were essentially social creatures animated by social instincts capable of disciplining egoism for the 'good of the whole.' This transformative power of sociality was missed by Bentham because he rooted his calculus in the activities of supposedly *discrete* individuals. Consequently, he failed to perceive that 'aggregating' these individual interests, bringing them together, so to speak, had the effect of transforming their character by activating the social instincts; and this, in turn, resulted in an 'organic whole,' the general interest of which was

23 *Veblen* (1936), 50
24 One answer Bentham (and James Mill) discovered was the mechanism of representative democracy. Subjects were to protect themselves from misrule by exercising their franchise as a veto power. But in a sense this only pushes the problem a step further back: why would rulers want to rule under these conditions? And what motivates the social reformer to introduce a system of representative democracy in the first place?

different from the sum of the particular interests of the separate parts. In subsequent chapters it will be shown that Hobson's 'organic calculus' provided him with a fruitful basis for criticizing what he considered to be the 'fallacy of composition' in both liberal economics and politics.

Finally, Hobson criticized conventional utilitarianism for failing to develop a gradation of values and therefore being unable or unwilling to confront the possibility of a distinction between 'the actually desired ... and the desirable, between what people want and what they ought to want, if they knew their true interests,' a distinction to which Hobson added the complication, as befitted his dynamic view of human nature, that 'the desirable [was] itself a moving object.'[25] In this light, Hobson criticized utilitarianism for condoning selfish and materialistic behaviour, and suggested instead that the highest values (i.e., the desirable) were those which stressed both the 'enrichment of self involving the whole personality,' and the enrichment of 'personality through the largest measure of sociality.'[26] Hobson grounded this assertion in the contemporary findings of biology:

No agreed decision is, perhaps, possible as to the hierarchy of values. But I ... hazard a criterion which is ultimately based upon the 'racial' or 'specific' trend of organic evolution. If Nature makes so much nisus (directive energy) towards the preservation and growth of a species, and if social coöeration plays the distinctive part it seems to do in human survival, then it may be argued that the highest value attaches to the conduct and the emotions which sustain society in the elaborate structure it has attained, and assist it to further useful modes of cooperation.[27]

Hobson further insisted that these 'complexes of values' were not to be regarded merely 'as forms of a single value.' They expressed 'differences in kind, not in quantity'; a preference for 'one way of living' or 'one group of values [as] better' and not merely 'bigger' than another.[28] Hobson therefore rejected the Benthamite calculus as inadequate because it dealt only with quantitative differences.

Hobson's commitment to the notion of a hierarchy of values, as will be shown in more detail later, also led him to break with orthodox utilitarianism by stressing the heuristic function of democracy, rather than its protective

25 *Free Thought*, 171
26 *Wealth and Life*, 72, 73
27 Ibid., 73
28 Ibid., 71

function.[29] Mass participation in politics was necessary in order to educate individuals in the fact and spirit of co-operation and thereby move them up the scale of values. For similar reasons Hobson reversed the usual priority given by the utilitarians to the production of material wealth and argued instead that leisure time was of first importance for the qualitative improvement of mankind.

Hobson was aware that in forwarding this critique of conventional utilitarianism he was covering much the same ground earlier traversed by J.S. Mill, noting that Mill's 'most explicitly ethical treatise, 'Utilitarianism,' virtually abandoned the Benthamite calculus of pleasures and pains by its admission of distinctions in the quality of pleasures.'[30] However, the fact that Hobson utilized the findings of contemporary naturalists like Kropotkin, Fabre, and Maeterlinck to undermine the hedonistic assumptions of Bentham's calculus, whereas Mill had looked to the teachings of Jesus of Nazareth for the completion of the 'spirit of the ethics of utility,'[31] gave rise to significant differences in their hierarchy of values. In particular, Hobson's hierarchy was much less puritanical than was Mill's. Thus he wrote, no doubt with Mill in mind, that,

There are those to whom this vision of a higher life signifies an evident subordination and depreciation of the simpler animal desires and the activities that gratify them, in favour of the cultivation of intellectual and spiritual goods. ... The hierarchy of values for which these votaries of the higher life contend, will be defended on the ... ground that, whereas the body is with us all and always, ... the life of the mind in its higher levels is only known to an enlightened few. ... [An] aristocracy of culture [is] thus ... designated for the delicate task of translating ... 'human welfare' into a changing hierarchy of values, in which things of the body and the mind take their appropriate places. But this is less convincing than appears at first sight. ... Common sense has always distrusted, perhaps with an instinctive wisdom, the withdrawn life of the ascetic and the scholar. ... Such mistrust cannot be rightly dismissed as mere ignorance and superstition. The common sense which it expresses may in this, as in other matters, have survival value. For the exclusive possessors of intellectual values must be accredited with a disposition to overrate them and to

29 Cf. chap. 7, sec. 1.
30 'John Stuart Mill,' *The Speaker*, 26 May 1906, 178
31 'Utilitarianism,' in *Utilitarianism, On Liberty and Considerations on Representative Government* (Everyman's Library ed., 1910), 16

underrate the material and popular values in forming their conception of a desirable life.[32]

This opinion did not lead Hobson to deny the need for enlightened leadership, but it did make him much more reluctant than Mill to assign this role to an élite of 'spiritually minded' intellectuals and other noble characters; the common man had something to contribute in his own right.

So far, Hobson's calculus of human welfare has been examined mainly in negative terms, by showing those ways in which it was not like Bentham's calculus. What it meant in more positive terms is best seen by considering Hobson's human valuation of work and consumption. Here the analysis focuses on Hobson's first major book on welfare economics, *Work and Wealth* (1914).

In Hobson's opinion classical economics had introduced a false antithesis into its doctrine of value by conceiving production as 'a process which rolls up costs into commodities' and 'consumption as a process that unrolls them into utilities.' Supply was said to be determined by the costs of production and demand by the satisfaction the product would give the consumer; the play of supply and demand, therefore, determined the value of the product. The key to Hobson's human valuation of work and wealth is his rejection of this classical assignment of costs and utilities:

An organic interpretation of industry cannot accept this mode of conceiving the productive and consumptive functions. Considerations of the organic origins of industry lend no support to the assumption that production is all 'cost' and no 'utility,' consumption all 'utility' and no 'cost.' On the contrary, in our human analysis of economic processes we shall rather expect to find costs and utilities, alike in their sense of pains and pleasures and of organic losses and organic gains, commingled in various degrees in all productive and consumptive processes.[33]

In order to find out roughly the human value of a stock of material wealth, it was necessary to know three things regarding its cost: '(1) the quality and kind of the various human efforts [i.e., physical and mental] involved; (2) the capacities of the human beings who give out these efforts; (3) the distribution of the effort among those who give it out.' Likewise it was necessary

32 *Wealth and Life*, xxiv-xxv; see also 60-4
33 *Work and Wealth*, 34

to know three things about its consumption: '(1) the quality and kind of satisfaction or utility yielded by the 'economic utility' that is sold to consumers; (2) the capacities of the consumers who get this economic utility; (3) the distribution of the economic utility among the consuming public.'[34] This was the basis of Hobson's welfare economics in a nutshell.

Turning first to the realm of production, Hobson determined that productive capacities could be divided into seven classes: art, invention, professional service, organization, management, labour, saving. Each of these activities varied in the amount of human cost and satisfaction incurred, depending on the conditions of work, the amount of time laboured, etc. But the major factor involved in grading the various sorts of human productive effort was the amount of 'creative and imitative character they seem to possess.'[35] Hobson was indebted to the French sociologist, M. Tarde, for this insight, although he also mentioned Morris' and Ruskin's indictment of the degrading effects of the division of labour on human character.[36] Indeed, so impressed was Hobson with the costs of imitative work that one scholar has concluded that his 'distaste for routine work amounted to a phobia.'[37]

Art was the most creative kind of work because it involved 'the freest expression of personality.' The net human cost of artistic work, therefore, was virtually nil: such work was 'varied, interesting and pleasurable' and consequently improved rather than depreciated the quality of life of the performer.[38] Routine specialized work, on the other hand, was dull, mechanical, and degrading. It denied the worker the 'opportunity for the exercise of his other productive faculties' and 'overtaxed' him in the 'servile repetition' of the 'single faculty that [was] employed.'[39] Imitative work bore a heavy human cost.

Having established these 'ideal types' Hobson then proceeded to use them as a yardstick for evaluating the reality of work under capitalism. Overall he detected an element of art in each of his various classifications of work. However, although no kind of work was totally 'alienating,' there were very

34 Ibid., 36
35 Ibid., 43
36 Ibid., 40, 62
37 H.B. Davis, 'Hobson and Human Welfare,' *Science and Society*, vol. 21 (1957), 304.
Along the same lines it has been suggested that 'perhaps Hobson saw Hobson in every one of [the] jobs he analysed.' P. Newman, *The Development of Economic Thought* (1952), 325. As will become evident, however, these comments are not entirely accurate since Hobson did believe that even routine work had some positive utility.
38 *Work and Wealth*, 44
39 Ibid., 62

significant differences in the degree to which creativity was blended with routine.

At the higher levels of management the employee was often called upon to exercise his personal skill, initiative, and judgement. Consequently, in these jobs there tended to be a large net sum of utility over cost. A certain discrimination was required, however, even when comparing these most favoured occupations. The manager of a 'well established business in staple trade' was not required to exercise 'much in the way of high intellectual skill, imagination or exploit,' and hence his work involved a 'good deal of dull routine,' carrying a 'distinct cost in mental wear and tear.' Financial speculators, on the other hand, had one of the best jobs capitalism had to offer, entailing, as it did, 'the finest business instincts, the most rapid, accurate, and complex powers of inference and prophecy, the best balance of audacity and caution, the largest and best informed imagination.'[40]

The situation was very different at the lower levels of white-collar work and factory labour. White-collar work, the work of clerks, nurses, secretaries, shop assistants, and others, although often quite varied in itself, was for the most part robbed of its artistic element, because the work was carried out under another's orders.

The work of a private secretary, clerk or other subordinate to a professional man or high official, may contain much ... novelty in detail or even in kind. ... But the subordinate does not reap these elements of personal interest because the initiation of the process does not rest with him. The essentials of the work are imposed upon him by the intellect and will of another: neither the design nor the mode of execution is his own. Though, therefore, his work may not consist in mere routine ... the fact that it is not properly 'his' work, the expression of 'his' personality, deprives it of all qualities of creation ... save such fragments as adhere to the details that are 'left to him.'[41]

This statement represents an important elaboration of Hobson's earlier criteria for evaluating the alienating aspects of work. The assessment had to be based not only on the technical nature of the job itself, but also on the degree of workers' participation allowed. Indeed in the case cited, the degree of participation would seem to be the weightier criterion, although, as will be shown, Hobson was more certain that lack of participation could lower the

40 Ibid., 55, 57
41 Ibid., 53

benefit to be gained from an otherwise rewarding task than he was of the contrary proposition, viz. that an unrewarding job could be made satisfying through the practice of workers' participation.

The heaviest 'human costs' were born by the ordinary 'machine tender in a factory.'[42] Not only was he subordinate, but the technical nature of his work was exceedingly monotonous. Hobson pointed to various studies which indicated the extent of the factory workers' physical and mental fatigue, and how these contributed to industrial accidents and nervous disorders. The high cost of routine work was also evident in the factory hands' weakness for alcohol and 'other sensational excesses,' the 'normal reactions of a lowered morale.'[43]

Again, a certain discrimination was required when evaluating the alienating effects of factory labour. For example, Hobson considered that, in so far as the worker was responsible for checking and regulating his machine, then his skills resembled those of an engineer and contained an element of creativity.[44] Indeed, even the most routine labour could not be seen as all cost and sacrifice; the identification of repetition and human costs, in Hobson's opinion, could 'not be pressed into a general law.' Reflection showed that 'healthy organic life permits, indeed requires, a certain admixture of routine ... with its more creative functions.'[45] The crux of the problem was really one of the duration rather than specialisation: 'it is only when repetition is extended so far as to engage too large a share of the time and energy of a human being that it involves a cost.'[46] Hence the importance of reforms designed to shorten the working day.

It seemed evident to Hobson that the human costs of repetitive work were greatest during the later hours of the working day. To shorten work hours, therefore, would more than proportionately diminish these costs. Provided that precautions were taken to ensure that a reduction in labour time was not accompanied by a speeding-up of the work process, the labourer would have sufficient energy to use his leisure time not only to replenish his labour power but also to 'exercise neglected faculties' and to 'cultivate neglected tastes.' Leisure time could then provide a 'counterpoise to specialisation' at the work-place.[47]

42 Ibid., 62
43 Ibid., 70
44 Cf. 'Character and Society,' in P. Parker, ed., *Character and Life* (1912), 86.
45 *Work and Wealth*, 83
46 Ibid., 84
47 Ibid., 233, 237

Hobson's remarks on the importance of leisure time indicate a certain ambivalence in his approach to the human costs of work. As has been shown, his basic objection to the classical economists' analysis of labour was that they assumed labour to be burdensome and costly. Hobson's own analysis suggested that this was not necessarily the case. Some labour under capitalism was creative. Moreover, even labour that was toilsome could be made more fulfilling, given certain reforms in the production process. However, the contrast of labour with leisure would seem to suggest that this de-alienization of labour could proceed only so far; it could not be wholly eliminated. A certain amount of disagreeable labour was unavoidable, for the division and routinization of labour was to some extent an inescapable condition of social life. Hobson's analysis, therefore, falls somewhere between the classical economist's position that alienation is inevitable and the Marxian position that it can be eradicated. While he trusted that individuals might willingly come to accept this work out of a 'sense of social service,'[48] he also felt compelled to look outside the productive sphere for alternate sources of contentment, placing great faith in the fact that capitalism 'for the first time in history' had developed a level of material wealth sufficient to provide a new fund of leisure time 'not for a little class but for whole peoples.'[49] But Hobson did not make clear the balance between his argument that labour was a means of self-expression and his concession to the classical economists' argument that labour was intrinsically toilsome and costly.

Having ascertained the kinds of human effort expended in work and the conditions under which this work was done, Hobson gave consideration to the manner in which this workload was distributed. A human valuation of work required that human costs be economized 'by distributing the burden proportionately to the power to bear it':

In endeavouring to estimate the human costs of labour in terms of physical wear and tear and the conscious pains and penalties entailed by the conditions under which many industrial processes are carried on ... it is evident that a given strain upon muscles and nerves over a period of time will vary greatly, both in the organic cost and in the conscious pain which it entails, according to the strength and endurance, nervous structure, physical and moral sensitiveness, of the different sorts of workers. Indeed, a given output of productive energy will evidently entail a different human

48 Ibid., 88
49 Ibid., 237

cost in every person called upon to give it out: for every difference of
strength, skill, capacity and character must to some extent affect the
organic burden of the task.[50]

Obviously such considerations as these would involve an extremely complex system of job evaluation. In fact, Hobson never developed a set of criteria sufficiently discriminatory positively to apply this principle, but had to
content himself with its use as a piece of negative critique.

Hobson's analysis of the human utility of consumption proceeded along
the same lines. He began by criticizing the classical economists for wrongly
identifying the human utility of an article or service with its economic utility;
simply because an item sold, this was no proof of its usefulness. To begin
with, there were many goods which possessed use value but little or no sale
value; a distinction that had been often noted in the past but one rarely
examined further since the classical economists were primarily interested in
marketable goods. It was thus possible for a nation to be rich in utilities but
have this wealth untallied in the ledgers of the economists. This 'grave fallacy' in the political economists' account of wealth was best exhibited in the
case of 'free goods':

'Those goods are "free" [said J.S. Mill], which are not appropriated and
are afforded by nature without requiring the effort of man.' Air, sunshine,
scenery – so far as they are accessible – certain fragments of land, are still
'free.' Should we not be disposed to say that the more of these free goods
a nation has, the wealthier it is, *caeteris paribus?* Yet the poorer it is,
according to political economy. For when a free good ceases to be free,
and to serve the use and enjoyment of all, and becomes private property,
it ranks for the first time as wealth and swells the national assets![51]

However, if there were goods possessing use value, but no exchange
value, which did not figure in 'ordinary economic book-keeping,' the converse was also true. There were many marketable goods which possessed
little or no use value, indeed were positively noxious; yet these were entered
on the credit side of the ledger. Here the orthodox economist's view was
equally shallow, for he identified use value by the act of purchase, on the
assumption that no good would be bought unless it had some utility for the
consumer. His interest in the consumer, however, went no further than the

shop counter. These noxious products, in Hobson's opinion, should not have been classified as wealth but as 'illth' (a term coined by Ruskin),[52] so as to recognize the possibility of a nation's material wealth expanding while its 'human wealth' declined.

It followed that the market valuation of a product was not trustworthy as a guide to its human worth. In order to determine the quality and kind of human utility yielded by a product, it was essential to refer to a standard which measured the 'life-sustaining and life-improving qualities' of a product.[53] To give substance to this criterion (for which he was indebted to Ruskin), Hobson attempted to sketch the development of the arts of consumption, and in doing so he once more utilized the distinction between creation and imitation.

Hobson maintained that in the early stages of evolution it was inevitable that the standard of consumption was set in terms of its survival value. Primitive man's instincts guided him in the selection of the basic necessities of his maintenance and so long as what he consumed was dictated by these 'strong definite needs' there was 'little scope for grave errors and waste.' Consequently, there were 'substantial guarantees for the organic [i.e., human] utility of most articles which enter[ed] the primitive standard of consumption.'[54]

However, man not only lived to exist but to advance his life by adapting 'the changing environment to his vital purposes.' In this way he evolved 'new needs and new modes of satisfying old needs';[55] but he also lost his immunity from serious error in forming a standard of consumption. For what he wasted now was his 'potential' and this pressed on him much less closely than did the issue of his biological survival:

In the earlier evolution of wants, when changes, alike of ways of living and ways of work, are few and slow and have a close bearing on survival, a standard of consumption will have a very high organic value. But when man passes into a more progressive era ... we seem to lose the earlier guarantees of organic utility ... and a standard of civilised human life contains ever larger and more numerous elements which carry little or no 'survival value,' the possibilities of error and of disutility appear to multiply.[56]

---

52 *Work and Wealth*, 106
53 *The Social Problem*, 48
54 *Work and Wealth*, 115
55 Ibid., 116
56 Ibid., 117

In this way Hobson drew a distinction between consumption needs that were urgent and had to be attended to first – the 'survival needs' – and those that followed. The latter might be more important in an ontological sense, but the former were more basic. As will be shown later, Hobson believed that this temporal ordering of needs had an important bearing on the approach to social reform.

However, Hobson was wary of drawing a sharp distinction between physiological and cultural needs. Such a distinction was too abstract, the dichotomy too forced, even for primitive societies. The savages' selection of foods was a case in point: it was part instinctive, part determined by the given physical environment, but it was also in part guided 'through some early conscious cunning of selection and of cultivation' which served to 'improve and increase the supplies.'[57] The biological and cultural dimension of needs, therefore, were mixed: even the savage experimented, albeit on a simple and restricted empirical basis. What was required, then, was a means by which to determine when such experimentation was a legitimate progressive extension of man's needs, and when it falsified and perverted those needs, so that their realization did not lead to an improvement in the quality of human life. Hobson's aim was not so much to draw a conceptual distinction between biological and other needs, or between natural and artificial needs, as other theorists had done by utilizing some fixed, ahistorical notion of what constitutes basic human nature,[58] but to show the difference between needs that are genuinely expressed and arrived at, and those superimposed on the individual at the behest of profit-seeking businessmen.

It was in an attempt to meet this requirement that Hobson reverted to his distinction between creation and imitation. He utilized this distinction to show the difference between the way in which new wants were discovered and assimilated in primitive societies, as compared with capitalist societies. Hobson suggested that in primitive societies, though consumption patterns were mostly customary, such individual experimentation in consumables as did take place was largely the result of chance, and that the results of these experiments were usually adopted or imitated by other members of the tribe 'on their merits' i.e., according to whether the properties of the item in question delivered the satisfaction promised. It was this condition of experimentation – the absence of ulterior motive – which provided the grounds for recognizing the naturalness of the need expressed. Thus, in referring to the consumption of sugar-cane, tobacco, and cinchona bark (a source of quinine) by primitive tribes, Hobson contended that:

---

57 Ibid., 114
58 See, for example, Hobson's comment on the work of Edward Carpenter, ibid., 118.

Such accretions to a standard of consumption may be regarded as possessing guarantees of utility or safeguards against strong positive disutility in their method of adoption. They have grown into the conventional standard 'on their merits.' Those 'merits' may indeed be variously estimated from the 'organic' standpoint. Quinine has high organic virtue ... while ... tobacco may [have] ... considerable organic demerits. But both the discovery and propagation have been in all these cases 'natural' and 'reasonable' processes, in the plain ordinary acceptation of these terms. Some actual utility has been discovered and recognised, and new articles thus incorporated in a standard of consumption ... have at any rate satisfied a preliminary test of organic welfare.[59]

Despite the reservations in this statement regarding the organic utility of tobacco, it is clear from the rest of Hobson's analysis that he assumed that needs and organic utility tended to converge under conditions of free experimentation. He did not, however, attempt to prove this correlation positively. Instead he focused on the negative case, namely that needs became perverted under the domination of capitalism.

With the emergence of capitalism it seemed to Hobson that a certain amount of falsification of human needs had been built into the system. This was primarily the result of two factors. First, capitalists produced in response to profit rather than needs. In order to make sales, the capitalist would often attempt to stimulate 'new wasteful modes of conventional consumption' by *needlessly* duplicating articles already accepted as having some human utility.[60] Consequently, capitalism had intensified 'the arts of adulteration and of advertising' in an attempt to palm off false substitutes on the public with the result that 'in a commercial society every standard of class comfort [was] certain to contain large ingredients of useless or noxious consumption.' In other words, under capitalism, creative experiments in consumption were frequently 'vitiated by an extraneous motive.'[61]

Capitalism's second detrimental effect on the standard of consumption was the outcome of its breaking down the cultural barriers between classes. Utilizing Veblen's findings in *The Theory of the Leisure Class*, Hobson showed that the rich had always valued their goods not merely according to their utility but also in terms of the prestige they conferred. Prior to capitalism, the lower classes had only stood in awe of such obstentation, but with

59 Ibid., 131. In Hobson's other major work on welfare economics, *Wealth and Life*, these reservations are given fresh emphasis and the role of the expert is reconsidered, but not in a fashion which fundamentally alters his analysis. See *Wealth and Life*, part 1, chap. IV.
60 *Work and Wealth*, 139
61 Ibid., 133, 131

the mass production of cheap substitutes for luxurious articles it was now possible for the poorer classes actively to imitate the consumption habits of their 'betters.' But this had the damaging effect of adding to the confusion between the actual properties of an item of consumption and the satisfaction associated with it: commodities now carried a host of false promises. Imitation was no longer based upon the merits of the case, but was converted by the authority and prestige of the ruling class into a snobbish imitation, both wasteful and futile. In this way not only did large elements of disutility enter into the standard of consumption of the masses, but that standard itself was perverted. The lower classes were in fact trying to identify, through their purchase of status goods, with the lifestyle of a parasitic and flatulent ruling class:

The actual expenditure of the income of every class in [modern industrialized] ... countries is very largely determined, not by organic needs, but by imitation of the conventional consumption of the class immediately above in income or in social esteem. ... Now even if it were a real aristocracy, a company of the best, it by no means follows that a standard of living good for them would be equally good for other social grades. ... But where the whole forces of prestige and imitation are set on a sham aristocracy ... incalculable damage and waste may ensue. For the defects in the standard of the upper few will, by imitation, be magnified as well as multiplied in the lower standards of the many. ... [For example], if the inconvenience of decorative dress is bad for rich women, who live a life of ease and leisure, its imitation by the active housewives of the middle, and the women workers of the lower classes, inflicts a graver disutility. For the waste of income is more injurious and the physical impediments to liberty of movement are more onerous.[62]

Hobson concluded that, overall, capitalism was perhaps unique in its power to corrupt both the creative and the imitative aspects of consumption behaviour.

Hobson's observations regarding the possibility of false standards also makes it clear that for him the evaluation of the 'life-improving' qualities of a product involved more than an examination of its intrinsic worth. Human utility also varied according to distribution. The ruling class was debauched in large part because the quantity of articles they could purchase made them indifferent to the utility of things:

62 Ibid., 140-1

Food will vary in true utility from infinity to a minus quantity according as it goes to feed a starving person or a glutton. Estimating the whole bread supply according to human 'utility' it is evident that, while the first portion of the supply has an infinite value, the last portion has no value, since servants throw it into dustbins.[63]

By the time of Hobson's writing, neoclassical economists, especially Marshall and Jevons, had already developed an analysis of demand schedules based on this notion of diminishing marginal utility and, later, welfare economists from within the same school, like A.C. Pigou, argued for a redistribution of income on this basis. Hobson's remarks here may be considered an early anticipation of this line of argument, although it should also be noted that he criticized Jevons' marginalism for being too simplistic in its mode of calculus. He similarly condemned Pigou's welfare economics for failing to 'go beyond existing standards' of the desirable; for using the measuring rod of money; and for neglecting to discuss the utilities of production along with consumption.[64]

Hobson's third and final criterion for evaluating the human utility of an article of consumption was to relate it to the capacity of the consumer who received it:

In order to ascertain the real 'utility' contained in a stock of commodities, we must know not merely how they are to be distributed, but what kind of persons they are who will consume them. None of the higher or more refined kinds of modern commodities would have any 'value' for a barbarous race, however rightly distributed. You may increase the wealth of a nation far more effectively by educating the consumer than by increasing the efficiency of the producer. All true education raises value by increasing the vital service to be got out of something. This common-place is often overlooked by political economy.[65]

Hobson illustrated his point by suggesting that a painting valued in money terms at £1000, if bought by a 'vulgar plutocrat' for his private gallery, could be written off as illth, since it only served to feed 'certain evil propensities of greed and ostentation.' But if it was located in a public gallery, where the people had been educated and endowed with a sense of beauty, then a value

63 *The Social Problem*, 49
64 Hobson discussed Pigou's book, *The Economics of Welfare* in *Free Thought*, 99-105
65 *The Social Problem*, 49

would be imparted to the picture which was 'incalculably great,' since it was now a 'formative influence on national character.'[66]

Hobson's analysis of the human utility of production and consumption undoubtedly constituted a sharp indictment of the ills of capitalism. But whether it also constituted a *calculus* for the human valuation of wealth is much less certain. Because the market imperfectly valued costs and utilities, Hobson would not allow money, the instrument of exchange, to stand as the measure of wealth; yet he was unable to find an alternate means of comparing one man's subjective efforts and satisfactions with those of another. This point has been hammered home by all of Hobson's critics, who view his welfare economics as essentially subjectivist. The remarks of W.H. Hamilton are typical: 'it must be insisted that in enumerating the pleasures and pains connected with various activities [Hobson] is not calculating. A catalogue, no matter how exhaustive, is not a scientific calculus.'[67] There is a good deal of validity to this criticism. Indeed, as will be shown later with reference to Hobson's reform program, Hobson himself confessed his inability to substitute measurement for argument in his analysis.

There is also a difficulty with Hobson's attempt to link his analysis of the human worth of production and consumption. His aim was to ensure that any costs incurred were borne by those best capable of sustaining the burden, while the benefits were to go to those who were best able to appreciate them. Hobson regarded this as being the essential meaning of the socialist formula, 'from each according to his capacity to work, to each according to his needs,' and he adopted this standard as his own.[68] What he did not seem fully to appreciate was that this formula was not intended to link work and consumption. It contains, in fact, a set of dual premises. Hobson managed to adapt the formula to his purposes only by belittling the notion of 'needs.' Without acknowledging the fact, he reinterpreted the doctrine to mean, 'from each according to his work, to each according to his work.' This transformation is evident in the following passage from Hobson's *The Social Problem* (pp. 164-5):

The active members of society who claim individual property according to their needs will not ... claim equal property. Individual needs ... will tend to vary directly and even proportionately with productivity, which is no more than saying that a larger output of energy requires a larger replacement

66 Ibid., 50
67 'Economic Theory and Social Reform,' *Journal of Political Economy*, vol. 23 (1915), 572
68 See, for example, *The Industrial System* (1909; 2nd ed., 1910), 329-30.

through consumption. ... [And] in proportion as the work calls upon higher mental qualities, it requires provision should be made for the continuous stimulation and satisfaction of new powers and interests. ... Put into simple language, this means that a higher grade worker should have a higher rate of pay than a low grade worker, because his needs are greater.

It is difficult to see, for example, how this narrow identification of needs with productivity could encompass Hobson's analysis of the importance of leisure time, where it seemed that it was the low-grade worker who was in *need* of a greater variety of interests and pursuits to compensate him for his routine labour.

None the less, it would be a mistake to dismiss Hobson's analysis as a mere *petit bourgeois* interpretation of human needs. In the next and subsequent chapters, it will be shown that he considered 'work' and 'needs' to be not only individual but social and, therefore, insisted that individual claims based on productivity had to be adjusted so as to take into action social needs and social rights to property. In Hobson's own words, he was 'not concerned with a society in which completeness of the individual life is the sole end, but with a society in which the desires, purposes, and welfare of the individuals are comprised in the achievement of a common life; [for man] ... is a social being and this social nature demands expression in economic processes.'[69] In sum, welfare had to be appreciated as an organic entity.

69 *Work and Wealth*, 160

3

Society as a Maker of Values

1 THE THEORY OF ORGANIC SURPLUS VALUE

The individualist notion of production ... regards the immediate producers of an
article as the rightful owners of that article and of the money it will fetch on the
market, disregarding all social determinants of value.

The Conditions of Industrial Peace, 55

One obvious thesis of economic analysis has been that the cooperation of
individuals within society, their combination as parts in a social whole,
produces far greater results than would be secured by the same individuals
working in isolation. Adam Smith, the founder of the discipline, began
with the proposition that the nation's income is a function of the labour
devoted to its production, and the productivity of such labour is in turn
positively associated with the extent of free division and specialisation of
labour, and so on. It follows from these elementary propositions that the
wider the division of labour, the wider the collaboration of the comple-
mentary parts, the greater the excess product of the whole over the hypo-
thetical output of the component parts operating in isolation. ... *Yet the
world has paid only scanty tribute to such inferences.*[1]

Hobson was one of the few economists to pay close attention to these 'inferences' of Adam Smith's analysis; ironically, in doing so, he overturned many
of the key elements of classical economics.

---

1 Simon Kuznets, 'Parts and Wholes in Economics,' in D. Lerner, *Parts and Wholes*
(1963), 53 (emphasis added)

Hobson had a high regard for the 'comprehensiveness and impartiality' of Adam Smith's *Wealth of Nations*.[2] None the less, he discovered within this seminal work of liberal economics an improper perspective, which ultimately 'legitimated' the private mulcting of public wealth. The source of Smith's error, according to Hobson, was to be found in his assumption that production was individual, rather than social:

Adam Smith, by opening his *Wealth of Nations* with a dissertation upon the economy of division of labour, without explaining that this economy rests upon a prior conception of coöperation, unwittingly assisted to set English Political Economy upon a wrong foundation.[3]

Now, it would be tempting to dismiss this comment on Smith as being simply incorrect. After all, Smith closed his first chapter, 'Of the Division of Labour,' with the remark that he hoped he had made his readers sensible to the fact that 'without the ... coöperation of many thousands, the very meanest person in a civilised country could not be provided, even according to what we very falsely imagine the easy and simple manner in which he is commonly accommodated.'[4] However, the real point of Hobson's comment was not to suggest that Smith was ignorant of the benefits of associated labour, for clearly he was not, but rather to argue that Smith failed to appreciate that this co-operation gave rise to social property rights, in addition to those individual rights which he adumbrated. In neglecting these social rights Smith inevitably overextended individual claims to the economic product. It was not surprising, therefore, that he had to warn his readers that it was 'not from the benevolence of the butcher, the brewer or the baker that we must expect our dinner, but from their regard to their own self-interest.'[5] This statement was merely a reflection of the fact that in Smith's analysis individual producers were allowed to lay claim to an economic product which was not strictly of their own making. In Hobson's opinion, society's contribution to production provided legitimate grounds for the abridgement of these private claims and a corresponding curtailment of the system of self-interest. This contention, as will become evident, is the lynchpin in Hobson's critique of classical economics.

Hobson presented two lines of argument for rejecting the 'individualist notion of production.' First, he pointed out that from a generic standpoint

2 *Free Thought in the Social Sciences* (1926), 69
3 *Work and Wealth* (1914), 251
4 Adam Smith, *Wealth of Nations* (1776; Everyman's ed., 1910) vol. 1, 11
5 Ibid., 13

neither the baker nor the brewer began work as 'self-made men': they were already the products of a social heritage for which a 'social lien' could be justifiably affixed to their property and incomes:

An individual acting by himself can create no wealth. [First] the material and tools with which he works are supplied to him by elaborate processes of social co-operation. [Second] the skill he applies to their use has been labouriously acquired by past generations of men and communicated to him by education and training. ... Finally, the organised community, as a State, protects and assists both the individual producer and the various institutions and processes which help him to produce. Thus society co-operates everywhere with the individual producer.[6]

Yet when the classical economists specified the factors of production, these community services, according to Hobson, were 'almost entirely ignored.' Wealth was treated 'as if it were entirely the product of private personal effort' and the community was left to 'live on suffrance.' Clearly these remarks implied a very vigorous rejection of Adam Smith's identification of state activities with unproductive labour:

If the question were posed plainly: 'Do not the public services of the [state] ... for the defence and security of citizens, for their health, morals, and education, for their personal happiness, efficiency, and progress, perform work that is directly conducive to the efficient operation of the economic system?' an affirmative answer could not be refused.[7]

Hobson's second line of argument was that even if production was considered from a static viewpoint, i.e., solely with regard to current productive efforts, it still could be shown that the productive process was intrinsically social and consequently that the value of a commodity was something bestowed upon it not only by the individual labourer but also by the 'collective labourer.' This social value became evident as soon as the individual producer began to make commodities for the market:

While value in use is strictly personal, value in exchange is distinctively social. A market, however crudely formed, is a social institution; the value of our [individual's] produce is now partly determined by the personal

6 *Taxation in the New State* (1919), 71. See also *Veblen* (1936), 67, where this notion is used to criticize Marxian economics.
7 *Wealth and Life* (1929), 162

labour he has put into them, but partly by the needs and capacities of others; and not even by the needs and capacities of any definite individual, but by a great variety of needs and capacities expressed socially through the instrument of market price. ... So, when our [individual] ... is enabled by the creation of this social institution ... to give special attention to [producing certain goods and exchanging them] for other commodities which he no longer raises, the productivity of his [business] ... has increased. *But part of this increment is not due to his 'personal labour' but to the labours and needs of others expressed through the market.*[8]

The co-operation of an unspecifiable number of others, therefore, was the prerequisite for the specialization of the immediate producer, and this placed a bridle on the latter's claim to the economic product as his exclusive property.

Faced with this critique of the individualistic assumptions of classical economics, the defenders of that system could still reply that, although it might be granted that this original private possession of bits of the economic surplus was of dubious right, this situation was only temporary, for there were forces of competition at work which ensured that eventually each producer was rewarded strictly according to his productive worth to society. Regardless of the merits of Hobson's argument that Adam Smith had allowed the social basis of production to slip from view in the early chapters of the *Wealth of Nations*, was it not evident that Smith intended to reinstate the notion by using the metaphor of the 'hidden hand' to indicate that the market mechanism had harmonized individual interests so as to bring about the social good?

This was, in effect, the answer given by J.B. Clark, the leading American exponent of the doctrine of 'marginalism' – a neologism for which Hobson is responsible.[9] Clark and other marginalists attempted, in Hobson's words, to

8 *The Social Problem* (1901), 144 (emphasis added)
9 Cf. R.S. Howey, 'The Origins of Marginalism,' in R. Black, A. Coats, C. Goodwin, eds., *The Marginal Revolution in Economics* (1973). This neologism was meant as a term of abuse. Throughout his life Hobson was unremitting in his attack on the individualistic premises of marginalism, its abstractness, and its service to 'ruling interests.' In the main his critique focused on the works of J.B. Clark and Philip Wicksteed. See, for example, *Free Thought*, 106-30. Alfred Marshall, on the other hand, was saved from marginalist excesses by his 'hankering after humanity' which continually broke 'the rigour of his mathematical proclivities.' *The Social Problem*, 58. Indeed, Hobson's book *The Economics of Distribution* (1900) shows considerable indebtedness to Marshall. Marshall, in turn, referred to Hobson as a 'suggestive writer on the realistic and social side of economics: but, as a critic of Ricardian doctrines [from whence marginalism springs] he is perhaps apt to underrate the difficulty of the problems which he discusses.' *Principles of Economics*, 8th ed., 339. A good account of Marshall's 'welfare economics' is to be found in Donald Winch, *Economics and Policy* (1969), chap. 2.

74 New Liberalism

fortify classical economics by focusing on the 'equalising process' which they supposed went on 'at the margin of each employment of the factors of production.'[10] Clark argued that, given the conditions of perfect competition, a rational employer would utilize each of the three factors of production to the point at which the price of the last unit of each factor was equal to its marginal product. This break-even point would establish a marginal rate of wages (or interest or rent) which contained no element of surplus. Any additional revenue earned by a factor would simply be a reward for its above-marginal productivity. On this basis Clark claimed that in a perfect market the social product would be completely and equitably distributed among the productive units, in accordance with what each was individually worth. Hobson admitted that this theory had a certain superficial attractiveness, especially for those interested in re-establishing confidence in the equity of the market system:

For if everybody gets for his labour, or any other factor of production, just what it is worth, and can only get more by making it more productive, since the payment to each 'of what he is worth' exhausts the entire product, leaving no surplus over which to quarrel, – why, we are living in the best of all possible economic worlds, and anyone who, by agitation and wilful misrepresentation, tries to incite envy or stir up discontent is as foolish as he is wicked.[11]

It was in formulating a reply to this theory of equivalence that Hobson developed the most distinctive and significant aspect of his critique of classical postulates, namely his theory of organic surplus value. From this perspective he was to argue that the distribution of the economic product in proportion to the individual contributions of the several agents of production was neither logical nor just.

The essential fault in marginalism and, indeed, in classical economics overall was its failure to credit the distinctive quality of economic co-operation. Hobson was convinced that co-operation produced a material result or effect which was 'different both in quantity *and in character* from that which the unorganised activities of the individual participants could compass.'[12] Co-operation was qualitatively different because its effect was organic: co-operation generated a 'whole [that was] more productive than the mere sum

10 *Work and Wealth*, 173
11 *Free Thought*, 110
12 *Wealth and Life*, 27 (emphasis added)

of the productive value of the parts.'[13] This was the source of surplus value. Hobson elaborated his argument as follows:

Brown, Smith, and Jones working together ... build a boat. Does the value of this boat, when made, represent the value made by Brown, *and* that made by Smith, *and* that made by Jones? No such thing. Why, Brown, by himself, could not have lifted the log to make the keel. Or suppose he could have made a boat, could he, in a given time, have made a boat worth one-third as much as the joint product of all three during the same time? Obviously not. Supposing all three to be equally efficient workmen, it is evident that their joint product, in a given time, will be worth more than three times the product of Brown alone. *Organised co-operation is a productive power.* The associated or 'social' productivity of Brown, Smith, and Jones, is not the mere addition of their productivity as individuals. ... If we set Brown, Smith, and Jones to work, first separately and then together, *the difference in value between their added and their joint product might rank as the quantity of social value.*[14]

Surplus value, then, was the difference between 'several' and 'joint' production. The total economic product necessarily exceeded the contributions of the individual factors. This was a difference which could not be comprehended except in organic terms. Here, Hobson and the classical economists definitely parted company, for as F.A. Hayek, in another context, has observed, the 'true individualist' argues that 'there is no other way toward an understanding of social phenomena, but through [an] understanding of individual actions.'[15] Hobson, on the other hand, believed that the 'real underlying error' of the classical liberals was precisely that they persisted in 'regarding society as an aggregate of individuals.' In order to see the surplus in organic terms, it was necessary to expose the 'fallacy of composition' involved in this way of thinking:

It seems to them a 'mere superstition to look upon society as anything other than the members who compose it'. This declaration sounds final, and yet its very language carries its refutation. 'Compose it.' Composition

13 *The Science of Wealth* (1911), 145
14 *The Social Problem*, 146-7 (emphasis added)
15 'Individualism: True and False' (1945) in *Individualism and the Economic Order* (1972), 6. See also Steven Lukes, *Individualism* (1973), chap. 17, 'Methodological Individualism,' for a brief survey of other social philosophers who have taken this approach to social explanation.

implies an orderly relation of parts. This relation is not found adhering to the individuals, as such. ... If society is a composition, it must have a unity consisting of the relations of its members. *The maintenance and activity of these relations can be shown to be a source of value.*[16]

In the economic sphere these 'relations' were the source of surplus value. The classical economists' theory of value, on the other hand, was based on the 'sheer denial of society as a working unity'[17] – and it is now possible to see that Hobson meant 'working' in the literal sense of the word – with the consequence that the value or product of that work was dissipated in a welter of individual possessiveness.

It was upon the basis of his analysis of the organic value of economic relations that Hobson reached the striking conclusion that capitalism, *even at its most ideal*,[18] was an unjust system of distribution. Hobson could accept *prima facie* the classical economists' vision of an equivalency of exchange, yet still indicate the exploitative potential of the system: even after all the individual factors had been paid their full economic worth, there would remain a surplus which belonged to none of the factors, this surplus having been created during the process of production by organic cooperation. A proper equivalency of exchange, therefore, would require, as will be shown in detail later, that this surplus be returned to the community as 'common-wealth,' to be used for the support of public welfare programs. It followed that in so far as classical political economy remained true to its ideals, rewarding factors only according to their individual productive efforts, it furnished 'no thinkable theory of distribution,' because the surplus was of definitely social origin and character:

Under the conditions of absolutely free competition, with payments of all factors at a minimum, no provision exists for securing ... any apportionment of the surplus. There would be an annual surplus which belonged to none of the factors, and which none of them was any better able to take

16 *The Social Problem*, 146 (emphasis added)
17 Ibid., 141
18 Adam Smith expressed this ideal as follows: 'When the price of any commodity is neither more nor less than what is sufficient to pay for the rent of the land, the wages of the labour, the profits of the stock employed in raising, preparing, and bringing it to market, according to their natural [costs], ... the commodity is then sold for its ... natural price. The commodity is then sold precisely for what it is worth.' *The Wealth of Nations*, 48-9.

than the others. This unappropriated surplus ... would ... wander ... owner-less and [run] ... to waste.[19]

The fact that this did not happen made it reasonable to assume that the teachings of the classical economists were obscuring the fact that appropriation was taking place on some basis other than as a reward for productivity.

Commentaries on Hobson's theory of surplus value, such as those made by Kemp, Winslow, Nemmers, and Naylor, often fail to appreciate the depth of Hobson's critique of classical economics.[20] They suggest, to cite Naylor, that Hobson believed that the 'industrial system *per se* was perfectly healthy provided it could be freed [of] monopoly control.'[21] Hobson's critique, in this view, amounts to little more than a simple reminder that the model of 'perfect competition' used by the classical economists had little or no relation to reality. Now, whilst this latter claim definitely reflects Hobson's opinion, and the next section will show this in detail, the foregoing analysis makes it clear that such an interpretation is inadequate, for it leaves Hobson sharing the same free-market ideal as the classics. Hobson, in fact, penetrated below the level of market relations in order to establish the real starting point of his critique of classical economics, namely its failure to specify 'co-operation' as a separate factor of production.

2 COSTS AND SURPLUS: THE REALITY OF IMPERFECT COMPETITION

The failure ... to make a clear distinction between the right and wrong sorts of property, between the sorts which in their origin and uses are expressive of personal effort and personal satisfaction, and the sorts which proceed from looting, oppressive bargains, ... and are put to luxurious expenditure or waste, is the chief barrier to sound economic reform. *Property and Impropriety*, 11

Just how far did capitalism actually depart from the standard of a proper equivalency of exchange as adumbrated by Hobson? Clearly this question was of paramount importance in evaluating any proposals for reforming the economic system. It is not surprising, therefore, that Hobson's major attempt

19 *The Industrial System* (1909; 2nd ed., 1910), 136
20 Cf. T. Kemp, *Theories of Imperialism* (1967), 34; E. Winslow, *The Pattern of Imperialism* (1948), 95-6; E. Nemmers, *Hobson and Underconsumption* (1956), passim; and R.T. Naylor, 'The Ideological Foundations of Social Democracy and Social Credit,' in G. Teeple, ed., *Capitalism and the National Question in Canada* (1972), 252-6.
21 Naylor, 'Ideological Foundations,' 254

at elaborating the component aspects of industrial costs and their allocation was done around the same time that Lloyd George, as Chancellor of the Exchequer with Asquith's Liberal administration (1908-15), was attempting to reform the national system of taxation so as better to levy the income and property of the wealthy classes.

As noted in Chapter 1, Lloyd George's 'Peoples' budget' created much dissension both within and outside Parliament. But it was not so much the size of the levies he imposed that created the furore, as the fact that it was sensed that the budget provided a direct challenge to the doctrine that property was an absolute right, by taxing certain forms of income on the grounds that it was undeserved by the recipient. This, however, was precisely the Budget's appeal to Hobson, and it was upon this basis that he chose to defend it:

The moral and intellectual defence of the Budget rests on the validity of a general distinction between earned and unearned wealth, that is, between those elements of income which are necessary to evoke the powers of mental or physical labour and the application of capital, and those which are not necessary, but which constitute surplus incomes taken because they can be got.[22]

The discovery of the forms and magnitude of the unproductive surplus was the major task Hobson set himself in his work, *The Industrial System* (1909).[23] In earlier books, like *The Economics of Distribution* (1900), he had categorized these distinctions simply in terms of necessary costs and forced gains. In *The Industrial System* he attempted a much more sophisticated and exhaustive classification.

Hobson began his analysis by dividing the industrial product into three categories: maintenance costs, productive surplus, and unproductive surplus. Essentially this division marked the difference between property acquired on the basis of economic service and that taken through the exercise of economic clout. Maintenance and productivity payments fell into the former category, while the unproductive surplus was made up of 'unearned income.' The goal of Hobson's analysis, then, was not to abolish private property rights, but to establish a clear demarcation between 'right and

---

22 'The Significance of the Budget,' *English Review* (July 1909), 800, cited in P. Clarke's 'Introduction' to Hobson's *Crisis of Liberalism* (new ed., 1974)

23 This work was published within a few weeks of Lloyd George's budget speech. A second edition, with minor revisions, was published in 1910. All quotations are taken from this later edition.

wrong' sorts of property, between property and 'improperty,' to use another neologism coined by Hobson. Other liberal reformers shared in this aim, likewise claiming that it marked the essential difference between New Liberalism and Socialism, but Hobson was exceptional in the degree to which he developed this aspect of the New Liberal platform. Thus, even though Hobhouse's book, *The Labour Movement*, first published in 1898, presents an early exposition of this distinction, none the less by the time of the third edition (1907) he had conceded the doctrine to Hobson – 'this most original and independent of our economists.' *The Industrial System* established Hobson's title beyond dispute.[24]

Maintenance costs were defined by Hobson as those charges made upon the industrial product which were necessary to provide against the future depreciation of productive factors. Included in these costs were:

1) minimum wages necessary to support the various sorts of labour and ability [i.e., both manual and mental labour];
2) depreciation for wear and tear of ... fixed capital;
3) a wear and tear provision for land;
4) a provision for the upkeep of the public services which the state renders to industry.[25]

But a dynamic economy had to do more than subsist; it had to summon additional productive energy in order to expand output and progress. The 'productive surplus' consisted of payments made for various 'costs of growth.' These included:

1) minimum wages of progressive efficiency to evoke a larger quantity and better quality of labour;
2) such a minimum of interest as suffices to evoke the supply of new capital needed to co-operate with the enlarged and improved supply of labour;
3) a provision for the improved size and efficiency of the public services rendered by the State to industry.[26]

24 *The Labour Movement*, 7. See also J. and B. Hammond, *The Village Labourer* (1913), viii, 166.
25 *The Science of Wealth*, 86. This work is a popularized version of *The Industrial System*. It has been used in this particular instance, because it defines more precisely the categories of costs and thus is more suitable for citation. However, the substance of the definitions is identical.
26 Ibid.

Several points of interest emerge from the consideration of these catego-ries. First, they clearly affirm Hobson's intention to place social co-operation on par with the other factors of production. Thus the cost of state services is included along with the other costs of industry. Second, it should be noted that land rent is excluded from the category of productive surplus. The pay-ment of rent beyond mere maintenance costs was fruitless, because it would not call forth extra productive output. Hobson apparently considered this proposition to be generally accepted among economists and did not argue the point at length. His main interest was in measuring the size of land rents, and here his views differed considerably from those of other economists, as will be shown later, when his recommendations for economic reforms are dis-cussed.

Much more contentious, in Hobson's opinion, was his defence of inter-est as a reward for productivity. This placed him in opposition not only to his mentor, Ruskin, but also to many socialist thinkers, both Fabian[27] and Marxist.

Hobson was especially critical of the Marxist argument that interest was mere tribute taken from the fund of surplus value created by labour. He attacked this position on two grounds. First, he argued that Marx was mis-taken in claiming that labour was the exclusive source of surplus value. Capi-tal was also productive and therefore the suppliers of capital had a right to share in the surplus. Hobson's clearest statement of his position in this regard is to be found in one of his last works, *Property and Improperty* (1937), although the criticism is suggested as early as 1900:[28]

Socialism ... regards all labour as productive, all capital as predatory. ... [It is said] that the gain which accrues from the use of the spade ... simply renders [the] labour [of digging] more productive. ... [Indeed] this can be said (and is said by Marx) to apply to all machinery and other technical equipment. It does not produce itself but only increases the productivity of labour. But such a contention leaves us in a morass of sophistry. A factor which makes another factor productive must have productivity imputed to it. It is idle to pretend that a ... machine is not productive and therefore has no claim to the increased productivity of labour it has brought about.[29]

27 *John Ruskin* (1898), 143f. L.G. Chiozza Money, for example, in the *Daily News* (1 June 1909) [Hobson Papers, Hull University], criticized Hobson for including interest in earned income. See also Maurice Dobb, 'Shaw as an Economist,' in S. Winsen *G.B.S. 90* (1946), for a brief comparison of Shaw's and Hobson's views on interest.
28 *The Economics of Distribution*, 353-4
29 *Property and Improperty* (1937), 73-4

By raising the productivity of labour, a machine had the capacity to save more labour time than the cost to produce it. It thus, in Hobson's terms, helped create a productive surplus above its maintenance costs and its input, therefore, had to be considered variable not constant, as Marx had argued. In Hobson's opinion, Marx had confounded this point because, in his desire to attack the capitalists, he failed to keep clear the crucial distinction between 'capital as a productive factor and the question of its ownership.'[30]

The second aspect of Hobson's critique was based on the contention that the supply of capital involved a certain kind of work or effort that was unaccounted for in the Marxian scheme. This was the effort of abstinence, upon which the classical economists had placed so much emphasis. Capital was peculiar in that it was entirely man-made. It had its origin in savings generated through non-consumption.

We may ... attribute to the free bounty of Nature an original stock of labour-power, as of land. ... There is, however, no such free original supply of capital. Whatever capital forms part of our industrial structure must have been brought into existence by the stimulus of ... interest.[31]

The refusal to recognize the creativity of abstinence stemmed from a crude materialist bias in the analysis of work:

That abstinence alone, in the sense of a refusal to consume existing goods, will not cause an increase of those goods is true enough; but neither will labour alone ... be effectual, except in co-operation with other forces. The notion which sometimes crops up ... that abstinence ... cannot

---

30 Ibid., 74. It is noteworthy that Hobson's formulation of this defect in the Marxian analysis prefigures an influential critique by Joan Robinson. Robinson argues that Marx's contention that only labour is productive 'in itself' is 'nothing but a verbal point.' Capital 'produce no *value* for *value* is the product of labour time.' But 'efficient machines enhance the productivity of labour. ... [However], whether we choose to say that capital is productive, or that capital is necessary to make labour productive, is not a matter of much importance. What is important to say is that *owning* capital is not a productive activity.' *An Essay on Marxian Economics* (1942; 2nd ed., 1966), 18. To this it might be replied that for Marx the distinction was important, in that he saw a crisis of profitability for capitalism arising out of the tendency for machinery not only to raise the productivity of labour but also to *displace* labour at the point of production. In this way capitalism would ultimately destroy its surplus-creating capacity, by creating a huge army of unemployed. Marx termed this the crisis of a 'rising organic composition of capital.' In Hobson's case, however, there is no indication he was aware of this theory of crisis in Marx's work.

31 *The Industrial System*, 69

be a productive activity, rests upon an unconscious materialism in the conception of productivity, as if no action were productive except by direct physical operation in shaping ... goods. The ... [abstinence] of the capitalist is productive in much the same sense as the inspection of the overlooker in a mill; it is a condition of the effective functioning of capital as the latter is of the effective functioning of labour.[32]

Abstinence, therefore, was a prerequisite of production. The original act of abstinence provided a fund of capital; continuing abstinence kept that capital in operation. Capital was 'not merely crystallised labour.'[33] Hobson thus felt justified in rewarding abstinence with interest.

However, having defended the classical economists' notion of abstinence from the ridicule of the Marxists, Hobson then willingly conceded that not all those who owned capital had gone through the effort of supplying it. Indeed he claimed that it was a 'legitimate presumption that capital, the saving of which involves no real sacrifice, has been acquired not by honest labour, but by some form of economic oppression.'[34] This presumption was to have a key part in Hobson's own analysis of capitalism. Nevertheless, Hobson believed that the Marxists, in impugning the principle of interest, had pressed this grievance too far:

The real gravamen of the charge, against those whose interest is un-attended by any 'cost' of abstinence, has reference, not to the payment of interest, but to the modes by which they have come into possession of the capital. ... [The] frequent assertion that the 'real abstinence is that of the worker and not the capitalist' does not meet the point at issue. Supposing it be true that the capitalist steals from the worker a portion of the product and uses it for capital, receiving interest for its use, a true bill of indictment against him would rest, not upon the wrongful receipt of interest, but upon the prior act of stealing the product of labour.[35]

The eradication of this swirl of misappropriation would not abolish the need for interest payments; rather it would re-establish the proper connection between effort and reward, abstinence and interest. In this light, Hobson was later to argue that the Soviet experience had more to teach socialists

32 *John Ruskin*, 146
33 *The Industrial System*, 71
34 *John Ruskin*, 147
35 *The Economics of Distribution*, 253-4

than it had the liberal economists, who had always recognized the cost of supplying capital, whether they had been sufficiently sensitive to the possibilities of misappropriation or not:

[In] a socialist ... planned economy, we find the need of [an] ... adjustment between present and future enjoyment. How much labour shall be applied to producing immediately consumable goods, how much to the enlargement and improvement of the capital structure so as to improve the future supply of consumable goods? Such is the problem that confronted the Soviet Government at the outset of its career, and still confronts it. ... Saving in a socialist society continues to be a 'cost' or sacrifice; it is, however, no longer an individual cost but a social cost, and the interest paid for individual saving is no longer payable.[36]

In Hobson's opinion, then, the Soviet example confirmed his analysis of the exaggeration of the Marxian attack on the principle of interest. In failing to 'distinguish between payments economically necessary ... to the providers of capital' and 'payments in excess of these amounts.' Marxism 'served to obscure the vital distinction between costs and surplus,' which Hobson was attempting to clarify.[37]

The unproductive surplus – the canker of the industrial system – comprised the final charge upon the industrial product. It consisted of,

1) economic rents of land and other natural resources;
2) all interest in excess of [the costs of growth];
3) all profits, salaries and other payments in ... excess of what would ... suffice to evoke the sufficient use of these factors.[38]

36 *Property and Improperty*, 81-2. Also of interest in this regard is Hobson's defence of the idea of abstinence as a cost from Simon Patten's criticism that since the abstainer always possesses a surplus of pleasure resulting from the imagination of the relief of his sacrifice, saving is costless. See 'The Subjective and Objective View of Distribution,' *Annals of the American Academy*, vol. 4 (1893). It might be noted, however, that Hobson does allow that, in what might be termed an egalitarian post-scarcity society, saving could become effortless and thus costless. This suggests that Hobson did not consider man's consumption desires to be insatiable, thus making abstinence always a sacrifice. See *The Science of Wealth*, 72, and *John Ruskin*, 151
37 *Wealth and Life*, 193. The continuing relevance of Hobson's remarks here may be traced in the various debates on economic policy that have taken place in the Soviet Union, dating from the period of War Communism through to the Liberman Debate of the early 1960s and Kosygin's economic reforms of 1965. For details see Alec Nove's books, *The Soviet Economy* (1969), and *An Economic History of the U.S.S.R.* (1972).
38 *The Science of Wealth*, 86

These payments were taken because they could be got, not because they were economically functional.

Here it is important to recall that, although Hobson considered these unproductive surpluses to be unearned, he did not intend by this, as is sometimes supposed, to convey the weak notion that this surplus was somehow provided gratuitously.[39] On the contrary, Hobson insisted that though the surplus might be 'unearned by its owners,' it was 'not for all that unearned':[40]

In the language of political economy this [surplus] ... consists of increments which, not being in their origin assignable to individual activities are called 'unearned,' but which, in sober fact, are the earnings of society, arising from public work.[41]

To suggest that Hobson limited his consideration of the ills of the economic system to the problems of misspending, i.e., the mismanagement of wealth, is seriously to underestimate the radical nature of his critique. Indeed, there are several occasions when Hobson himself criticized the superficiality of various proposals for social reform precisely on the grounds that they failed to make the connection between the misapplication of funds and their mode of acquisition.[42]

The significance of Hobson's separation of costs and surplus is that it provides a means of identifying the point at which the market system of distribution becomes inequitous and inefficient. Hobson pinpointed his own innovation in this matter as follows:

The distinctive character of this doctrine of distribution consists in assigning the priority of significance to the division of the product into costs and surplus instead of into wages, interest and rent. Not until the surplus has been separated from the full subsistence fund of costs does any real problem of distribution as between the several factors arise.[43]

39 For example, Alvin S. Johnson in his review of *The Industrial System* in the *Journal of Political Economy*, vol. 17 (1909), 646, mistakenly suggests that the unproductive surplus referred 'not to the way one makes his income, but the way he spends it.' William Tien-Chen Liu, 'A Study in Hobson's Welfare Economics' Ph.D thesis, Northwestern University (1934), 137-8, repeats this error.
40 *The Problem of the Unemployed*, 99
41 *The Social Problem*, 149
42 Cf. *Wealth and Life*, 155-7. Later it will be shown that this relationship also provided Hobson with an important insight into the causes of industrial depression.
43 *The Industrial System*, 80

Prior to the generation of surplus value, strong laws of necessity prevented the maldistribution of income, and generally ensured that the various agents were paid their maintenance costs. To this extent Adam Smith was vindicated. The capitalist system did have a certain capacity for self-regulation, and in the past, when the size of the economic surplus was smaller, the system was correspondingly less crisis-ridden. In a statement that clearly indicates the ambit of his reformism, Hobson warned that more radical opponents of capitalism 'often underestimated [this] ... genuine and substantial basis of orderly co-operation' within the economic system.[44]

Hobson's favourable opinion of the competitive system's capacity to regulate maintenance costs was based on an examination of its operations under 'normal conditions.' However, there were exceptions to this norm. For example, Hobson recognized that certain trades were able to escape market imperatives and pay wages below the subsistence level, at least in the short run. One of his early works, *Problems of Poverty* (1891), was largely devoted to examining the causes and consequences of the 'sweating system,' particularly in the clothing trade. The victims of this system of sweating were usually low-skill, unorganized female workers, forced to work excessive hours at low wages and in unsanitary conditions. When physically exhausted, they were replaced rather than replenished. Market higgling, then, could provide no solid assurance that maintenance costs would be met in full. None the less, Hobson contended that an outright condemnation of the market system was not warranted.

The real defects of the market system only became evident with the distribution of the surplus product. Here could be found 'the source of every sort of trouble or malady of the industrial system.'[45] The slap of the hidden hand might be felt when failure to support maintenance costs was in question, but with costs of growth the question was not so much one of economic survival as the pace and direction of economic activity. Hobson contended that for waste in this sense the competitive system provided no ongoing safeguards:

[Although] it is not possible for the owners of one factor of production to encroach far upon the subsistence fund of any of the others, ... it is possible for one section or interest ... to effect a considerable separate gain by encroaching upon the portion of surplus required to furnish growth to some other part of the system. There exists no close harmony in the system as shall furnish an automatic check on such depradations. An indus-

44 Ibid., 79
45 Ibid., 78

trial system may still survive and even grow, though not as freely or so rapidly, if a land-lord class claims a large piece of the 'surplus,' the payment of which is not essential to evoke the use of his land, or if a class of capitalists draw an interest or profit larger than is sufficient to induce the application of their capital or ability, or if some favoured and protected professions or trades take salaries or wages which are more than sufficient to stimulate any improved efficiency they give out. In these ways 'surplus' may be diverted from its proper work of furnishing growing-power and become unearned income. It is notorious that combination is primarily directed to secure some such element of superfluous gain.[46]

On this last point, Hobson, of course, recognized that classical economics did take these 'combinatory elements' into account in its consideration of the distribution of the industrial product. It considered them temporary frictions which functioned as signposts for the further stimulation of competition, the rise in price calling forth additional resources so as to eliminate the scarcity and re-establish an equivalence of exchange.[47] The difficulties with this classical analysis, according to Hobson, were three-fold. First, it was irrelevant as a mechanism for guarding the productive efforts of 'society'; the private acquisition of social wealth, as has already been noted, was not recognized as a depradation in classical economics. Second, it rested upon assumptions that at best had only limited applicability in a number of markets. Thus competitive bargaining worked imperfectly when the goods in question had a 'narrow time market,' because this put pressure to sell on the supplier. Nor did the market function freely when there was a 'place limit' restricting the portability of the goods supplied. Again, the market was necessarily imperfect when the goods sold were not easily and minutely divisible; or when there were no 'reliable standards of goods,' so that 'each portion of the supply' formed a 'separate centre for bargaining.' In each of these cases there was an opportunity for an element of 'force or bluff' to enter into the bargaining process.[48]

But even more disconcerting for the adherents of an 'ideal' of perfect competition was the fact that actual developments within the capitalist economy were making this ideal an ever-diminishing possibility, even in those areas where it once might have had some application. The present economic reality, according to Hobson, was no longer one of competition qualified by

46 Ibid.
47 Ibid., 137-8
48 Ibid., 160-1

combination, but one of combination qualified by competition. The various economic interests in society were organizing in cartels, trade unions, etc., so as better to exploit situations of natural and fortuitous scarcity and wherever possible actually create situations of scarcity favourable to themselves.

In these new circumstances it was necessary to confront classical economics with the question: 'Is the distribution of the surplus according to the relative pulls of natural and contrived scarcity of the factors an economical method of stimulating improved productivity?' Hobson's answer was no. This system now had the very reverse effect of that intended, directing 'much of the surplus into payments which check instead of stimulating efficiency and progress.'[49]

Summarizing the various aspects of Hobson's critique of the classical analysis of distribution, it can be said that he considered it based on a faulty ideal, of limited applicability, which increasingly failed to reflect economic realities. This conclusion naturally led Hobson to re-evaluate the role of force in the economy, with a view to determining who were the mighty and what were the consequences of their victory. This first consideration is examined in the next section. The major consequences of their victory were economic crises, imperialism, and the impoverishment of public life – the subject matter of the rest of this book.

3 WHO GETS WHAT?
THE STRUGGLE FOR THE DISTRIBUTION OF THE SURPLUS

According to Hobson, the struggle for the surplus took place largely outside the economic harmonies envisaged by the classical economists. Force prevailed over equity and in consequence, as H.B. Acton has noted (disapprovingly), 'Hobson's account of bargaining in a market is ... more like politics than trade.'[50] the spoils of the contest going to the stronger party. In his *Confessions*, Hobson wrote that he considered his analysis of the intrusion of force into bargaining processes to be his 'most destructive heresy.'[51]

In *The Physiology of Industry* (1889), Hobson argued that the distribution of the surplus was governed by the 'Law of the Limiting Requisite.'[52] By this Hobson simply meant that, given an increase in general demand, the bulk of the rise in price that would result would be taken by that factor which was

---

49 Ibid., 138, 142
50 *The Morals of Markets* (1971), 27
51 168
52 Cf. *The Physiology of Industry* (1889), chap. v.

least easily supplied. This 'law' was then examined in the context of a short analysis of what happened to factor prices during the Franco-German War of 1871. Hobson (and Mummery) concluded that no one factor had a permanent advantage in attaching scarcity value to itself. This conclusion had important ramifications for Hobson's theory of distribution. He saw it as a basis for rejecting various class analyses of distribution and substituting for them a *generalized* concept of rent (i.e., unearned income).

Hobson considered his own account of the Law of the Limiting Requisite so obvious a truth that it could not have failed to secure an earlier recognition among economists, had political economy not been dominated by a narrow and hard class bias, bent on exposing one special group of producers as the residual claimants of the economic surplus. This approach was described by Hobson as consisting in

Taking the aggregate product, the object of distribution, showing that two of the three claimants are entitled to a fixed minimum charge on the product, and thus placing the third claimant in the position of the residual claimant to whatever remains.[53]

It seemed to Hobson that by the close of the 1880s variations on this theme had been exhausted: land, labour, capital, each in turn had been named the sole recipient of surplus value. Thus Henry George, the radical Ricardian, had claimed that 'natural agents' were far less capable of 'easy and indefinite increase' than were capital and labour; consequently he supposed that land acted as the 'limit to increase in production.' The 'whole increase in [the] price of commodities was said to be swallowed up in increased rent.' On the other hand, 'Marx and Lasalle' (sic) had been no less convinced that it was not land but capital that functioned as the privileged factor of production. They argued, according to Hobson, that the 'natural agents' were 'practically without limit as to quantity and easy access,' and that the 'growth of population and the increased economy of labour due to the inventiveness of man' also made it 'easy to get fresh labour.' Capital, however, was not so readily accessible. It followed that 'Capital forms the limiting Requisite of Production, and that all increase in prices will eventually fall to Capital in increased Profits.' Finally Hobson noted that General Walker (later to become president of Massachusetts Institute of Technology) had played the only remaining hand, by suggesting that 'Natural Agents and Capital admit

53 'The Law of Three Rents,' *Quarterly Journal of Economics*, vol. v (1891), 279

of easy increase at a more rapid rate than Labour'; therefore Labour was the residual legatee.[54]

Hobson believed that his own account of the Law of the Limiting Requisite completely destroyed the residual theory of distribution and put an end to the simplistic panaceas that invariably accompanied it.[55] A more discriminating approach was required, but for this it was necessary to recognize that the concept of rent was of general applicability:

Investigation of the actual course of modern industry shows that ... sometimes it will be a particular sort of land, sometimes of capital, sometimes of ability, or even of manual labour, that will take this surplus. *No single factor can be regarded as the residual claimant.* The 'surplus' passes in innumerable fragments to the owners of a scarce factor wherever it is found. The 'natural' scarcity of land does not secure for its owners any power to take a larger share of the surplus than the artificial scarcities which capital or specialised ability are able to enjoy in many fields of industry. Only by following closely the actual course of each stream of industry ... can we ascertain the different forms and sizes of extra payments or surplus that emerge.[56]

Aside from believing that his approach to the issue of distribution was a better guide to empirical reality than the alternate theories he discussed, Hobson also considered his position to have tactical significance. Hobson was fearful that a failure to discriminate carefully between the various claimants to the surplus would serve to 'bind in a common bond of instinctive self-defence all owners of property or 'unearned' incomes irrespective of size, origin, or use.'[57] A solid front of reactionary forces would seriously impede any chances of social reform – hence Hobson's concern about distinguishing the 'forms and sizes' of unearned incomes taken by the various economic bargainers.[58]

However, once having cleared the ground of 'deterministic' theories, Hobson subsequently introduced a number of important considerations designed to show that, as a matter of probability rather than necessity, the institutions of capitalism were such that the capitalist was in the best position

54 *The Physiology of Industry*, 171-2
55 'The Law of Three Rents,' 279
56 *The Industrial System*, vii (emphasis added)
57 *Free Thought*, 154
58 See below, chap. 7, sec. 5.

to stake his claim to the surplus, particularly in comparison with labour. Both aspects of Hobson's position are summarized in the following passage from *The Economics of Distribution*:

Surplus value ... is not something which emerges in the dealings of capital with labour; ... it emerges in every competitive bargain and adheres to the stronger bargainer ... [In] modern industry the owner of capital ... is normally found to be the stronger bargainer, [so] he obtains most of the surplus. ... [But] the fact that the labourer gets so little as compared with the capitalist ... ought not to lead us to adopt a false or one sided theory of the ... nature of surplus value.[59]

It is not clear what prompted Hobson to examine the Law of the Limiting Requisite in a less abstract or generalized framework than he had in *The Physiology of Industry*. In one of his later books he recalled how the dock strike of 1889 'dramatised the situation of the underworld of East London and the demands of 'unskilled' labour,'[60] and this might have had the effect of directing his attention to the special difficulties workers faced in organizing to promote their demands. Certainly Hobson's friends in the Fabian Society were working in this area, having realized, in Sidney Webb's words, that the original Fabian essays had attached 'quite insufficient attention to Trade Unionism.'[61] But whatever the cause or influence, the important point is that Hobson became increasingly interested in specifying those institutions that fixed the conditions under which the agents of production bargained.

Hobson primarily focused on two features of capitalism which he considered worked to the disadvantage of labour in its contest with capital. The one reflected the changing face of capitalism, the other its enduring nature. First, Hobson observed that as the economy advanced so capital became collected in trusts, and labour sought to combine in trade unions, but overall capital was far more advanced in this process than was labour. This obviously enhanced capital's bargaining power vis-à-vis labour. Second, Hobson contended that under capitalism the separation of the worker from the instruments of production – the means of livelihood – meant that the conditions under which labour contracted with the owners of capital often resembled

59 357
60 *Wealth and Life*, xiii
61 'Introduction to the 1920 Reprint,' *The Fabian Essays*, 1889 (6th ed., 1962), 272. The product of the Fabians' research in this area was the Webbs' *History of Trade Unionism* published in 1894.

those of a 'forced sale' rather than a free contract. Again, such duress could function only to bolster the capitalists' position as a 'strong bargainer.'

Unlike the classical economists, who either ignored or minimized the development of cartels and other monopoly elements in the economy,[62] Hobson was quick to appreciate their significance. His awareness was no doubt sharpened by his visits to the United States during the eighteen-eighties where the growth of syndicates was more prodigious than in England; some five thousand companies were consolidated into about three hundred trusts in this period.[63] Furthermore, it was in America that Hobson met and became friends with Henry D. Lloyd, who was then preparing an exposé of the practices of the Standard Oil Company, considered by Hobson to be the 'leading example of a successful trust.'[64] Thus by the time Hobson published his first solo work, *Problems of Poverty* in 1891, he was willing to attribute much of the 'labour problem' to the development of business cartels and trusts. And in his next book, *The Evolution of Modern Capitalism* (1894), the growth of monopoly elements in the economy was firmly established as being of prime importance in appreciating the progress of capitalist economic relations.

The combination of capital, in Hobson's opinion, was part of the natural evolution of capitalism; it grew directly out of the forces of competition whereby 'surviving competitors have crushed or absorbed their weaker rivals, and have grown big by feeding on their carcases.' In this light the trust or syndicate, which took advantage of these centralizing forces, could be viewed as the 'highest reach of capitalist evolution.'[65]

Hobson was aware that the combination of capital brought with it many economic advantages of scale, but he was concerned that, without strict social control, these economies would be used to further the private profits of the monopolists, rather than to benefit the workers in the trusts, or least

---

62 Alfred Marshall, for example, described the profits of monopolies as quasi-rents in order to denote their *temporary* significance. For Hobson's critique of Marshall in this regard, see *The Economics of Distribution*, 341-4.

63 These facts are cited in J. Hutcheson, *Dominance and Dependency* (1978), 55.

64 *Problems of Poverty* (1891; 2nd. ed., 1895), 210. Sometime later Hobson was appointed, along with John Hilton and Sidney Webb, to membership on the Committee on Trusts, set up by the Ministry of Reconstruction in 1918. The Committee found that there had been a considerable increase in the number of trade combinations during the war. In a supplementary chapter to the 1926 edition of *The Evolution of Modern Capitalism*, 447-9, Hobson utilized the findings of this committee to reinforce his argument regarding the concentration of industry.

65 *Problems of Poverty*, 207, 213

of all the general public. Indeed, he considered that 'one of the special economies which a large capital possesses over a small, and which a trust possesses *par excellence* is the power of making advantageous bargains with its employees.' Big corporations, earning super-profits, might well be able to afford to pay their workers more, but at the same time there was less chance of compelling them to do so. Hobson gave two reasons for this. First, the combination of capital had narrowed the range of options open to the worker:

The more or less complete control of the capital engaged in an industry, and of the market, involves an enormous power over the labour engaged in that industry. So long as competition survives, the employee or group of employees are able to obtain wages and other terms of employment determined in some measure by the conflicting interests of different em- ployers. But when there is only one employer, the Trust, the workman who seeks employment has no option but to accept the terms offered by the Trust. ... The Standard Oil Company or the Linseed Oil Trust are the owners of their employees almost to the same extent as they are owners of their mills and machinery, so subservient has modern labour become to the fixed capital under which it works.[66]

The second advantage that trusts had over labour was less direct, but in Hobson's opinion, no less effective. The centralization of capital tended to create a 'reserve army of the unemployed' (to use Marx's phrase), which helped depress the general level of wages:

The Trust came into existence in order to restrict production and so raise prices, [it follows that] ... the aggregate output of the business will be either reduced or its rate of increase will be less than under open compe- tition. The chief economy of the Trust will in fact arise from the net diminution of employment of labour. As the Trust grows stronger ... the reduction of employment will as a rule continue. ... The ability to choose [the workmen it does require] out of an artificially made oversupply of labour, rid of the competition of other employers, gives the Trust a well- nigh absolute power to fix wages ... and generally to dictate terms of employment and conditions of life.[67]

66 *The Evolution of Modern Capitalism* (1894), 148, and chap. v, 'The Formation of Monopolies in Capital,' and *Rationalisation and Unemployment* (1930), passim
67 *The Evolution of Modern Capitalism*, 151

When examining the trend towards the combination of capital, Hobson observed what he considered to be a 'closely correspondent' trade-union movement within the ranks of labour.[68] However, with certain significant exceptions, which will be discussed later,[69] Hobson was not very optimistic about the capacity of the trade-union movement as a whole to keep pace with and match the power of the trusts. This was not, Hobson insisted, because an 'iron law of wages' operated to defeat all efforts to redistribute income in favour of the working class. On the contrary, Hobson believed that his theory of surplus value clearly refuted such a contention:

The failure of most economists to recognise the large proportion of 'forced gains' ... which are included in the net profits of a trade, is chiefly responsible for the tone of disparagement in which even the most liberal minded amongst them speak of the economic efficacy of trade unions to raise wages. ... Our analysis ... involves the recognition of a great fund of surplus profits, which is available for higher wages. ... Forced gains ... are not permanently necessary payments to the owners of capital who take them, and may be transferred ... to the workers.[70]

The fact that Hobson none the less remained sceptical with regard to trade-union efforts to redistribute income was a reflection of his sharp appreciation of a second major institutional feature of capitalism, namely that the labouring class had been 'deprived of the means of earning an independent livelihood.[71]

68 *Problems of Poverty*, 216
69 See below, chap. 7, sec. 5.
70 *The Economics of Distribution*, 337-8. See also *The Industrial System*, chap. XIII. This work, according to P. Ford, had 'a very large readership among the working class.' Ford, *Social Theory and Social Practice* (1968), 118. This, no doubt, can be attributed to its defence of trade unionism. However, it should also be noted that Hobson had serious objections to the politics of trade unionism. See below, chap. 7, sec. 4.
71 *The Evolution of Modern Capitalism* (1894; 2nd ed., 1906), 2. It is noteworthy that in the first edition of this book this feature of capitalism received scant attention. The emphasis was on 'the study of machine production.' In the second edition, Hobson wrote a new introductory chapter in which he stated that the existence of a proletariat deprived of the means of production was a basic structural feature of capitalism. The main influence in this regard was not Marx's *Das Kapital*, which Hobson had read prior to writing the first edition, but Werner Sombart's *Der Moderne Kapitalismus* (1902). Cf. Hobson's 'Preface to the Revised Edition.' However, it should be noted that Hobson had already examined this feature of capitalism in *The Economics of Distribution*, which was published prior to Sombart's work. The two editions of *The Evolution of Modern Capitalism* capsulate Hobson's movement from the abstract to the specific.

The moment labour was divorced from the means of production it suffered a special enfeeblement which tilted the wage-bargaining situation in favour of the capitalist. Adam Smith[72] (and of course Marx) had recognized this bias in the system, but later classical economists had obfuscated the fact by ever more readily assuming, from the first, a separatist treatment of the factors of production. Hobson reinstated the notion of unequal bargaining power at the forefront of his analysis:

There are certain special considerations affecting the sale of labour-power which make the sellers of that commodity normally weaker than the buyers. ... A supply of goods or of land which, if it is placed upon the market, would bring down prices to an unprofitable level, can in most cases be withheld from the market without sustaining irreparable damage. This is not the case with labour-power. It must be sold; if not sold for a week, not only is the week's supply wasted, but the aggregate of labour-power ... [i.e.] the labourer himself, perishes. This labour-power must be sold continuously ... [and] it must be sold to a buyer who knows the necessity under which the seller stands to effect a sale. In a word, the labourer is selling his labour-power under conditions of a forced sale. ... These weaknesses of bargaining attach to labour-power, as distinct from other things because labour-power cannot be detached from the vitality of which it is a function. ... [i.e.] while the worker is selling a portion of his labour-power, he is also buying permission to live. ... The power to starve labour into submission [is] the final economic arbiter.[73]

This enfeeblement would have disadvantaged labour in its contest with capital, even in the most perfect of markets – 'For all that a man hath will he give for his life' – let alone one riddled with elements of business monopoly.[74]

Hobson's closer inspection of the institutions of capitalism, then, had disclosed two areas in which measures of social reform had to be undertaken if labour's normal position as a weak-bargainer was to be redressed. First, the worker had to be protected from the trusts and other monopolistic elements in the economy; second, he had to be protected from his own perishability. Hobson's response to these problems of labour will be examined later as part of the analysis of his reform program.

72 See *The Wealth of Nations*, 60
73 *The Economics of Distribution*, 218-22
74 *Wealth and Life*, 202. The phrase is Ruskin's.

4 CONCLUSION

This chapter has examined Hobson's theory of the organic generation of surplus value. This theory placed Hobson beyond the pale of classical liberal economics, but did not push him into the embrace of Marxian socialists. He argued against the premise of classical political economy that production is a composite of individual efforts, suggesting instead that production is organic and that a significant part of the industrial product belongs not to particular individuals but to the public as a whole, to be used for shared projects. On the other hand, he withstood the embrace of Marxian socialists on the grounds that socialist doctrine, although recognizing the existence of social surplus, did not correctly appreciate its organic nature and thus erred in assigning it to the proletariat rather than the public;[75] nor did it give credence to the full economy of costs involved in production, in particular neglecting the costs of abstinence and refusing to assign interest payments as recompense. In short, both classical and socialist doctrine promoted claims to public property which Hobson considered to be unjust.

Hobson's own prescription for economic justice involved a major re-evaluation of the role of the state in economic affairs. But before turning to this matter, it is first necessary to examine Hobson's theory of underconsumption and imperialism, for it is important to recognize that Hobson considered the existing system of distribution to be not only unjust but woefully inefficient. Hobson wanted to show not only the faulty ideals of a system which failed to credit the organic value of social relations, but also the fact that the private possession of social values could not be defended economically. Economic depression rather than the public good was the path along which the hidden hand guided the possessive individuals of classical political economy.

75 The British Communist party, in turn, labelled Hobson's doctrine of the organic surplus, or 'pool of wealth,' as they described it, as a 'Social Fascist theory.' See *Political Economy: Marxist Study Courses*, Lesson v, 1976 (originally published in 1933).

4

The Theory of Underconsumption

The basis on which all economic teaching since Adam Smith has stood, viz., that the quantity annually produced is determined by the aggregates of Natural Agents, Capital, and Labour, is erroneous, ... on the contrary, the quantity produced, while it can never exceed [these] limits ... may be ... reduced far below this maximum by the check that undue saving and consequent accumulation of over-supply exerts on production; i.e., ... consumption limits production and not production consumption. Mummery and Hobson, *The Physiology of Industry*, vi.

Underconsumption theory had a longer history than Hobson first realized. As Keynes was to write,[1] Hobson brought the underconsumptionist critique out from hibernation, but Hobson himself was barely aware of this earlier 'winter of discontent.'[2] When he and his associate, A.F. Mummery, first expounded their theory of underconsumption in *The Physiology of Industry* in 1889, only Malthus and Chalmers received brief mention as intellectual forebears.[3]

---

1 J.M. Keynes, *The General Theory of Employment, Interest and Money* (1936), 364
2 *Confessions* (1938), 31
3 *The Physiology of Industry* (1889), 101. Other names that might have been mentioned are: Lauderdale, Sismondi, Rodbertus, Fourier, and perhaps Marx. The most recent history of underconsumption doctrines is Michael Bleaney's *Underconsumption Theories*, (1976). This is not, however, the first history of underconsumptionism, as Bleaney claims, for it was preceded by J.M. Robertson, *The Fallacy of Saving* (1892), which includes a review of such theories up to and including Mummery and Hobson's first work. The best statement on Marx as an underconsumptionist is Paul Sweezy, *The Theory of Capital Development* (1942). On the other hand, Paul Mattick, *Marx and Keynes* (1969), denies that Marx was an underconsumptionist.

Yet almost from its inception, classical political economy had to be defended from the contention that capitalism was incapable of sustaining a market for its products because it tended to compress consumer spending below the level necessary to absorb the industrial product. In short, capitalism was said to suffer from a lack of effective demand. By the time of Hobson's writing this underconsumptionist critique had tenuously established two main variants, the first associated with the ideas of Thomas Malthus, the second with those of Simonde de Sismondi. It is interesting that both of these variants are present in Hobson's works.

Malthus, in correspondence with Ricardo and in *Principles of Political Economy* [1820], attributed the likelihood of industrial glut to the excessive saving habits of the bourgeoisie. He considered Adam Smith responsible for this erroneous stress on the economic virtue of thrift. Smith was the first economist to appreciate that what was distinctive about capitalism was that the capitalist, unlike the feudal landlord, was continuously faced with the dilemma as to whether to consume his profits or save and invest them. The latter course was the one advocated by Smith, for only further capital accumulation, to his mind, could advance the wealth of nations. The following passage makes Smith's position clear.

Capitals are increased by parsimony, and diminished by prodigality and misconduct. Whatever a person saves from his revenue he adds to his capital. ... As the capital of an individual can be increased only by what he saves from his annual revenue ... so the capital of a society, which is the same with that of all the individuals who compose it, can be increased only in the same manner ... That portion of his revenue which a rich man annually spends is in most cases consumed by idle guests and menial servants, who leave nothing behind them in return for their consumption. That portion which he annually saves, as for the sake of profit it is immediately employed as capital, is consumed in the same manner, and nearly in the same time too, but by a different set of people, by labourers, manufacturers, and artificers, who reproduce with a profit the value of their annual consumption.[4]

Malthus countered Smith's focus on thrift, with a defence of consumption expenditure and in particular that expenditure made by the landed aristocracy. He argued, in his *Principles of Political Economy*, that too much saving could destroy the incentive to produce. 'It is quite obvious that [these propositions of Smith] are not true to an indefinite extent, and that the principle of

4 *The Wealth of Nations* (1776, Everyman's ed., 1910), vol. 2, 301-2

saving, pushed to excess, would destroy the motive of production ... If production be in great excess above consumption, the motive to accumulate and produce must cease from the want of will to consume.'[5] Elsewhere, Malthus attempted to give substance to this contention by suggesting that Smith and his followers had supposed that 'accumulation ensures demand; or that the consumption of the labourers employed by those whose object is to save, will create such an effective demand for commodities as to encourage a continued increase of produce.'[6] This Malthus denied. Investment might create some additional demand, but not enough to realize a profit. The effective demand created within the capitalist process of production would only be equal to the additional cost of employing new workers. The extra demand needed in order to secure a profit, therefore, had to come, according to Malthus, from the prodigality of the landlord class, who stood outside the capitalist investment process. If such 'luxurious expenditure' was not forthcoming, then the market would be glutted with commodities.

The details of the debate between Malthus and Ricardo – the latter being the main spokesman for the new orthodoxy – need not be reiterated here, save to say that Malthus was refuted, at least to the satisfaction of the next several generations of liberal economists up to and including J.S. Mill. In England, at least, the weight of orthodoxy, assisted by England's dominant industrial position in foreign markets, stilled all disquiet about the problems of 'effective demand' until Hobson once more picked up the debate in 1889, by which time, he remarked, the idea of underconsumption was 'considered ... as equivalent in rationality to an attempt to prove the flatness of the earth.'[7]

But although all was quiet in England, on the continent a second variant of the underconsumptionist critique had been developed by the Swiss historian and economist, Simonde de Sismondi. Whereas Malthus had placed primary emphasis on 'oversaving' as the cause of economic disturbances, Sismondi believed the fault lay with the maldistribution of income.

Sismondi's disillusionment with Adam Smith's generally optimistic prognosis for industrial society was occasioned by a visit to England in 1819, one of the worst years of the post-Napoleonic depression, where he witnessed the appalling social conditions of the new industrial 'proletarii.' Sismondi was the first economist to take this term out of its ancient Roman context and apply

---

5 Cited in M. Bleaney, *Underconsumption Theories* (1976), 49
6 Ibid., 53
7 *Confessions* 30; cf. also 34, where Hobson remarks, 'If Britain had been an isolated economic community ... we should have been brought up against the limit of effective saving long ago.'

it to modern wage labour. It is significant that he chose a word which originally meant 'those who had nothing, who paid no taxes and could contribute only their offspring – the proles – to the country,' since he believed it was the impoverishment of the workers that was at the root of economic slumps. Sismondi argued that competition in production had kept labour costs at a minimum and maximized output, just as Adam Smith predicted, but that in the realm of distribution such a system created havoc; subsistence wages meant that the workers could not buy back the full stock of goods they produced. On the other hand, the rich were not interested in mass-produced goods but in luxury items, and thus failed to pick up the slack in the market. The surplus accumulated until a crisis set in and then the unsold stock was liquidated in a depression. Sismondi granted that capitalists could delay this eventuality by opening foreign markets for their surplus goods, but he considered the more humane solution was for the state to advance the workers' level of consumption by setting up public works – whose products do not bear upon the market and do not increase the general glut – thereby reducing the competition for jobs, one of the prime causes of low wages.[8] Sismondi also proposed that the state should encourage small-scale businesses so as to improve the workers' chances of becoming self-supporting.

Although Sismondi seems to have had even less influence on Hobson than did Malthus, in many ways their affinity is greater. While Hobson's key variable in explaining economic depression is the level of savings, which is the Malthusian line, he sides with Sismondi on the important question as to whether the crisis can be averted by reforms operating within the system (by diverting income from the capitalists to the workers), or whether, because wages are fixed 'as if by some iron law,' reliance has to be placed on the prodigality of the landed aristocracy or some other 'third person' who exists on the periphery of the capitalist accumulative process, as Malthus contended. Hobson and Malthus may begin their analysis on the same note, but overall the tone of Hobson's work is closer to that of Sismondi.

2 THE EVOLUTION OF HOBSON'S THEORY OF UNDERCONSUMPTION

It took some time before Hobson firmly linked the idea of income maldistribution to his theory of economic crisis. It is a notable feature of *The Physiology of Industry* (1889) that maldistribution of income receives at best only implied recognition as a cause of unemployment. There are sections of the book which could have easily accommodated a critique of the process of

8 J. Oser and W. Blanchfield, *The Evolution of Economic Thought* (1975), 161

income distribution under capitalism.[9] However, this was not the way in which the argument was actually developed. Instead, emphasis was placed upon the saving *habits* of the rich as the key to explaining economic depressions. The premise of Mummery and Hobson's theory is stated as follows:

If increased *thrift* or *caution* induces people to save more in the present, they must consent to consume more in the future. If they refuse to assent to this condition, they may persist in heaping up new material forms of capital, but the real effective capital will be absolutely limited by the actual extent of their future consumption [and the rest will go to waste].[10]

Later, when directly considering the plight of workers in an economic depression, they write:

The labourers ... are the chief sufferers from the saving *habits* of the rich, and in so far as the evil proceeds from poverty, the highly extolled virtues of thrift, parsimony and saving are the cause.[11]

These two statements make it clear that in *The Physiology of Industry* attention was focused on peoples' propensity to save more as their income increased.

In Hobson's subsequent works, beginning with *The Problem of the Unemployed* (1896), this emphasis on oversaving as the critical factor in generating underconsumption crises was retained, but the origin of these savings was made an increasingly significant part of the analysis. The rich were identified as capitalists rather than as a somewhat amorphous body of savers and the ills of the economic system were located in specific institutions fostering the maldistribution of income. Consequently, savings were largely redefined to mean 'unearned incomes,' the fruit of exploitation rather than thrift, since monies originating from this source were especially likely to be overinvested. By concentrating on savings derived from unearned income, Hobson synthesized the separate contributions that Malthus and Sismondi had made to underconsumption theory.

Hobson's analysis of the origins of unearned income was largely worked out by 1900, in *The Economics of Distribution*. However, the connection between these 'unproductive surpluses' and the tendency to oversave was not fully articulated until the publication of *The Industrial System* in 1909. In

9 See, for example, chap. VI, 'The Law of the Limiting Requisite,' and chap. VIII, sec. IV.
10 *The Physiology of Industry* (1889), 51 (emphasis added)
11 Ibid., 182 (emphasis added)

this work, the major aspects of Hobson's conceptual apparatus for analysing underconsumption crises was brought to a completion. This did not prevent him from repeating his thesis in later works, notably in *The Economics of Unemployment* (1922), *Rationalisation and Unemployment* (1930), and *Property and Impropery* (1937), but no major conceptual innovations took place after 1909. Hence, it is now possible to give a general account of Hobson's theory taking in the full range of his works.

3 HOBSON'S GENERAL THEORY OF EMPLOYMENT, SAVINGS, AND CONSUMPTION

The failure to give proper recognition to the obvious fact that the quantity of serviceable forms of capital at the several stages of production is absolutely limited by the rates at which consumable goods are drawn out of the industrial machine, arises from the refusal to consider industry from the *social organic* viewpoint. *The Problem of the Unemployed*, 82 (emphasis added)

In Hobson's opinion, the reason why orthodox economists of his time continued to deny the possibility of underconsumption crises amidst mounting evidence that industrial depression was a recurring feature of the capitalist economy, was that they still, in effect, analysed capitalism as if it were a barter economy. In this they were only reaffirming Jean Baptiste Say's celebrated 'Law of Markets.' This law stated, in Hobson's words, that 'since all business is the exchange of commodities for commodities, it is evident that someone possesses the power to consume whatever can be produced ... [and] since the desires of man are unlimited ... there exists the desire to consume whatever can be produced':[12] consequently, neither too much can be produced, nor too little consumed. The normal state of the economy was one of equilibrium.

It is sometimes suggested that Hobson completely demolished Say's Law.[13] As the following analysis will show that opinion is substantially correct, but with one or two reservations which should be noted at the outset. First, Hobson agreed with Say that production and consumption were ultimately bound together.[14] In his own words, he accepted that 'there must be a

---

12 *The Problem of the Unemployed* (1896), 72-3
13 Cf. Horace B. Davis, 'Hobson and Human Welfare,' *Science and Society*, vol. 21, no. 4 (1957), 296.
14 The best-known exponent of the view that under capitalism production and consumption are independent economic functions is Tugan-Baranowsky. See P. Sweezy, *The Theory of Capitalist Development*, chap. x.

definite quantitative relation between the rate of production and the rate of consumption.'[15] The equilibrating of these two rates expressed Hobson's ideal of a well-ordered economy. Moreover, Hobson also accepted the proposition that when saving and consumption rates were in balance, there would be full employment. Hobson's concurrence in this matter stems from the fact that, like Say and the classical economists, he identified the act of saving with the act of investment:

The real economic function of saving must be clearly kept in mind. It does not consist in not spending. ... It consists in paying producers to make more non-consumable goods for use as capital.[16]

This definition of saving has resulted in a good deal of 'post-Keynesian' criticism of Hobson's work, as will be shown later. But it should be immediately noted that Keynes' *ex ante* and *ex post* distinctions regarding both savings and investments, and his related contention that savings and investment could be in balance at less than full employment provided a more thorough subversion of Say's Law than did Hobson's critique.

What Hobson seriously doubted about Say's Law was its general applicability in a capitalist economy. There, Say's Law did not work automatically: it was the exception rather than the rule. 'Though it must be admitted,' Hobson wrote, 'that a desire to consume is in general the motive force behind production, it does not operate so closely ... as to preclude the waste of overproduction.[17] Say and his followers had badly misconceived the real dynamic of capital accumulation and especially how under capitalism the organic connection between consumption and production had been split asunder. Capitalism thwarted Say's Law because essentially it was a planless mode of production. Thus there could be both oversaving (overproduction) and underconsumption; indeed these imbalances are merely the convex and concave of this same fact.

a / The Causes of Oversaving (Overproduction)
One of Hobson's most significant contributions to the critique of classical economics was his exposure of its underpinnings in erroneous individualist assumptions, and in particular its attachment to the fallacy of composition – the fallacy, as the Oxford English Dictionary defines it, 'of arguing that

15 *The Industrial System* (1909; 2nd ed., 1910), 41
16 *The Economics of Unemployment* (1922), 34
17 *The Problem of the Unemployed*, 74

what is true of each of several things is true of all taken together.' It has already been shown that Hobson believed that it was the classical economists' failure to see through this fallacy that blinded them to the social origins and character of surplus value. Likewise, in his analysis of the causes of oversaving, Hobson concluded that the classical economists' approach to this problem was dogged by the same fallacy:

The statement of Adam Smith, 'What is prudence in the conduct of a private family can scarce be folly in that of a great nation' has been taken too generally for a gospel truth. This view, that the community means nothing more than the addition of a number of individual units, and that the interest of Society can be obtained by adding together the interests of individual members, has led to ... grave errors in Economics. ... [This] confident assumption ... is the true explanation of the indifference with which students of the mechanism of commerce have regarded all such criticism of the construction of that machine as is contained in the theories of Over-production. ... The disclosure of the falsehood on which the assumption rests will also disclose the existence and nature of that force which gives to Over-Supply an actual existence in the world of commerce. ... *It is, in fact, the clash of interests between the community as a whole and the individual members in respect to Saving, that is the cause of Over-Supply.*[18]

Adam Smith's 'hidden hand,' then, has become lost in a paradox, namely that the interest of each saver did not add up to the general interest.

Hobson began his attempt to uncover the causes behind his paradox of thrift by examining the conditions under which an individual saved. When an individual reduced his level of consumption and took the savings thus generated and invested them (as Hobson claimed was bound to happen), he created an additional supply of productive power. The individual's thrift would be rewarded provided others could be induced to consume the extra supply of commodities the industrial system was now capable of delivering. Given this prerequisite, there was no limit on the level of individual saving.

Could this situation of limitless thrift, valid from the individual standpoint, be generalized so as to apply to the community as a whole? Hobson's answer was no. If too many individuals in society were intent on saving, then there would be too few left to consume the extra products these savings generated and the excess would go to waste. It followed that while it was true that 'the individual need not increase his Consumption in order to increase his Capital,' none the less 'if the Community wished to increase its Capital, it must consent to increase its Consumption.'[19] In other words, the concept of 'other,' which was valid from the individualistic standpoint, was not available to the collective: others could not be left responsible for advancing the level of consumption. It followed that unless the community itself took on the responsibility of regulating savings, then the limitless character of individual saving was bound to upset that balance between investment and consumption, which Hobson had earlier determined was crucial in establishing the amount of saving that was *socially* useful. Hobson therefore concluded that there was good reason to reject the 'accepted dogmas that the saving of the individual must always and necessarily enrich the Community' and that 'the individual seeking his own advantage necessarily works for the Community.'[20]

At this point Hobson's attack on the individualist underpinnings of Say's Law was significantly deepened by his consideration of what might be termed the paradox of profits. Thus far, the dilemma he had been examining had the appearance of being accidental in nature, the outcome of unintended consequences. But the malady was more serious than that. Oversaving was the consequence of something other than mere miscalculation and ignorance. The sickness in fact went to the heart of the competitive system. Competition compelled entrepreneurs and financiers, whose job it was to apply the stock of individual savings to industry, to do this in a manner which necessarily sacrificed the social interest to private gain.[21] Thus even if trade statistics and other social guidelines for investment decisions were provided, each capitalist would still attempt 'to do himself the largest portion of useful saving' in the hope that any waste of overproduction would be borne by his competitors. It was 'just this spirit of competition,' according to Hobson, which supplied, 'the force that operates to bring about Overproduction.'[22] Behind the paradox of thrift, then, stood a more determinant motive force,

19 Ibid., 112
20 Ibid., viii
21 Here it is evident that, in assuming that all savings were invested, Hobson discounted the possibility of any basic discord between entrepreneurial decisions as to how much to invest and household decisions as to how much to save. This distinction, of course, was important to Keynes' analysis of the interaction between the level of desired savings and the level of actual savings. To what extent this distinction is still important is debatable. See, for example, J.K. Galbraith, *The New Industrial State* (1967), where stress is placed on corporations providing their own savings from retained profits. Here saver and investor are the same person.
22 *The Physiology of Industry*, 112

the struggle for private profit, which was driving a wedge between private benefit and public good. Hobson elaborated as follows:

In manufacture it is often in the interest of a capitalist to set up and work new spinning-mills or iron-works, although there may already exist enough mills and works to supply every possible demand, provided he sees a fair prospect of getting away from his competitors a sufficient proportion of trade. Nor is it an adequate response to say that the new-comer can only get the trade by producing a better or cheaper article, and that in this way the community, as a body of consumers, is advantaged by his action. In the first place, this statement is not true; it is commonly by superiority in the arts of competition, which do not necessarily involve superiority in production, that the modern business firm is able to get business. Secondly, even supposing that the new capital is made effective by some trifling economy in methods of production, it by no means follows that the consuming public gains ... to a corresponding extent ... Lastly, the fall in retail prices to the consuming public must not be taken as the just and final test and measure of the net gain to the community. The gain may be bought too dearly if it involves, as it often does, a large and unforeseen displacement of capital and labour in earlier use, the vested interests of which receive neither compensation nor consideration under the stern rule of competitive trade.[23]

Investment decisions taken by individual firms operating within a market system were unlikely to include considerations such as these, not because of imperfect knowledge of trade conditions or other 'accidents,' but because capitalists never took regard of 'the interests of capitalism as a whole.' The conditions of survival in the market ensured that a businessman 'seldom' looked further than the 'early profitable sales' of the goods he produced.[24]

The economic taproot of oversaving, therefore, was to be found in the independent nature of corporate decision-making in a market economy. The composite of each capitalist's efforts to accumulate capital and maximize profits did not necessarily add up to the social interest but instead was a dangerous excitation to oversaving.

---

23 *The Problem of the Unemployed*, 84. See also *The Physiology of Industry*, 112-16.
24 'Underconsumption and Its Remedies,' in G. Hutton, ed., *The Burden of Plenty?* (1935), 55-6

It has already been noted that Hobson's original account of oversaving, as presented in *The Physiology of Industry* contained no mention of the concept of unearned income. Once this concept was introduced into Hobson's subsequent works, it provided him with two additional explanations of the phenomenon of oversaving/overinvestment.

According to Hobson, saving that involved some kind of sacrifice in its creation was regulated by a careful calculation relating this sacrifice to the amount of future benefit to be secured from its investment. On the other hand, saving derived from unearned income escaped this limitation, because its acquisition involved no cost or sacrifice, at least to the recipient. Such savings tended to accumulate. To illustrate his point, Hobson contrasted the process of saving in a Crusoe economy and a communist economy with that of a capitalist economy.

In a single man, or Crusoe economy, the proportion between consumption and saving, i.e. between the amount of energy given to making consumables and that given to making new tools ... would be determined by a close comparison between present and future pleasures and pains. Crusoe would find himself willing to give so much energy to making provision for increased consumption next year, but no more. So with a completely communistic society ... it would regulate the portion of its savings to its spending by a careful calculus of present and future satisfactions. The rightness of such calculations would be based upon the fact that all saving required a proportionate effort on the part of the individual or community that made it. ... But if, as regards any large portion of savings, this condition is not present, there is no automatic guarantee of the maintenance of the right proportion between spending and saving. ... [And] that saving which is made out of unproductive surplus income is not amenable to this calculus.[25]

Not savings *per se*, but only savings which represent unearned income, tend to be saved to excess. These savings, when invested, are likely to create a volume of productive power superfluous to consumption demand.

This, then, was an additional reason why profiteers saved too much, but Hobson also used the idea of unearned income to explain why those savings were invested rather than spent on consumables. The whip of competition would seem to provide one answer, but Hobson also had a second explanation. He suggested that those who lived off unearned income had not only

25 *The Industrial System*, 294

broken the tie between saving and abstinence, but also the link between consumption and effort.[26] The workingman knew what he was saving for, since each unit of saving represented a real want deferred. Consequently, he was eager to advance his level of consumption once his hard-earned savings started bringing in a return as investments. But the rich man did not sustain the effort of saving by anticipating the additional stocks of consumables to be had in the future. On the contrary, he saved from a fortuitous surplus for which no real want had been sacrificed. The rich man was thus ill-prepared to advance his consumption demands in line with the incoming flow of rents, dividends, and other surplus payments he received, and eventually he found himself in a position where he had 'the *power* to consume' but not 'the *desire*.'[27] The rich man's attempt to place himself above 'natural law' was self-defeating:

In spite of all attempts to make an artificial severance between a 'producing' and a 'consuming' class, the natural relation between production and consumption, between effort and satisfaction, exercises a strong influence in the ... economy. It is possible for individuals and for classes who draw large incomes *alieni vultus sudore*, or without any considerable contribution to effort, to be large and profuse consumers. But ... the law which relates effort to satisfaction is a 'natural' law, which, finding its simplest expression in the physical fact that a man cannot eat and digest a good dinner unless he has made some output of physical energy in exercise, penetrates in some unseen way the whole region of consumption, denying satisfaction that is not compensated by some corresponding personal effort. This 'natural' law finds an economical expression in the fact that an attempt to be a very large consumer and a very small producer in the long run defeats itself. ... This, interpreted into simple language, means that a man who draws a large income without working for it, cannot and does not spend it.[28]

Hobson's conclusion is that the rich are driven to invest from the 'sheer inability to make consumption keep pace with rising income.'[29]

One important corollary of Hobson's thesis should be noted. It provided him with grounds for rejecting Malthus' remedy for underconsumption. Not

26 *The Problem of the Unemployed*, 91
27 Ibid., 73
28 Ibid., 88-9
29 *The Industrial System*, 295

only was the advocacy of luxurious expenditure by the unproductive classes distasteful to Hobson's egalitarian sentiments, but it was also unrealistic:

Malthus saw that the over-saving of the wealthy was the direct economic force which kept trade back. His remedy was an increase of luxurious expenditure. But this, even were it otherwise desirable, is wholly impracticable. We have seen that the motives which induce the wealthy to withhold the present use of consuming-power are natural and necessary. A piece of academic advice, unbacked by any economic force, is absolutely futile. The owners of unearned ... income, as we see, *must* accumulate capital, which from the social standpoint is excess.[30]

Thus, going one better than St Paul, Hobson claimed that those who do not work, should not, indeed cannot, eat, and therefore could not be relied upon to maintain the level of consumption.

For some commentators, Hobson's assertion that consumption is related to the effort involved in earning an income is unconvincing. Professor Coppock, for example, finds the relation 'mysterious.'[31] Moreover, Hobson's contention that the rich accumulate much of their income from the 'sheer inability' to raise the level of their expenditure on luxuries, seems to underestimate their capacity in this regard, when examined alongside his own often incisive analysis of the capacity of the rich to indulge in conspicuous consumption. For one so skilled in Veblenist critique, indeed Hobson's friend Brailsford considered him better at it than Veblen himself,[32] Hobson does not appear fully to appreciate the implications of conspicuous consumption for his own thesis. The essence of conspicuous consumption, after all, is that it is expenditure for display, and the goods on show are designed precisely to advertise that their owner has superfluous income and thus can afford to disregard the utility of things. Conspicuous consumption has no direct, organic link with the personal needs of the spender, rather it is 'other-directed' and consequently less easily satiated. This kind of exhibitionism would seem to negate Hobson's 'natural law.'

In this light it seems reasonable to conclude that Hobson's earlier analysis of the *structural* barriers to consumption expenditure by capitalists, i.e., their need to capitalize savings in order to remain competitive, is little assisted by

---

30 *The Problem of the Unemployed*, 99
31 D.J. Coppock, 'A Reconsideration of Hobson's Theory of Unemployment,' *Manchester School of Economics and Social Studies*, vol. xxi (1953), 4
32 *The Life-Work of J.A. Hobson* (1948), 18

this later assertion that there exists a *natural* barrier to their consumption needs. On the other hand, it is possible that Hobson's own satisfaction with this 'Pauline' explanation of overinvestment, is the reason why he never attempted a full structural analysis of the process of capital accumulation under conditions of imperfect competition, as did later underconsumptionists, like Baran and Sweezy.[33]

b / The Causes of Underconsumption
Oversaving was the first stage of industrial depression, but the ultimate barrier to capitalist prosperity was the rate of consumption. The capitalist had continuously to accumulate (save) in order to survive, but the conditions of his survival opposed an even more fundamental law, namely that such accumulation had no validity except in terms of consumption. 'The end and object of commerce,' Hobson asserted, was to produce those 'necessaries and conveniences to which the term commodity is applied.'[34] Therefore, it was inevitable that the contradiction between the motive force of capitalism and the natural grounding of production in consumption would be resolved negatively in terms of an underconsumption crisis.

There were two specific reasons why the rate of consumption could not keep pace with the powers of production in a capitalist economy. The first was the result of what Hobson termed 'the conservative character of the arts of consumption.' In *Economics and Unemployment* he attributed this conservatism to capitalism's uneven development in its capacity to dominate all areas of economic life:

In primitive societies the standards or methods of work are almost as conservative as those of consumption. Of ... modern industrial nations, this is no longer true. Invention and business initiative, enlisted in the cause of

---

33 Cf. Baran and Sweezy, *Monopoly Capital*, 1966, chap. 3. In his books Sweezy nowhere indicates any indebtedness to Hobson. There is, however, an interesting and generally supportive review by Sweezy of Hobson's *Confessions* in the *Nation* (27 Aug. 1939) entitled, 'J.A. Hobson's Economic Heresies.'

It should be also noted that the fact that Hobson used this theory to reject the Malthusian solution to underconsumption does not mean that in objecting to it, the Malthusian alternative once more becomes viable. Hobson's analysis of the 'structural' imperative to invest also provides reasons for doubting Malthus' argument. Competition allows no sector of the economy to long remain both rich and unproductive. Even those who only wish to stand still must continuously reinvest simply to maintain their existing position. Thus Malthus' 'gentlemen farmers' are compelled to become 'agro-businessmen.'

34 *The Physiology of Industry*, 20

quick profiteering [raise] this productivity by leaps and bounds. Though modern man, in his capacity of consumer, is far more progressive than his ancestors, his power of taking on new economic needs and of raising rapidly the quantity, variety and quality of consumption, is limited by a narrowness of imagination and a servitude of habit which are far less dominant in production. There is in modern business ... a strong stimulus to the early imitation and adoption of new superior methods by the whole body of members of a trade, who are otherwise outcompeted and ruined by their conservatism. ... [On the other hand] a large part of consumption is carried on in the privacy of separate homes, under the bonds of custom and withdrawn from any strong continual stimulus to imitation and competition.[35]

The Industrial Revolution had not been attended by a commensurate revolution in the arts of consumption, with the consequence that a significant time lag had developed between the moment of increased production and the absorption of this product by consumers.

Although Hobson never rescinded his opinion that this 'conservatism in the arts of consumption' was a primary cause of economic slumps, it is clear from several of his works that he considered this to be a matter in a state of flux. Indeed as early as *The Problem of the Unemployed* (1896), Hobson had noted the increasing proportion of national income that was being devoted to the 'sales effort,' and sometime later he seems to have concluded that in certain ways this effort had paid off.[36] In *Wealth and Life* (1929) he qualified what could be termed his 'uneven development' thesis in so far as it applied to the rate of consumption. Consumption now appeared to be an increasingly conquered sphere; it had become chained to the realm of production:

The dominant economic forces of our time are employing all the resources of the physical sciences and of applied psychology, to produce large masses of identical goods, and to persuade large masses of persons to purchase and consume them. ... There is a serious attempt, partly in the interests of profitable business ... to standardise the mental processes of whole communities. If all the members of a community can be induced, not merely to buy the same foods, wear the same clothes, use the same furniture and other material appliances, but to learn the same facts, think the same thoughts, feel the same emotions, hold the same opinions, culti-

35 33. See also *The Problem of the Unemployed*, 65-6.
36 Cf. *The Problem of the Unemployed*, 66-72.

vate the same tastes and interests, all the machinery of life ... will run smoothly. ...

If the salesman of the mass-producers can tempt consumers ever to enlarge their demand for standard goods, they can gradually standardise the whole man and his family into servitude to a normal type ... with all the conventions and respectabilities moulded by the requirements of profitable business.[37]

It is probable, then, that Hobson's increasing awareness of the receptivity of the public to mass advertising, etc., explains why he makes little or no mention of the 'conservatism of consumption' as a cause of economic depression in his last few works. His silence perhaps indicates an emerging perception of the enormous changes capitalism was about to undergo in its attempt to oppose its ascetic origins and wage a war against the 'savings mentality.'

The second and more important reason why the level of consumption failed to keep pace with advances in productive capacity was related, in Hobson's opinion, to inequalities in the distribution of income. Hobson rejected the proposition, advanced by Major Douglas, that economic depression was a consequence of insufficient income in the economy as a whole. Indeed, this was one of the few issues upon which Hobson was in complete accord with the classical economists (including J.B. Say). They had argued that the act of production simultaneously created sufficient income to take all the goods off the market. In this sense, supply created its own demand. Similarly, Hobson wrote that, 'it is to be admitted that these final commodities could be sold, in the sense that someone possesses the money income capable of buying them.'[38]

What Hobson objected to was not this axiom of classical economics but the *petitio principii* involved, namely that if the money income existed, then so did the effective demand. In Hobson's words, it assumed that 'the power to consume and the desire to consume' were 'vested in the same person.'[39] In Hobson's opinion, the unfair bargaining processes within capitalism negated this assumption:

[The] failure to fully utilise consuming-power is due to the fact that much of it is owned by those who, having already satisfied their strong present

37 *Wealth and Life* (1929), 318, 321. See also *Rationalisation and Unemployment* (1930), 80-2.
38 *The Economics of Unemployment*, 69. The first edition of this work contained a chapter criticizing the underconsumption theories of Major Douglas, focusing on the fact that Douglas denied this contention.
39 *The Problem of the Unemployed*, 73

desires have no adequate motive for utilising it in the present, and therefore allow it to accumulate.[40]

Underconsumption crises, therefore, could not be understood unless it was
recognized that the propensity to consume from profit income was significantly different from the propensity to consume from wage income, and
hence must be given separate consideration in any analysis of effective
demand.

Hobson summarized the crux of his argument regarding the mal-distribu-
tion of income as follows:

A rapidly rising technique and improved organisation have undoubtedly
led to a rapid increase of the productive power of industry. But the inability to make full profitable use of this increased power must be imputed to
a failure to make full, continuous use of the purchasing power created and
distributed simultaneously with every act of production. This failure,
again, can only be imputed to a maldistribution of income of such a kind
as to place too much purchasing power in the hands of the rich classes,
who allow it to accumulate for investment, too little in the hands of those
who desire to raise their standard of living. The necessary effect is to
evoke a monetary saving which is found to be excessive, in that the
increased goods it is intended to produce cannot actually get produced,
because there is an insufficient market for them.[41]

4 THE TRADE CYCLE

The main features of Hobson's theory of underconsumption having been
described, it is now possible to fill in the details of the series of events which
Hobson saw as intervening between the moment of overproduction (the
boom stage of the cycle) and the moment of underconsumption (the slump).
It might be noted that Hobson's attempt to present his theory of underconsumption as a cyclical process also marks a difference between his and
earlier nineteenth-century accounts. Sismondi and Malthus, for example,
appear to have considered underconsumption the 'final' crisis of capitalism:
if the proper remedy was not administered, then the system would grind to a
halt. Hobson, on the other hand, argued that even though the crisis was
fundamental, it was not final; the system could recover, but only temporarily

40 Ibid., 92
41 *Rationalisation and Unemployment*, 55

and at great social cost. Bleaney is no doubt correct in ascribing this difference 'to the realisation that the new order of things had proven its durability in spite of periodic cataclysms, so that a theory of these fluctuations had to be provided' in order to 'round out' the theory of underconsumption.[42]

Although Hobson was one of the first underconsumptionists to attempt a systematic theory of the trade cycle, he was not, of course, the first to notice that trade fluctuated in this way; nor was his the first or only explanation of these cycles. In the analysis which follows, an attempt will be made to indicate Hobson's objections to competing theories of the trade cycle, although his comments on these theories are invariably brief and often not addressed to any theorist in particular; he was, after all, primarily concerned with criticizing those economists whose aim was not to explain but to explain away economic slumps.

Hobson described the basic movements of the trade cycle as follows:

first, the diversion of an excessive proportion of incomes into the creation of new capital;
second, the discovery of this excess as registered in unsold stocks of consumption and capital goods;
third, the shrinkage of incomes, both of workers and capitalists;
fourth, the reduction in the rate of saving and the letting down of existing plant;
fifth, the beginning of what might be called natural recovery. This last process does not, however, indicate that the disease has been diagnosed correctly and healed. For the recovery can only be temporary.[43]

Stage one, then, was initiated by a spate of overcapitalization. This contention immediately brought Hobson into dispute with two schools of thought: one minor, the other of major significance. The minor school comprised those economists who attributed the causes of industrial fluctuations to factors external to the economic system, whereas Hobson was arguing that there was a cycle-producing mechanism built into the system. In *The Industrial System* Hobson rejected the theory, first proposed by W.S. Jevons in 1875, that industrial depressions were the result of natural causes (in Jevons' case, fluctuations in sun-spots) leading to periodic failures in the wheat harvest.[44] Hobson could find no statistical evidence to link unemployment

42 *Underconsumption Theories*, 173
43 *Property and Impropery* (1937), 51
44 Cf. Gottfried von Haberler, *Prosperity and Depression* (1937), chap. 7.

and bad harvests, 'either in duration or in intensity.'[45] Further, he suggested that the theory overstated the repercussions of wheat shortages on the rest of the economy. Given that the demand for wheat was fairly inelastic, poor harvests would raise wheat prices and thus increase the spending power of the farming community 'by just as much as the general consuming public finds theirs reduced.' This reallocation might result in some dislocation of trade, 'but there was no reason to assume that the aggregate of spending, or unemployment will be less.'[46] This argument would seem to presuppose that the distribution of income in the farming community closely reflects that of the community as a whole. Hobson, however, gave no evidence that this in fact was the case.

Hobson also dismissed the idea that the trade cycle was dependent on the impact of technological innovations. Here the 'heroic inventor' was taken to be the critical 'external variable.'[47] According to Hobson, technological innovation accounted for some 'change in [the] locale' of certain industries and for the 'decline and eclipse' of others. But except in 'rare cases,' changes arising from new industrial processes were 'seldom so rapid and simultaneous as to cause great displacement of labour.' Most technological changes were 'gradual and foreseen.'[48] The contrary impression was the result of a romanticized' view that innovative ideas came 'flashing suddenly from the brain of a single genius and effect[ed] a rapid revolution in trade.' This gave an 'irregular and catastrophic appearance' to a process which was in reality quite orderly.[49]

The major opposition to Hobson's analysis of overcapitalization, however, came from the classical economists. They argued that the economic system had built-in safeguards to protect it from unhealthy excesses. In particular, they claimed, in Hobson's words, that 'over-saving was impossible because any tendency to it, leading to undue increase of capital, would straightway be corrected by a falling rate of interest.'[50] Hobson rejected this piece of conventional wisdom and instead maintained that the manipulation of the rate of

---

45 *The Industrial System*, 285
46 Ibid., 287
47 This was a notion that Joseph Schumpeter was later to utilize as the foundation of his theory of business cycles. Cf. Haberler, *Prosperity and Depression*, 77-8.
48 *The Industrial System*, 290. See also 'Underconsumption: An Exposition and a Reply,' *Economica*, vol. XIII (1933).
49 *The Evolution of Modern Capitalism* (1894), 57
50 *The Economics of Unemployment*, 51. See also *The Physiology of Industry*, 117ff. Hobson's identification of savings and investment resulted in him limiting his examination to the influence of interest rates on saving. Unlike Keynes, Hobson gave no separate consideration to the influence of the rate of interest on the decision to invest.

interest was largely ineffective in influencing the rate of saving; it operated too slowly and affected too little of the mass of savings generated in the industrial system.

First, Hobson pointed out that there were a number of institutions that had opted out of the money market, as it were. Many municipal corporations, for example, raised their capital 'not from the investment market but from taxation' and hence were 'not answerable to any rate-of-interest regulation.' Even more significant was the fact that a number of large corporations were financing their investment projects 'by building up reserves.' These, too, would not be 'much affected by consideration of the current rate of interest.'[51] Later economists have come to consider this as one of the most important developments in advanced capitalism.[52] Hobson, however, nowhere elaborated this point.

Turning next to the savings of individuals, Hobson based his analysis of the influence of the rate of interest upon a sharp appraisal of the various motivations that comprised the savings habit and how the play of these motives changed according to the size of income. The poor saved as a precautionary measure, i.e., as insurance against some future emergency. Such saving would be largely insensitive to changes in the rate of interest. Indeed, in so far as this kind of saving was affected by the rate of interest, the influence was probably in the opposite direction to that supposed by the classical economists: 'Some sort of conscious thrift, aiming to make definite provision for old age or other future contingency, may even be stimulated, instead of depressed, by a falling rate of interest, which demands a larger volume of saving to yield the required income.'[53]

Ironically, the indifference that the poor showed towards changes in the interest rate was shared by the rich. The rich, whose savings, of course, play a much more significant role in the economy, saved automatically. Any close calculation of cost and sacrifice that changes in the rate of interest was supposed to induce would not be effective, according to Hobson, where a large element of savings was made up of unearned income. A fall in the rate of interest would not motivate the rich to consume more (save less) because their consumption needs were already satiated.

Only the savings of the *lower* middle class were responsive to changes in the rate of interest. But in Hobson's opinion, this merely saved the classical theory from being totally redundant; it did not alter the fact that the rate of

51 *Wealth and Life*, 291. See also *From Capitalism to Socialism* (1932), 29.
52 See, for example, Galbraith, *The New Industrial State*, chap. IV.
53 *The Economics of Unemployment*, 52. See also *Work and Wealth* (1914), 89f.

interest was an 'exceedingly unreliable regulator' of savings.[54] Stage one of the trade cycle, then, reflected the fact that there existed a fund of savings which inexorably poured into investment, impervious to the nervous twitchings of the rate of interest.

Hobson's description of the second stage of the business cycle, i.e., the moment when the creation of excess capital is discovered, is especially important, for it is here that he attempts to pull together his analysis of over-saving and underconsumption.

The first stage consists in the excessive payment of income to the productive factors in the industries making capital goods. ... So long as this process continues, the portion of savings expended in these industries which go to labour other productive agents is available for the purchase of consumption goods and *no unemployment is created.* This is the element of truth in the commonly accepted doctrine that saving employs as much labour as spending. So it does, as long as it is invested without delay in payment for the production of capital goods. *But as soon as it is discovered that the increased fabric of capital exceeds the size required* ... to produce consumption goods at the rate they are being purchased by consumers, there is a necessary check upon the further creation of capital goods by investment of new savings, and these savings, so far as they continue to be made, lie uninvested. Then the depression, with its accompanying unemployment, actually begins.[55]

The depression, then, only begins when overinvestment ceases. Prior to that moment, investment in capital goods creates sufficient income to keep the demand for current consumer goods buoyant. Overinvestment is an erroneous policy from the beginning, but its effect is not immediate and for a while the economy appears to be in equilibrium.

Bleaney has suggested that Hobson's analysis of this early phase of the trade cycle actually reveals a major defect in his theory of underconsumption. By admitting the income-generating effect of investment, Hobson is supposedly hoisted with his own petard, for he is left trying to prove that there exists 'a deficiency of effective demand while retaining the classical assumption that all savings are at all times automatically invested, which of course removes any possibility of such a deficiency.'[56] If it is also realized that Hobson's statement clearly indicates that he had no notion of the 'multiplier'

54 *Wealth and Life*, 292
55 *Property and Impropery*, 48-9 (emphasis added)
56 *Underconsumption Theories*, 209. See also 180.

effect of new investment expenditure and was unable therefore to envisage occasions when investment could generate more than an equivalent expansion of consumptive capacity, then Bleaney's criticism is made to look even more damaging.[57]

None the less, Bleaney's evaluation badly misses the mark. This is essentially because Bleaney appears to assume that Hobson is describing a static economy, whereas in fact Hobson is describing a dynamic economy. The equilibrium between saving and spending is correctly described by Hobson as temporary, because he was arguing that investment not only replenishes income but also raises industrial capacity; and this, in turn, results in a significant quantitative change in the economy. It follows that when this new layer of capital fructifies, the extra commodities which now could be produced would be purchased only if there had been a corresponding increase in the rate of *prospective* demand.[58] In sum, the rise in wages had to keep pace with the rise in productive capacity.[59] The instability of the capitalist system arose from the fact that the income that should have been distributed to consumers to provide for this increase in future demand was misappropriated and applied to the capital goods industries, thus generating an excess in productive capacity. It can still be said that Hobson overstated this imbalance because of his ignorance of the 'multiplier,' but this is very different from saying (as does Bleaney) that he was unable to show why there should be any imbalance at all.

Hobson realized, of course, that his analysis of the second stage of the business cycle did not accord with the accounts of other economists, even those who agreed that overinvestment was a possibility. Some economists, for example, suggested that the rush for capital during the boom period had the effect of driving up wages, along with the price of machinery and interest

57 The concept of the multiplier was first developed by R.F. Kahn in 1931. Keynes incorporated the notion into his *General Theory* (see book III, chap. 10). It might be noted that Oser and Blanchfield, in *The Evolution of Economic Thought*, 409, cite a passage from Hobson's *The Industrial System*, which they suggest indicates that he had 'a clear, if rudimentary idea of the multiplier.' However, it is difficult to determine how they reached this conclusion, and, in any case, Hobson certainly never put the notion to use.

58 In modern economic parlance, the relationship between the growth of production capacity and the growth of output is known as the 'marginal capital-output ratio.' Major work in this area was done by Roy Harrod in the 1930s. Harrod considered Hobson's economic works to be 'full of wisdom.' See his 'Introduction' to Hobson's *Science of Wealth*, 4th ed. (1950). The specification of this ratio combined with a specification of the growth in demand resulting from the 'multiplier' constitute two of the major tools of macro-economics. Cf. R.L. Heilbroner, *Understanding Macro Economics* (1965), 227-34.

59 *Rationalisation and Unemployment*, 76

rates. These increased costs eventually pressured profit margins, and as a result investment declined. In this view, overinvestment created crises for altogether different reasons from those outlined by Hobson. In the 1920s and 1930s, variations on this theme were proposed by such noted economists as F.A. Hayek and Knut Wicksell.[60] Much earlier, Karl Marx had questioned underconsumption theory on the grounds that if it was argued 'that the working class receives too little a portion of its product and the evil would be remedied as soon as it receives a larger share of it and wages increase in consequence, one could only remark that crises are always prepared by precisely a period in which wages rise generally.'[61]

In so far as Hobson replied to such criticism, it was merely to deny that rising costs, incurred during the boom period of the cycle, put sufficient strain on profit margins to call a halt to investment. The crisis was essentially one of realization – selling the goods on an impoverished market – not production. Thus, although interest rates could be observed to rise during the boom, Hobson was satisfied, for reasons already given, that the rate of interest, whether rising or falling, was largely irrelevant as a cost of production. However, it is worth noting that Hobson's analysis left unexplained why interest rates increased at all, given his assumption that economic booms were generated by an excess of savings.[62] Similarly with regard to wages, Hobson argued that although wages tended to rise during the boom, they did so neither fast enough nor in sufficient amounts to jeopardize profit margins:

Though more employment will give higher aggregate wages, wage rates will not rise so fast as prices and profits. This wage-lag is generally admitted. It signifies ... the important fact that during rising prices and reviving trade the distribution of the product, i.e. of real incomes, is favourable to the employing and capitalist classes, unfavourable to labour. For though wages and even the real income of the workers may be rising with the enlargement of the product, this enhanced working-class income repre-

60 Cf. Harberler, *Prosperity and Depression*, chap. x, 'The Overinvestment Theories.' A brief, but not altogether reliable, comparison of the theories of Hayek and Hobson is given by John Stachey, *The Nature of the Capitalist Crisis* (1935), chaps. II and IV. See also, Leo Huberman, *Man's Worldly Goods* (1937), 277-80.

61 Karl Marx, *Capital*, vol. 3, cited in Tom Kemp, *Theories of Imperialism* (1967), 36. Kemp suggests that Marx's comment applies to Hobson.

62 Keynes did present an explanation for increases in the rate of interest, which took into account plentiful supplies of savings. He suggested that the rate of interest represented the price, not of saving, but of sacrificing liquidity and placing those savings at the disposal of others to invest. A succinct statement of Keynes' analysis of the rate of interest is given in William Barber, *A History of Economic Thought* (1967), 234-7.

sents a smaller proportion of the whole income. ... [As the boom] with rising prices goes on, ... the time lag for wages still keeps trade highly profitable. ... Only when the rise in prices had stopped for some time [i.e., stage two of the cycle], do wages catch up, and high wages are then held responsible for the failure to market goods at profitable prices.[63]

The real brunt of Hobson's analysis, however, was directed at the classical economists. The same spirit that moved these economists to declare oversaving impossible, because it would be prevented by a fall in the rate of interest, also led them to pronounce oversupply impossible because, in Hobson's words, 'any tendency to it would straight way be corrected by a fall in prices stimulating increased consumption.[64]

Hobson argued that there were at least three reasons why a fall in price would not bring about the result desired by the classical economists. First, Hobson thought it was likely that any firm which had sufficient monopoly power and a relatively inelastic demand for its products would refuse to cut prices by the disproportionately large amounts that would be required in order to shift additional supplies. Instead, it would seek to hold up prices by restricting output, even though this would leave its productive capacity underutilized. The existence of this monopoly power indicated that the classical economists' reliance on price reductions to check oversupply was increasingly anachronistic:

Since in each advanced industrial country an ever-increasing proportion of the industrial capital and labour comes under this combined dispensation, the check of price reduction is largely nullified. It may be noted that the conventional economic doctrine ... arose in an age of small businesses when the incentives to combined restraint of output, and the possibility of achieving it were weaker than is now the case.[65]

Second, Hobson claimed that 'though falling prices [might] stimulate some increased consumption,' probably among the hard-pressed poor, this increase would not be 'large or quick enough' to take the glut off the market, because of the countervailing tendency set in motion by the 'conservatism of consumption.' This cultural constraint meant that it was probable that 'when money incomes remain the same, falling prices will stimulate more saving, at

63 *The Economics of Unemployment*, 68-70
64 Ibid., 51
65 Ibid., 54

a time when more saving is not wanted, and so reduce the efficacy of this check on gluts.'

But money incomes did not 'remain the same' and Hobson's third indictment was that the classical economists' preoccupation with price cuts as a remedy for overproduction had blinded them to what was happening to the level of income:

This glut causes considerable stoppage of production and unemployment, usually accompanied by a fall in wage rates for those remaining in employment. This shrinkage of employment, whether wages be reduced or not, is reflected in a reduction of the money incomes of producers. This fall in money income, once set in, stops altogether the already defective operation of the falling prices check. *For purchasing power ... soon begins to shrink faster than the fall in prices.*[66]

Hobson was aware, of course, that falling prices probably meant an increase in real income for those who remained employed. But his point was that in the 'race' between the fall in income caused by a rise in the level of unemployment, as more and more companies failed to sell in a saturated market a prices which covered their costs, and the rise in real income that falling prices brought about, there was no mechanism which automatically guaranteed that the general level of effective demand would not decline. Indeed, all the evidence seemed to suggest that the 'play of the elasticity of demand' which falling prices might have encouraged was effectively 'inhibited by falling incomes.'[67] Here, Hobson's emphasis on the determining influence of the level of income on effective demand prefigured Keynes' approach to the problem of unemployment.

This last argument was also crucial in providing Hobson with grounds for encouraging labour to resist demands that wages be cut as a means of reducing costs, lowering prices, and thereby stimulating consumption. In this regard, Hobson was something of a maverick, since Pigou, Hayek, Robbins, and most other notable economists were agreed that wage reduction was a remedy for industrial depression, as were the vast majority of businessmen.[68]

66 Ibid., 55 (emphasis added)
67 *The Industrial System*, 296
68 Cf. Michael Stewart, *Keynes and After* (1967), 115-23, for a brief review of the ideas of Pigou, Robbins, and Hayek on wage reductions and unemployment. Also of interest in this regard is Hobson's lecture, 'Remaking the World' (1932), Hobson Papers, where he contrasts the responses of the orthodox economists, revolutionaries, and reformers towards the Depression.

It is not surprising, therefore, that it was during the late 1920s and early 1930s that Hobson had his greatest influence on the labour movement.

The ultimate folly of a policy of wage reductions was that it was self-defeating. It would fail because although 'the labour cost per unit' might fall, the capital cost would be increased 'by reason of the diminution in output and sales due to the reduced purchasing power of the general body of workers and consumers.[69] In pinpointing why this 'irony' was not recognized by other economists and businessmen, Hobson once more centred on the fallacious individualism of orthodox economics. Those advocating wage reductions had failed to discern the relation between unemployment and the aggregate level of income because they incorrectly assumed that what was in the interest of each individual firm was necessarily in the general interest. Hobson elaborated this argument, while at the same time advocating a policy of high wages:

To many business men and to some economists it will seem preposterous to propose high wages ... as a [remedy] for unemployment. ... To raise wage-rates in a business which can barely meet current costs is seen to be impractical. And so it is if the policy is tested by application to a single business, or even a single trade. For this separatist application does not provide the expansion of demand which alone can validate the policy. ... To raise wages in the motor industry ... would not cause workers in this trade to buy many more motors. ... But if ... the high wage policy were simultaneously applied to all or most occupations, the general increase in consuming power ... might easily provide a sufficient new fund to meet the higher wage bill out of the reduction in overhead costs due to the full continuous use of plant, etc.[70]

By a similar logic, although it might be in the interest of any one producer to lower his wage bill, it would not be in the interest of all producers to do so, since this would result in a general fall in national income. The advocacy of wage reductions, then, stemmed from the same erroneous reasoning that had originally led liberal economists to deny that industrial slump was a possibility. It was only to be expected that this same school of thought would be incapable of prescribing remedies for unemployment. The workers consequently were fully justified in ignoring their advice.

69 *Poverty in Plenty* (1931), 65. Among the lesser follies, Hobson suggested that wage reduction might encourage inefficient management by off-loading costs onto the workers; and where there was any element of monopoly, then there could be no guarantee that these economies would be passed on to the consumers.
70 Ibid., 64

The next two stages in the business cycle, i.e., stages three and four, represent the low point of the slump. Men and machines stand idle; hoarding for the first time becomes significant because savings can no longer find investment outlets;[71] and the bankers tighten their credit in the face of mounting business failures. Hobson's analysis of this period of slump is primarily designed to show, first, that the mental gloom that now grips the economy is the result of the industrial situation, not its cause. Facts precede feelings in Hobson's account of the trade cycle, and consequently he has little regard for theories like those proposed by J.S. Mill and A.C. Pigou which attribute industrial crises to 'want of commercial confidence':

Here [in J.S. Mill's *Unsettled Questions of Political Economy*] we have the explicit explanation of a purely objective phenomenon, an excess of unsaleable articles, by reference to what is properly and primarily a purely subjective phenomenon, want of confidence. *Want of commercial confidence can no more be a cause of an accumulation of unsaleable goods than a rise in the thermometer can be a cause of sunshine.* ... Want of confidence ... is nothing but a subjective interpretation of the already existing fact of a general excess of forms of capital, or productive power. It may be a convenient term to describe the attitude of mind of those who have money to invest and who refuse to place it, but it can furnish no explanation of the congested state of industry implied by the fact of general over-supply.[72]

Thus Hobson resisted the temptation to divert attention from the faults of the system by blaming instead the men who ran the system.

Closely allied to this argument was Hobson's rejection of all explanations which gave primary influence to monetary factors in regulating industrial activity. The fact that, at the onset of the slump, financiers and bankers could be seen pulling in the credit they had earlier extended and refusing to offer more did not provide grounds for 'imputing any independent causation to credit as a factor in trade fluctuations. Its operation only quickens, exaggerates, and facilitates industrial changes that are otherwise produced.'[73] However, this should not be read as meaning that Hobson discounted the importance of credit altogether. On the contrary, he considered that the secondary role it played was still sufficiently important to warrant the nationalization of credit facilities.[74]

71 Cf. *The Industrial System*, 50.
72 *The Problem of the Unemployed*, 121-2 (emphasis added)
73 *The Economics of Unemployment*, 66
74 Cf. 'The Social Control of Credit,' in Kirby Page, ed., *A New Economic Order* (1930), 289-300.

The recovery from this period of slump (stage five) depended upon the incomes of the rich being reduced sufficiently to lower the rate of saving. An excess of savings, after all, was the original cause of disequilibrium. Thus, as the depression deepens, 'the diminished market for new capital goods and for consumption goods reduces the amount of profits, interest and rent, ... which normally supply the bulk of savings.'[75] This trend continues until it is realized that there is 'insufficient provision of new productive capital to meet the reasonable calculations of future demands for commodities.'[76] Faced with this new situation of 'undersaving' capitalists feel encouraged to start reinvesting and the cycle begins anew.

Hobson's description of the moment of recovery never extends to more than a few short paragraphs in any of his works. This brevity of analysis is explained in part by his confidence that there was a process of natural recovery (here, Hobson clearly differs from Keynes) and in part by his reforming zeal, which made him impatient with that process and those economists who lingered over it. The latter argument is clearly illustrated by his comments on Professor Edwin Cannan's studies in this area: 'What is wanted,' Hobson proclaimed, 'is a remedy against unemployment and depression, not a declaration that when the disease has run its course the patient may – even must – recover!'[77] No better example could be given of Hobson's lack of fascination with theoretical niceties, if he thought that such analysis impeded social action. This impatience, of course, is to be understood as the impatience of a reformer not a revolutionary, for the fact that the system could recover reaffirmed Hobson's belief in reformism. The economic system was more resilient than revolutionary socialists supposed; whilst there had been crises there was no final crisis. Hobson's critique of capitalism, like that of many other social reformers in the first quarter of the century, focused primarily on the system's wastefulness and not upon its supposed fatal contradictions. In the final analysis Hobson did not consider capitalism to be self destructive.

5 CRITICISMS OF HOBSON'S UNDERCONSUMPTION THEORY

Hobson's theory of underconsumption has been criticized mainly from two perspectives. The best known of these critiques is the one offered by Keynes, who challenged Hobson's assumption that all savings are automatically invested. The other line of criticism calls into question Hobson's assumption

75 *Property and Improperty*, 49
76 *The Industrial System*, 303
77 *Rationalisation and Unemployment*, 44

as to the primacy of consumption demand. It is suggested, instead, that investment is less closely regulated by consumption demand than Hobson supposed.

Implicit in both criticisms is the suggestion that Hobson's theory of under-consumption did not incorporate certain developments that had taken place within advanced capitalism and thus had a definite nineteenth-century ring to it.

a / The Primacy of Consumption Demand

By 'consumers' here is signified consumers of final commodities. ... It is their purchases, and not the purchases of new capital goods by investment, that ultimately regulate the balance [between spending and saving]. *Rationalisation and Unemployment*, 76

Hobson generally assumed that the regulative control which the rate of consumption exercised on the rate of investment was a close one. This idea was best expressed in *The Industrial System*. There he argued that, although there were some forms of capital investment, for example, railroad building and mining exploration, 'the services of which will fructify in the shape of consumption goods a long time hence,' it was none the less a mistake to conclude that the limit which the 'prospective increase in consumption' imposed on investment was thereby entirely cancelled.' The reasons he gave were two fold:

In the first place, most forms of new capital, even in this age of elaborated indirect production by machinery, *very soon* result in promoting an increased flow of finished goods, and unless the proportion of spending and saving were speedily readjusted ... the machinery of industry must become conjested. ... Secondly, the proportion of new savings which can be so applied as to fructify at some far distant date is necessarily small, restricted principally by our inability to forecast far ahead either the needs of coming men, or the most economical modes of providing for them.[78]

However, in later works Hobson seems to have some doubts as to the validity of these arguments. For example, in *Property and Impropery,* Hobson contends that armaments expenditure might prove an exception to the regulatory effect of consumption.

78 *The Industrial System*, 52 (emphasis added)

Regarded as an application of large [funds] to non-productive goods and services, it appears to furnish an additional correction to the disequilibrium between spending and saving, by expanding the investment market so as to 'justify' a larger portion of saving. This is irrespective of whether increased armaments are a sound social service of national defence or not. Their immediate result is the absorption of some capital and labour, otherwise unemployed, in the production and operation of articles which lie outside the ordinary play of economic forces.[79]

What is especially interesting here is Hobson's remark that armaments expenditure somehow lies 'outside the ordinary play of economic forces.' Hobson does not elaborate, except to say that in order to reduce the level of unemployment, such expenditure would have to be financed by the capitalist class. However, if he did intend to suggest that investment in bombs, tanks, and other weapons of destruction provided a means of draining excess capital in a way that did not feed back into the productive system, and therefore, did not ultimately advance the output of consumables, but was pure economic waste, then this idea would seem to have profound consequences for his theory of underconsumption. It would mean that an 'arms economy' could continue the erroneous policy of oversaving indefinitely. By leaking excess capital into the military sector, capitalists could circumvent potential underconsumption crises. Those scholars who have interpreted the 'arms race' along these lines have serious doubts about the primacy of consumption demand as a regulator of economic activity,[80] although Hobson himself never traced these repercussions back to his original thesis, preferring instead to dismiss the possibility of a fully fledged arms economy as irrational and inhumane.

Hobson's later works also indicate a revealing change in emphasis with regard to those forms of investment which took a long time to fructify. In *The Industrial System*, as has already been noted, Hobson mentioned these investment outlets only to dismiss their overall significance, while in *Property and Improperty* Hobson grants that this form of investment had 'sensibly lightened the burdens of trade depression.'[81] Here, then, was an important

---

79 *Property and Improperty*, 185-6. See also, *Confessions*, 194-5. Hobson first made the connection between capitalist economic crises and armaments in *The Physiology of Industry*, 162. But there his stress was on the actual physical destruction of excess capital rather than an armaments expenditure *per se*.

80 See, for example, Joan Robinson's 'Introduction' to Rosa Luxembourg, *The Accumulation of Capital* (3rd ed., 1968), 27-8; and M. Kidron, *Western Capitalism since the War* (1968).

81 *Property and Improperty*, 185

branch of investment which on Hobson's own admittance was not closely regulated by consumption demand. Even so, Hobson did not concede that this seriously qualified his original thesis, though some of his contemporaries pressed him hard on this point. These critics were emboldened by what they had observed of the Soviet Union's drive to industrialization after 1929. Thus, as one scholar commented:

The experience of the Russian system [is] instructive. According to the Hobson theory, a society in which the mass of consumers are poor must not put up more than a strictly limited quantity of new plant and buildings, lest productive capacity outrun the power of consumers to purchase. In the Soviet Union ... it is clear that the proportion of the country's resources devoted to this kind of production during the first Five Year Plan is staggeringly large as compared with the standards of capitalist countries. The Russian consumers, on the other hand, are exceedingly poor. Yet there has been no suggestion that the enormously high rate of new investment in the U.S.S.R. has any result than the commonsense one of promising a higher standard of living in the future ... even though all the conditions of overinvestment ... are present in contemporary Russia.[82]

Hobson's response to this kind of criticism was not very satisfactory. Instead of pointing to any structural reasons why such an imbalance might have different consequences in Russia than in capitalist states (e.g., differences in income distribution, the size of the economic surplus, planning techniques, etc.), Hobson preferred to attack the Soviet five-year plans on moralistic grounds: these plans were a 'crazy miscalculation,' for it was not possible to 'forecast ... future ... needs and tastes and changes in productive technique' with sufficient accuracy so as to 'justify [a] policy of unlimited saving and capital creation.'[83]

Now, whatever the merits of this argument for favouring a more gradualist approach to planning, it is none the less clear that it left unanswered the important *quantitative* question that Hobson's critics were asking, namely: 'How much saving is too much?' If the Russians could save such a high percentage of their income without provoking an underconsumption crisis, it seemed only reasonable to conclude that the rate of consumption did not

82 Barbara Wootton, *Plan or No Plan* (1934), 129. In Canada, the same point was made by the League for Social Reconstruction: see *Social Planning for Canada* (1935), 190.
83 'Under-Production and Under-Consumption,' in *New Statesman* (24 March 1934), 441. See also 'Underconsumption: An Exposition and a Reply' (Nov. 1933), 408-9.

have the close regulatory effect that Hobson had originally attributed to it. This, combined with the qualifications Hobson himself had introduced with regard to investment leakages and long delays in fructification, suggested that much greater care was needed in specifying the ratio between savings and consumption. Hobson, however, never summoned the mental energy required to revise his original emphasis on the primacy of consumption demand.

b / Savings and Investment
It was mentioned earlier that Hobson's tendency to identify the activity of saving with the activity of investment resulted in a good deal of Keynesian criticism of his position. Keynes himself introduced this line of critique in 1930, when his *Treatise on Money* was published. In that work Keynes noted that there was 'some affinity' between his ideas and those of the under-consumptionists – affinity, it should be noted meaning something less than influence, for there is no evidence of any direct indebtedness of Keynes to Hobson or other economic heretics – but he was careful to point out that his analysis focused on underinvestment, 'an entirely different terrain' from theories emphasizing 'too large a production of consumption goods'.[84]

The *Treatise on Money* spoke very generally about 'a class of theories' of underconsumption, but six years later, in *The General Theory of Employment, Interest and Money*, Keynes devoted special attention to Hobson's analysis. This time he cited a passage from Mummery and Hobson's *Physiology of Industry*, where they had written, 'Any undue exercise of this habit [of saving] must ... cause an accumulation of capital in excess of what which is required for use, and this excess will exist in the form of general overproduction.' Keynes comments:

In [this] sentence ... appears the root of Hobson's mistake, namely, his supposing that it is a case of excessive saving causing the *actual* accumulation of capital in excess of what is required, which is, in fact, a secondary evil which only occurs through mistakes of foresight; whereas the primary evil is a propensity to save in conditions of full employment more than the equivalent of the capital which is required, thus preventing full employment except when there is a mistake of foresight.[85]

These statements make the basic difference between Hobson's and Keynes' approach very clear: for Hobson industrial crisis can be traced to savings that

84 1958 ed., vol. 1, 179
85 367-8

get invested; for Keynes to savings that do not. Hobson believed that over-investment was endemic to capitalism, Keynes believed that it was acciden-tal, and that 'throughout human history' the 'propensity to save' had been 'stronger than the inducement to invest.'[86] Thus, according to Keynes, any attempt by savers to hoard more money than businessmen *intended* to invest caused a gap in demand. As a result, company inventories piled up, and businessmen were likely to cut back on production. This would lead to an increase in unemployment and a fall in national income. As incomes fell, so did the propensity to save. Eventually, the *actual* level of savings would equal the businessmen's spending on investments, and the economy would be in equilibrium, although, as Keynes stressed, this point of equilibrium would usually be below the level required to ensure full employment.

Hobson, of course, was not unaware of Keynes' criticism of his position. Indeed, not only did Hobson read Keynes' works but they briefly corre-sponded on the meaning of 'oversaving' during the early 1930s.[87] Hobson, however, conceded remarkably little to Keynes. For example, in a lecture written in 1935, Hobson summarized what he considered to be Keynes' chief contribution to the study of trade cycles as follows:

Mr. Maynard Keynes has made a notable addition to the doctrine of over-saving, by stressing the notorious accumulation of uninvested and unin-vestable money savings which everywhere lie idle in bank deposits. Under sound trade conditions these money savings would [corrected to read: should] be invested. ... The fact that such investment no longer takes place is a direct testimony to the excessive creation of capital goods beyond the requirements of the final markets for consumable commo-dities.[88]

Hobson, then, could envisage a discrepancy between intended savings and realized investments only as an 'after-effect.' Money sitting idle in bank deposits was merely a *post factum* phenomenon of underconsumption: it was money that 'will not expend itself on consumables and ... cannot find an immediate outlet in stimulating the creation of more machinery of produc-tion.'[89] This was essentially the case stated by Hobson as early as 1909 in *The Industrial System*, and this remained his position even after his discussions

---

86 Ibid., 347
87 The correspondence between Keynes and Hobson is reprinted in *The Collected Writings of J.M. Keynes*, vol. XIII (1973).
88 'Lecture, no title,' Hobson Papers, 10-11
89 'Saving and Spending: Why Production Is Clogged,' *New Leader* reprint (n.d. 1932?), 8

with Keynes. The only difference was that now Hobson was more prone to attach the adjectives 'important' and 'significant' to this phenomenon than he had been in the past.

In the Keynesian analysis it is crucial to separate the acts of saving and investing at the outset, since discrepancies in the plans of those who perform these two economic functions is taken to be the norm rather than a secondary effect. The fact, however, that Hobson was unable to appreciate the centrality of this distinction should not be seen necessarily as indicating that he was unable to comprehend what Keynes was saying, as is sometimes implied, although, of course, it would be surprising if Hobson's forty or so years arguing the case about overinvestment had not cribbed the nimbleness of his mind somewhat.

Certainly with regard to the long-term trend of this discrepancy between saving and investment plans, there emerged a divergence of opinion which suggests that Hobson's analysis is a genuine alternative to Keynes, and not one merely by default. For Keynes, initiative in the economic system rests with the entrepreneur. If investment spending is active, savings will not prove abortive. But the capitalist portrayed in the *General Theory* is often a timid and increasingly dispirited creature whose willingness to invest weakens as the economy matures and the 'extent of existing accumulations' mount.[90] It is the lack of enterprise that is at the root of capitalism's crisis. For Hobson, on the other hand, capitalism was an inherently dynamic and innovative system, limited primarily by its mode of distribution. Hobson assumed that capitalists were forever striving to invest: it was this that pushed them 'over the top' during the boom and made them struggle for recovery during slumps.[91] Keynes believed that capitalists might at any moment settle for an equilibrium at which there would exist unused plant and unemployed workers. Essentially his capitalists were under-achievers, whereas in Hobson's analysis they were over-achievers.

This difference in their appreciation of capitalist behaviour explains why Hobson was not especially worried about further taxing profits (unproductive surpluses) in order to replenish consumption demand, whereas Keynes (although not opposed to some measure of redistribution) advocated enforced reductions in the rate of interest so as to raise the profit expectations of the industrial capitalists. Similarly, this contrast explains Keynes' promotion of the state as a surrogate investor, whereas public work programs play a much

90 See 348 and 31.
91 On this point see the interesting comment on Hobson by G.D.H. Cole in *The Means to Full Employment* (1943), 47.

smaller part in Hobson's policy proposals, which focus instead on the problems of underconsumption and misappropriation, not underinvestment.

In this broader perspective, it is not altogether certain that Hobson's position has nothing to be said for it. Certainly, Keynes has been criticized, even by his admirers, for discounting the long-term potential for technological change within capitalism and the new investment opportunities this would bring about.[92] In this regard, perhaps the conclusion of J.M. Clark, written in 1940 just before Keynesianism became firmly established as the new orthodoxy, is the most reasonable:

Hobson's views differed ... from present theories, which emphasise underinvestment relative to savings. Hobson concentrated on excessive investment relative to demand. ... Yet this feature is not to be rejected merely because the present emphasis lies elsewhere. As a step in the process leading to a falling-off in investment it may deserve a place in a balanced synthesis.[93]

6 CONCLUSION

In Hobson's opinion, trade depressions could be eliminated by the application of a variety of economic reforms designed to eliminate the 'unproductive surplus' by way of redistributing income from the rich to the poor. But before examining Hobson's reform program, it is preferable to look at his analysis of imperialism, for here was a practical policy for ameliorating the problem of excess capital, already on the agenda, but one which Hobson bitterly opposed.

92 See, for example, H.L. McCraken, *Keynesian Economics in the Stream of Economic Thought* (1961), chap. 9, and M. Stewart, *Keynes and After*, 125. A useful overview of this debate is given in Eric Roll, *A History of Economic Thought* (1953), 504-8.
93 'J.A. Hobson, Heretic and Pioneer (1858-1940),' *Journal of Social Philosophy* (July 1940), 357

5

Hobson's Theory of Imperialism

1 THE BOER WAR

Hobson's interest in the motivations behind Britain's rapid addition of some 4,750,000 square miles of territory to her empire between 1870 and 1900[1] was primarily aroused by the events in South Africa immediately preceding the Boer War.[2] The circumstances surrounding Hobson's visit to South Africa at this time have already been described in chapter 1.

The first intellectual product of Hobson's visit was *The War in South Africa: Its Causes and Effects* (1900), consisting of articles Hobson had originally published in the *Manchester Guardian* and the *Speaker*. Written in the heat of battle, as it were, *The War in South Africa* did not explore any general theoretical perspective on imperialism. Hobson did make an attempt to uncover the machinations of businessmen and financiers behind the cloak of paternalism and good intentions with which the war was swathed, but with little time for considered reflection he failed to sustain a high level of analysis and lapsed into simplistic notions of economic conspiracy and dark forebodings about a supposed Jewish confederacy. The following quotation gives a sense of the level of analysis contained in this work:

For whom are we fighting? It is difficult to state the truth about our doings in South Africa without seeming to appeal to the ignominious passion of Judenhetze. Nevertheless a plain account of the personal and eco-

---

1 Figures cited in *Imperialism* (1902; 3rd ed., 1938), 18. All future references are taken from the 1938 edition.
2 As already noted, the rudiments of Hobson's theory of imperialism can be found in an article he wrote for the *Contemporary Review* in 1898, in which events in South Africa do not play a significant part.

nomic forces operative in the Transvaal is essential ... and must not be shirked. A few of the financial pioneers in South Africa have been Englishmen ... [but recent developments] have thrown the economic resources of the country more and more into the hands of a small group of international financiers, chiefly German in origin and Jewish in race. ... The first and incomparably the most important industry, the gold mines of the Rand, are almost entirely in their hands ... But while the power of this capitalism is built on gold, it is by no means confined to it. Whatever large or profitable interest we approach, we find the same control. The interests are often entirely severed from, even hostile to, the mining industry, but they are in the hands of the same [race]. ... This is the case with the dynamite monopoly. ... The rich and powerful liquor trade ... is entirely in the hands of Jews. ... The stock exchange is, needless to say, mostly Jewish. ... The press of Johannesburg is chiefly their property. ... Nor has the Jew been backward in developing those forms of loan and mortgage business which have made his fame the world over. ... A consideration of these points throws a clear light upon the nature of the conflict in South Africa. We are fighting in order to place a small international oligarchy of mineowners and speculators in power at Pretoria.[3]

The conspirators, then, were the Rand Jews. On this basis, and with little more evidence to go on than the number of Jewish-sounding names listed in company prospectuses, public census records, and above shop doors, Hobson felt able to reconcile what at first appeared to be a diverse variety of interests.[4] The dynamite monopolists, the mine owners, the dealers in liquor, slaves, and gambling, were supposedly united in their desire to increase, not so much their own private profits, but the total fund of Jewish profits. Perhaps the caveat which Hobson himself entered at the start of his analysis, claiming that his references were not to Jews as such, but to the 'class of financial capitalist of which the foreign Jew [is] the leading type,'[5] indicates his own discomfort with this shallow form of argument, although as Arendt has pointed out, Hobson was not alone in drawing these conclusions.[6] Anti-Jewish remarks were frequently voiced by radical opponents of the Boer War. Certainly very few of the many reviews that Hobson's book received in the press noted with any disdain this aspect of his argument.[7]

3 *The War in South Africa* (1900), 189-97
4 Ibid., 11f
5 Ibid., 189
6 H. Arendt, *The Origins of Totalitarianism* (1958), 135ff
7 Of the 72 reviews of this work to be found in the *Hobson Papers*, only one, in a journal called *The Jewish World*, suggests that Hobson was biased against Jews.

Whether it was because Hobson was uneasy with the form of his analysis from the beginning, as Harvey Mitchell suggests,[8] or whether, as Arendt claims, Hobson came to consider the Jewish factor of little significance in establishing a general theory of economic imperialism,[9] the fact remains that Hobson quickly dropped almost all references to Jews in his subsequent analyses.

In some ways, then, Hobson probably felt that the analysis given in *The War in South Africa* was inadequate. He had tried to persuade the British public that British companies operating in the Rand had fallen under the control of Jewish financiers, and that it was irrational to make war sacrifices for the sake of these men, 'most of whom are foreigners by origin ... and whose trade interests are not chiefly British.'[10] Still convinced of the irrationality of imperialism, Hobson none the less realized that this was too narrow a basis upon which to make his appeal. What if the beneficiaries of the next imperialist drive were not German Jews in origin but 'native' British manufacturers? Could imperialism then be considered in the national interest?

In 1902, Hobson published *Imperialism: A Study*, in answer to this query. Here he once more argued that imperialism was irrational – 'a depraved choice of national life, imposed by self-seeking interests' – but this time the argument is presented from a different perspective, namely that imperialism *per se* did not make good business sense; it had little commercial value for the nation. Ledgers replaced Levites as grounds for condemning imperialism.

2 THE ECONOMIC FOUNDATION OF IMPERIALISM

The chief economic source of imperialism [is to be] ... found in the inequality of industrial opportunities by which a favoured class accumulates superfluous elements of income which, in their search for profitable investments, press ever farther afield. *Imperialism*, 361

Hobson viewed the tremendous expansion in the size of the British Empire during the last quarter of the nineteenth century as the most visible manifestation of a new aggressiveness in British foreign trade policy. The pull of profit, of course, had always proven good cause for capitalists to scurry over the globe, but in the past they always had the option of withdrawing when the risks seemed too great. Hobson was one of the first to argue that this option was no longer available to the capitalist. The capitalist was now com-

8 'Hobson Revisited,' *Journal of the History of Ideas*, vol. 26 (1965)
9 *The Origins of Totalitarianism*, 135
10 *The War in South Africa*, 197

pelled, for definite economic reasons, to send his capital overseas. Thus pushed into foreign ventures, the capitalist's only course was to eliminate the risks involved by rendering the 'host' nation safe as an investment project – hence, the aggressiveness of the New Imperialism.

This new push to invest abroad had combined with the old pull of profit with momentous consequences: it was now assumed by businessmen and politicians alike that England required the 'continual expansion' of its foreign trade; that this expansion could 'only be adequately secured by increased armaments and an extension of the area of empire'; and that it was 'sound economy to undergo ... these expenses in order to promote foreign trade.'[11] From this combination of ideas flowed the whole gamut of imperialist practices.

Furthermore, Hobson perceived that there was a special relationship between capital exports and this new type of aggressive imperialism. He argued that this aggression stemmed from the fact that capital investment, unlike trade in commodities, took time to fructify and hence required close and frequent supervision on behalf of the creditor-nation:

The stake which a trader has in the material prosperity and the good government of a foreign country to which he sells cotton, cloth, guns, gin, ... is limited and fluctuating. If he finds his market falling off in one country, he can push for a market in another. ... But when trade in the narrow sense has developed into 'peaceful penetration' of an area of Africa, or a South Sea island, trade begins to be supplemented by factories and collecting stations. ... The stake established in this foreign country is far bigger, more solid and more permanent. ... The acquisition, protection and enlargement of these solid permanent stakes in backward countries have furnished the greater part of the inflammatory material in modern foreign policy.[12]

In this regard, T. Lloyd has suggested that Hobson's special contribution to the theory of imperialism was 'to point out the important role of investment – trade with no investment would not be a permanent matter.'[13]

Hobson attributed this new 'push' to invest abroad to changes taking place within the economies of advanced capitalist nations. In effect, he restated his thesis on underconsumption crises and suggested that one of the options

11 'Free Trade and Foreign Policy,' *Contemporary Review* (1898), 169
12 *Richard Cobden: The International Man* (1919), 403-4
13 T. Lloyd, 'Africa and Hobson's Imperialism,' *Past and Present*, no. 55 (1972), 152

facing capitalists embarrassed by surplus capital was to invest it abroad. But this in itself did not explain why capitalists were so eager and so forceful in exercising this option in the late nineteenth century in comparison with earlier periods. To answer this question, Hobson focused on the growth of monopolies, cartels, and trusts in advanced capitalism and argued that imperialism was a policy especially favoured by such elements. In other words, the New Imperialism signified the difference between the effects of overcapitalization in early as compared with late capitalism. The following quotation makes this difference clear:

In the free competition of the manufacturers *preceding combination* the chronic condition is one of 'overproduction,' in the sense that all the mills or factories can only be kept at work by cutting prices down to a point where the weaker competitors are forced to close down. ... This concentration of industry ... at once limits the quantity of capital which can be effectively employed. ... It is quite evident that a trust which is [potentially] motivated by cut-throat competition, due to an excess of capital, cannot normally find inside the 'trusted' industry employment for that portion of the profits which the trust-makers desire to save and invest. ... Two economic courses were open to them, *both leading towards an abandonment of the political isolation of the past and the adoption of imperialist methods in the future.* ... [First], they might employ their full productive power ... and while still regulating output and prices for the home market, may 'hustle' for foreign markets, dumping down their surplus goods at prices which would not be possible save for the profitable nature of their home market. [Second], they might employ their savings in seeking investments outside their country ... becoming ... a creditor class to foreign countries. It was this sudden demand for foreign markets ... which was avowedley responsible for the adoption of Imperialism.[14]

B. Sutcliffe has argued that Hobson 'hardly saw [imperial expansion] as a special stage of capitalist development.' This statement is useful in so far as it serves as a reminder of the differences between Hobson's approach and that of Lenin, as will be shown shortly, but, as the above quotation makes clear, Sutcliffe's statement is misleading if it is taken to mean that Hobson was not fully cognizant of the emergence of monopoly capitalism around the turn of the century – and this is what Sutcliffe seems to imply. For Hobson the New

14 *Imperialism*, 75-7

Imperialism was the monopolists' response to the threat of overproduction crises on the domestic market.[15]

3 THE COSTS OF IMPERIALISM

Hobson measured the costs of imperialism on two different (but related) scales. First, there were the human costs, which he calculated in terms of the loss involved in the abandonment of the liberal credo; second, there were the more strictly commercial costs.

a / The Human Costs

The true nature of imperialism is best seen by confronting it with the watchwords of progress ... – peace, economy, reform, and popular self-government. ... A large section of professed liberals believe ... that Imperialism is consistent with the maintenance of all these virtues. This contention, however, is belied by the facts. *Imperialism*, 126

Hobson considered imperialism to be a betrayal of liberal principles and he viewed the effort of the Liberal party to come to terms with imperialism as selling its birthright 'for a mess of pottage.'[16] Consequently, Hobson attempted to describe the plight of subject races faced with imperial power in a way deliberately designed to prick the liberal conscience and stem the missionary's zeal.

i / Liberalism, imperialism, and peace

Hobson began his analysis with a brief discussion of the liberal heritage on matters of internationalism, nationalism, and colonialism. He argued that early liberal thinkers were genuinely internationalist in their outlook and cited, approvingly, the asseveration of his friend William Clarke that 'the eve of the French Revolution found every wise man in Europe – Lessing, Kant, Goethe, Rousseau, Lavater, Condorcet, Priestley, Gibbon, Franklin – more a citizen of the world than of any particular country.'[17] Genuine sentiments of internationalism could also be found in the later writings of the theorists of free trade up to and including J.S. Mill. Significantly, Hobson entitled his

15 B. Sutcliffe 'Conclusion' in R. Owen and B. Sutcliffe, eds., *Studies in the Theory of Imperialism* (1972), 315
16 *Imperialism*, 144
17 Ibid., 9

own edited work on one of the leading advocates of free trade *Richard Cobden: The International Man.*

Alongside this liberal cosmopolitan outlook could be found a sense of 'genuine nationalism,' best stated, in Hobson's opinion, by J.S. Mill, as a sense of national self-respect, based on an 'identity of political antecedents, the possession of a national history and consequent community of recollections, collective pride and humiliation, pleasure and regret, connected with the same incidents in the past.[18] Since self-respect was the prerequisite of respect for others, this sense of nationalism was viewed by Hobson as being quite compatible with internationalism.

Nationalism, in turn, helped to foster a 'genuine colonialism' which represented a 'natural overflow of nationality' into 'vacant or sparsely peopled foreign lands.'[19] Hobson cited Australia and Canada as examples. Colonialism in its best sense caused little or no offence to liberal principles.

These genuine sentiments of internationalism, nationalism, and colonialism, however, were soon to wither before the onslaught of the New Imperialism. Whereas liberal philosophers like Kant had once 'speculated on an empire as the only feasible security for peace,'[20] now liberals had to be warned about sentimentalizing empires, for they had become the battlegrounds of nations. The peaceful hegemony that had been associated with *Pax Romana* and even with *Pax Britannica* was a thing of the past. An entirely novel situation had emerged in which there were now a number of competing empires. By the end of the nineteenth century, not only Britain but also the United States, Germany, France, and other advanced industrial nations were facing overcapitalization crises. It was this struggle for markets that was responsible, in Hobson's opinion, for transforming the 'wholesome stimulative rivalry of varied national types into the cut-throat competition of empires.' Nationalism now glowed with the 'animus of greed and self aggrandisement,' and the areas of conflict between nations had multiplied accordingly.[21] Thus, 'where thirty years ago there existed one sensitive spot in [Britain's] relations with France, Germany, or Russia,' there were 'a dozen now.'[22] Elsewhere Hobson cited the following cases:

Through the entanglements of Anglo-French political policy in Egypt runs the clear, determinant streak of bondholding interests. The kernal of the

18 Ibid., 5
19 Ibid., 6
20 Ibid., 9
21 Ibid., 11
22 Ibid., 126

Moroccan trouble was the competition of the Mannesmann and the Schneider firms over the 'richest iron ores in the world.' Mining financiers moulded the policy of South Africa. ... In Mexico['s] history [we] find a leading clue to recent disturbances in the contest of two commercial potentates for the control of oil fields. Persia came into modern politics as an arena of struggle between Russian and British bankers. ... In China it was the competition for leases. ... Turkey and the Balkans became an incendiary issue to Western Europe because they lay along the route of German economic penetration in Asia, a project fatally antagonised by Russian needs for 'free' Southern waters.[23]

Events such as these made the prospect of peace among the empire builders look bleak. Hobson was to view the First World War as a tragic confirmation of his thesis.[24]

But if war between empires was a possibility, war within empires was already a fact. Unlike the old colonialism, the New Imperialism made claims to lands where the natives were 'too foreign to be absorbed and too compact to be permanently crushed.'[25] Imperialism thus generated its own forces of opposition in the form of nationalist movements which sought to defend native cultures and interests. Consequently, 'the decades of imperialism' had been 'prolific in wars ... directly motivated by aggression of white races on lower races.'[26]

The emergence of these nationalist forces led Hobson to speculate on an alternative future for Western capitalist nations. He was among the first to suggest that, in the future, the subject peoples of the 'third world' might assume the major initiative in opposing capitalism, rather than the domestic proletariat of the industrialized nations. Given the right circumstances, the imperialist nations would likely decide that rather than face conflicts on three fronts – viz. between themselves, the foreign nationalists, and their own working class – it would be more profitable for them to unite. In Imperialism, Hobson suggested that the lure of China's huge untapped market might prove sufficient inducement to unite the imperialists in a common cause:

[It is] reasonable to suppose that capitalism, having failed to gain its way by national separatist policies issuing in strife of Western peoples, may

23 The New Protectionism (1916), 119-20
24 Problems of a New World (1921), chap. 1. It should be noted, however, that Hobson never claimed that the economic rivalry between nations was the sole cause of the First World War. Cf. 'Introduction' to the 1938 edition of Imperialism.
25 Imperialism, 11
26 Ibid., 126

learn the art of combination, and that the power of international capitalism, which has been growing apace, may make its great crucial experiment in the exploitation of China. ...

Such an experiment may revolutionise the methods of Imperialism; the pressure of working-class movements in politics and industry in the West can be met by a flood of China goods, so as to keep down wages and compel industry, or, where the power of imperialist oligarchy is well set, by menaces of yellow workmen or of yellow mercenary troops, while collaboration in this huge Eastern development may involve an understanding between the groups of business politicians in the Western States close enough and strong enough to secure international peace in Europe.[27]

This warning about inter-imperialism and the suppression of democracy was written for liberals who failed to see the domestic repercussions of imperialism, but there is little doubt that this passage, combined with others where Hobson spoke of elements within the 'lower classes' being 'bribed into acquiescence' with monies taken from imperialist exploits,[28] also had its impact on Lenin, who had his own reasons for looking elsewhere than Europe for the 'spark' that would ignite a world-wide proletarian revolution.

27 Ibid., 311, 313-14. Interestingly, the scare of 'cheap Chinese labour' was soon to become a major election issue arousing wide spread working-class agitation, and providing a basis for Socialist and Liberal co-operation in the 1906 election. See A.K. Russell, *Liberal Landslide* (1973), chap. 7.

28 *Imperialism*, 194. See also Lenin, *Imperialism: The Highest Stage of Capitalism* (1917), in *Selected Works* (New World ed., 1967), 756-8.

Hobson was not optimistic about the likelihood of a successful challenge to Western imperialism emanating from the backward nations. For example, in *Imperialism*, 311, he wrote: 'the notion of China organising an army of six millions under some great general and driving the "foreign devil" out of the country ... is the least likely of all early issues in the East.' If 1949, the year of Mao's takeover in China is considered 'early,' then this is one occasion when Hobson's prescience failed him.

It should also be noted that Hobson varied his emphasis on the future of imperialism, sometimes stressing competition between the Western powers and at other times talking of a federacy of imperial nations lined up against the third world. Either way the discussion usually revolved around some aspect of the conflict between nations and classes. The one short-lived exception to this was his book *An Economic Interpretation of Investment* (1911), which seems to have been written under the influence of Norman Angell. Here Hobson pays close attention to the possibility that the 'interdependence' of those Western financiers who invested in one another's countries, afforded a 'considerable guarantee of peace' (cf. 117-24); and he noted only in passing the possibility of race and class conflicts. Thus the conflictual element was minimized. However, the events leading up to the First World War seemed to Hobson to confound this analysis, and thereafter he was much more wary about the chances of 'peaceful imperialism.' See, for example, *Problems of a New World*, 29, and *Rationalisation and Unemployment* (1930), 116-17.

ii / Liberalism, imperialism, and self-government

Hobson contended that the number of Liberals who genuinely believed the commonplace that 'England's imperial mission was to spread the arts of free government' was already rapidly diminishing by the turn of the century, so patent was the evidence to the contrary about this mission. Certainly very few British officials any longer retained the notion that the populations they ruled were 'capable of being trained for effective free government.'[29] Many of these officials had lapsed into a pure unvarnished racism. The fundamental cause of this early failure of even well-intentioned efforts to spread democracy in the colonies was the Liberal imperialist's inability to appreciate the presence and potential of indigenous cultures. This failure was especially apparent, according to Hobson, when examining imperialism in Asia:

The races of Africa it has been possible to regard as savages or children, 'backward' in their progress along the same general road of civilisation in which Anglo-Saxondom represents the vanguard, and requiring the help of more forward races. It is not so easy to make a specious case for Western control over India, China, and other Asiatic peoples upon the same ground. Save in the more recent developments of the physical sciences and their application to industrial arts, it cannot be contended that these peoples are 'backward.'[30]

For Liberal Imperialists to lay claim to a civilizing mission in such cases indicated a state of mind unable to see in the world they had conquered any image but their own.

This contention led Hobson to a discussion of cultural relativism. As Bernard Porter has commented, this concern for cultural diversity, though not original to Hobson, was unusual.[31] In an earlier work Hobson indicated that his insights on cultural relativism were indebted to the studies of Gustave Le Bon, whose conclusion, in the *Psychology of Peoples*, that each race was strongly resistant to foreign sentiments and ideas, was one for which Hobson saw much confirmation in British imperial practices.[32] In *Imperialism* Hobson does not mention Le Bon, but he does commend the study of Mary Kingley's work, another noted cultural relativist, as a 'move in the right direction.'[33] Following this line of thought, Hobson claimed that it was essential to

29 *Imperialism*, 118, 119
30 Ibid., 285
31 *Critics of Empire*, 181
32 *The Social Problem* (1901), 276. An English translation of Le Bon's *The Psychology of Peoples* was published in 1899.
33 *Imperialism*, 244

recognize that 'there may be many paths to civilisation,' and that 'strong racial and environmental differences preclude a hasty grafting of alien institutions.'[34] Subject cultures, therefore, had to be approached empathetically and in a democratic spirit committed to the ideal of self-development:

If we or any other nation really undertook the care and education of a 'lower race' as a trust, how should we set about the execution of the trust? By studying the religions, political and other social institutions and the habits of the people, and by endeavouring to penetrate into their present mind and capacities of adaptation, by learning their language and their history, we should seek to place them in the natural history of man; by similar close attention to the country in which they live ... we should get a real grip upon their environment ... Our first aim [is] to understand and to promote the healthy free operations of all internal forces for progress which we might discover.[35]

The Liberal imperialist, on the other hand, even when not solely bent on exploiting the labour and minerals of a territory, was so transfixed by the idea of the superiority of his own culture that he invariably approached subject cultures convinced that they have nothing worthwhile to contribute. Such liberals were captives of the idea:

that there exists one sound, just, rational system of government, suitable for all sorts and conditions of men, embodied in the elective representative institutions of Great Britain, and that [their] duty was to impose this system as soon as possible ... upon lower races, without any regard to their past history.[36]

Only in the administration of Basutoland did Hobson detect a 'saner imperialism,' but this example merely served to 'point the path by which most of our imperialism has diverged from the ideal of a "trust for civilisation."'[37] As for British rule elsewhere in the Empire, the evidence clearly showed that British institutions were failing to win the attachment of the subject races:

When British authority has been forcibly fastened upon large populations of alien race and colour, with habits of life and thought which do not

34 Ibid., 245
35 Ibid., 243
36 Ibid., 245
37 Ibid., 246

blend with ours, it is found impossible to graft the tender plants of free representative government, and at the same time preserve good order ... We are obliged in practice to make a choice between good order and justice administered autocratically ... on the one hand, and delicate, costly, doubtful and disorderly experiments in self-government ... upon the other, and we have practically everywhere decided to adopt the former alternative.[38]

Overall Hobson estimated that of the 376 millions of British subjects in the Empire, 'not more than eleven millions, or one in thirty-four' had any 'real self-government' for purposes of legislation and administration. Self-rule prevailed in the older white colonies, but in the new territories imperialism had been an 'expansion of autocracy.'[39]

To drive this point home, Hobson went on to outline the ramifications of imperialism on domestic politics. Imperialism represented an attempt to avert and 'frustrate' domestic struggles for 'economic reform,' but more than this it operated 'to paralyse' the machinery of British parliamentary institutions.[40] Hobson's analysis of British democracy is the subject of a later chapter, but the gist of his argument in this regard can be culled from the following portmanteau quotation:

The government of a great heterogeneous medley of lower races by departmental officials in London ... lies outside the scope of popular knowledge and popular control. ... This subordination of the legislative to the executive, and the concentration of executive power in an autocracy [i.e. the cabinet] are necessary consequences of the predominance of foreign over domestic politics. The process is attended by a decay of party spirit. ... At elections the electorate is no longer invited to exercise a free, conscious, rational choice between the representatives of different intelligible policies ... Imperialism poisons the springs of democracy in the mind and character of the people. ... Our despotically ruled dependencies have ever served to damage the character of our people by feeding the habits of snobbish subservience, the admiration of wealth and rank. ... It is, indeed, a nemesis of Imperialism that the arts and crafts of tyranny, acquired and exercised in our unfree Empire, should be turned against our liberties at home.[41]

38 Ibid., 122
39 Ibid., 114. These figures refer to the situation in 1905. In the first edition the ratio is stated as 1 in 37.
40 *Imperialism*, 145
41 Ibid., 145, 147-52

Imperialism, then, was the enemy of democracy, both at home and abroad.

iii / Liberalism, imperialism, and progress

Hobson was perhaps the first theorist of imperialism to point out the possibility that the third world's contact with industrial nations might not lead to their eventual emergence as mature industrial states. It was, of course, the assumption of many orthodox liberals at the time that imperial rule was a form of tutelage that would eventually bestow the benefits of an industrial civilization upon the dependent nations. Indeed, this was a view shared by many Fabians and socialist groups of a more radical bent. Thus, as Irving Zeitlin has pointed out, 'Even Marx ... believed that British construction of railways in India would unavoidably lead to India's industrialisation to the point where the colony eventually would mirror the mother country'[42] – a reflection also to be endorsed later by Lenin.[43]

Although Hobson did not hold to the contrary thesis in all his works,[44] and given the complexity of the issue this is, perhaps, not surprising, in his major work *Imperialism* there is a strong suggestion that the more likely outcome of imperialist rule would be the skewed development of colonial economies in ways specifically tailored to enhance the industrial superiority of capitalists in the imperialist nations. Imperialism would not spread the fruits of industrialization, even inadvertently, but simply increase the dependency of the colonies on the advanced nations they were set up to service.

Hobson's discussion of this thesis resolves around the fact that the imperialists were interested in investing in the colonies primarily as resource bases and as markets for finished goods. He pictured the consequences of this for the colonial economy from two different angles. First, he suggested that the imperialists, either through neglect or design, would inhibit or crush colonial manufactures and trades, that might compete with their own industries for raw materials and markets. The classic example he used to illustrate this point was the British destruction of the Indian handweaving industry:

Industrial revolution is one thing when it is the natural movement of internal forces ... and another thing when it is imposed by foreign conquerors looking primarily to present gains for themselves. ... The story of the

42 *Capitalism and Imperialism* (1972), 95
43 'The export of capital influences and greatly accelerates the development of capitalism in those countries to which it is exported.' Lenin, *Imperialism: The Highest Stage of Capitalism*, 725
44 See, for example, *An Economic Interpretation of Investment* (1911), 100-1. For a recent review of the debate see J. Petras, *Critical Perspectives on Imperialism and Social Classes in the Third World* (1978), chap. 4.

destruction of the native weaving industry by the [East India] Company ... illustrate[s] the selfish, short-sighted economic policy of the late eighteenth and early nineteenth centuries. ... The effect ... was the irreparable ruin of many of the most valuable and characteristic arts of Indian industry.[45]

There was also substantial British investment in Indian roads, railways, irrigation works, and mines, yet the conclusion of British officials, even those 'strongly favourable' to British rule, was that such investment had not given 'any considerable economic prosperity to India.'[46] Indeed, one of the more prosperous regions of India, Bengal, was prosperous at least in part, according to Hobson, because it staved off close British rule. Overall, Hobson concluded that even though British administration in India had been carried out with considerable goodwill, there remained ample 'testimony to the injury inflicted ... by sudden ill-advised application of Western economic ... methods.'[47]

Pictured from another angle, the destructiveness of imperialism, Hobson supposed, would be evident once the colonies' raw materials and minerals ran out. In South Africa, he suggested, 'after a single generation of gold-getting,' the 'industrial strength of the country must steadily and surely decline.' The mines once exhausted would be abandoned, and the 'Hebrew mining speculators, American and Scottish engineers, Chinese miners, German traders' would evacuate 'the country they have sacked.' The colony, however, would not return to its 'primitive condition of wholesome agriculture,' for once touched by modern imperialism a country was changed thereafter. Its working population, now 'broken from their customary life of agriculture' would degenerate into a lumpen-proletariat – 'a chronic pest of vagabonds and unemployed.'[48] Agriculture, as a result, would continue to decline, whilst no new industry would rise to take its place, for the imperialists, interested only in exploiting the mines, had furnished no foundation upon which to build 'a secure fabric of industrial ... civilisation.' Imperialist penetration of the Transvaal, therefore, had the effect of substituting 'for normal gradual and natural development, a hasty artificial abnormal development.'[49]

Hobson's comments on Japan, written in 1905 for the second edition of *Imperialism*, are also interesting in this regard, for they suggest that Japan

45 *Imperialism*, 292
46 Ibid., 288-9
47 Ibid., 294
48 Ibid., 277
49 Ibid., 276

was the exception that proved the rule. By the turn of the century Japan could be ranked as a major industrial nation, and one already showing tendencies towards imperialism. 'The wonderful success of Japan,' Hobson wrote, 'appears to be in large measure due to ... *inner* sources of economy.' One of these sources was the Japanese capacity for 'cerebral work,' the other was their 'intense patriotism.' This latter sentiment assisted not only to produce 'a better co-operation' of industrial activities in Japan, but also helped to safeguard Japanese culture and territory from Western capitalism.[50] A marked contrast with the fate of most of Africa! However, if Japan was to remain a great industrial power, it could do so, in Hobson's opinion, only if it continued to develop its economy mainly with its '*own* resources of capital and organising skill.' Otherwise Japan likely would become 'a catspaw of cosmopolitan capitalism.'[51] Too close contact with Western imperialists carried the threat of deindustrialization.

All told the evidence seemed to suggest that:

The relations subsisting between the superior and the inferior nations, commonly established by pure force, and resting on that basis, are such as to preclude the genuine sympathy essential to the operation of the best civilising influences, and usually resolve themselves into the maintenance of external good order so as to forward the profitable development of certain natural resources of land, under 'forced' native labour, primarily for the benefit of white traders and investors, and secondarily for the benefit of the world of white western consumers.

This failure to justify by results the forcible rule over alien peoples is ... inherent in the nature of such domination.[52]

In Hobson's view the widening gap between the economies of Western nations and those of Africa and Asia was essentially a consequence of power structures which locked underdeveloped countries into positions of continuous dependency.

Several commentators have suggested that this part of Hobson's analysis contradicts his main thesis. Michael Barrat Brown, for example, argues that Hobson is involved in the following dilemma: 'Profits were supposed to be declining at home ... because of the impoverishment of the masses at home, while super-profits were to be earned overseas through still greater impover-

50 Ibid., 315-16 (emphasis added)
51 Ibid., 317 (emphasis added)
52 Ibid., 283-4

ishment of the masses overseas.'[53] Now, it is interesting that Hobson recognized this contradiction (a fact of which Barratt Brown does not seem aware), but he saw it as a long-term problem that would have to be faced by capitalists; in other words, the contradiction was viewed by him, not as a defect of his theory, but as a reflection of the irrationality of the capitalist mode of income distribution:

The world-market seemed to the Lancashire and Birmingham exporters of the early nineteenth century illimitable. ... But just as the manufacturers and traders of each nation found their home markets limited, so they found the world-market also limited. ... Nor is it really surprising that this should be so. ... The profits of the foreign trade and of the foreign industries which it sustained were distributed so unequally, and the gains of the masses of the peoples in the newly developed countries were relatively so small, that the same incapacity to purchase for consumption the whole volume of exported goods competing for sale was exhibited. Closely linked with this practical restriction of the expansion of markets for goods is the restriction of profitable fields of investment. ... The supply of competing capital from different investing countries has shown the same tendency to exceed effective demand.[54]

This, of course, does not dispose of Barratt Brown's critique, but it does indicate that for Hobson to be consistent it would not be necessary for him to abandon altogether his theory regarding the impoverishment of colonial markets; rather, he had only to develop a two-stage theory of imperialism, indicating that although in the long run the imperialists' profit margins must fall as a consequence of underconsumption abroad, in the short run there were reasons why this was not the case. Unfortunately, although Hobson's *Imperialism* does contain a number of statements regarding the immediate profit to be gained from capital investment overseas, these are not tied into his general theory of underconsumption. In another of his works, *Gold, Prices and Wages* (1913), he does, however, present the gist of what would be required to explain this first stage of imperial expansion:

The general effect of opening up of rich new areas of investment would seem to be an increase in supply. For what else is meant by the develop-

53 M. Barrat Brown, *After Imperialism* (1978), 96. The same point is made by G. Lichtheim, *Imperialism* (1971), 117.
54 *Democracy after the War* (1917; 4th ed. 1919), 77-9. See also *Rationalisation and Unemployment*, 115-18.

ment of these new areas except the bringing of new productive agents into the commercial system, and so increasing the world supply of goods?

This is, no doubt, the ultimate effect. But there are interim effects. In the case of new countries in the course of being opened up, a long period of initial development may occur before the harvest of goods begins to be reaped. During this period large masses of capital raised by the investors in the older industrial countries are devoted to making roads and railways, docks and harbours, to clearing land, to irrigation, to building and planting processes, to prospecting and other initial stages of mining, to all those kinds of experimental work necessary to discover and test the real resources of a country. Though the object of all this expenditure is to produce marketable goods, a long period of capital expenditure, unaccompanied by any considerable immediate yield of marketable goods, is likely to occur.[55]

Here, then, was the beginnings of a two-step theory of imperialism, quite compatible (*pace* Barrat Brown) with Hobson's general theory of underconsumption.

b / Liberalism, Imperialism, and Economy:
The Commercial Value of Imperialism

The imperialism of the last six decades is clearly condemned as a business policy in that at enormous expense it has procured a small, bad, unsafe increase of markets. *Imperialism*, 46

To appeal to the conscience of liberals to resist the forces of imperialism was a major part of Hobson's study, but he made no less strong an appeal to their wallets. In Hobson's estimation, imperialism could be proven to be bad business for the nation. Indeed, Bernard Porter has gone so far as to suggest that the orginality of Hobson's analysis did not rest with his theory of underconsumption, but with his argument that the new empire did not even constitute a profitable enterprise.

Porter points out that the contention that the empire was being built in order to avert economic slump at home made its first appeal not to radical dissenters but to the advocates of imperialism. Cecil Rhodes, for example, viewed imperialism as the solution to the social problem of unemployment:

---

55 *Gold, Prices and Wages*, 98-9. Hobson's comments here appear to develop out of his earlier analysis of the differing rates at which capital fructifies. See *The Industrial System* (1909; 2nd ed., 1910), 53.

'My cherished ideal,' he said, 'in order to save the 40,000,000 inhabitants of the United Kingdom from a bloody civil war, [is that] our colonial statesmen ... acquire new lands for settling the surplus population, to provide new markets for the goods produced in the factories and mines. The Empire ... is a bread and butter question. If you want to avoid civil war, you must become imperialists.' Joseph Chamberlain also courted support for imperialism on the basis of its commercial benefits. 'Is there any man in his senses,' he inquired, 'who believes that the crowded population of the [British] islands could exist for a single day if it were to cut adrift from us the great dependencies ... which are the natural outlets of our trade.'[56] Porter concludes from this and other evidence that the novelty of Hobson's theory of imperialism

did not lie in its mere attribution of imperialism to economic factors, nor even in its assertion that 'over-production' was the root cause. ... The chief difference was that the 'surplus capital' theory before [Hobson wrote *Imperialism*] was an argument in *support* of imperialism, rather than against it.[57]

[Opponents of imperialism] would make no kind of impression merely by pointing to its roots in 'over-production.' Over-production was its excuse. What anti-imperialists had to do was, somehow, to counter the 'economic theory' offered by the imperialists themselves.[58]

This is an interesting historical perspective on the nature of the challenge facing Hobson in his effort to refute imperialist arguments. Porter tends to gloss over the fact that Hobson was also innovative in relating the particular aggressive character of late Victorian imperialism to the 'push' of over-production; none the less, his comments do help to explain why Hobson was keen to tackle the imperialist on his own ground, i.e., to assess whether imperialism was a viable policy for keeping British industry working, regardless of whether it was incompatible with the pacific, humanist aspirations of liberalism.

Hobson's analysis of statistics put out by the Colonial office and other official sources revealed that one-third of the total British Empire of some

56 Cited in Bernard Porter, *Critics of Empire*, 45, 46. Lenin quotes the same speech in his pamphlet, *Imperialism: The Highest Stage of Capitalism*.
57 *Critics of Empire*, 41
58 Ibid., 47

13,000,000 square miles had been added between 1870 and 1900, and that the vast majority of this territorial expansion had taken place in Africa and Asia.[59] The volume of Britain's external trade also increased considerably during this period. Was it right, then, to assume, as did the pro-imperialist, that 'trade follows the flag?' According to Hobson, nothing was further from the truth, for the statistics also revealed that most of this trade by-passed these newly acquired territories in favour of other industrial nations. Indeed, colonial trade with Britain, despite these mass annexations, showed a relative decline over the years 1868-99. The conclusion was irresistible: 'it is clear that while imperial expansion was attended by no increase in the value of our trade with our colonies and dependencies, a considerable increase in the value of our trade with foreign nations had taken place.'[60] In particular, trade had increased with the major industrial nations – France, Germany, Russia, and the United States – the very nations 'whose political enmity [Britain] was in danger of arousing by its policy of expansion.' The folly of this policy was only enhanced by the fact that trade with the new tropical and subtropical regions of the empire was 'small, precarious and unprogressive.'[61]

The limited and fluctuating benefits of imperial trade, in Hobson's estimation, could not bear the cost of maintaining an imperial presence in these new protectorates: 'At whatever figure we estimate the profits in this trade, it forms an utterly insignificant part of our national income, while the expenses connected directly and indirectly with the acquisition, administration and defence of these possessions must swallow an immeasurably large sum.'[62]

The case against imperialism as a business policy seemed so overwhelming that Hobson sympathized with the 'disinterested spectator' who was 'apt to despair' and regard imperialism as testimony to 'some ultimate irrationalism in politics.' Irrationalism there was, but in Hobson's opinion, not as much as

59 *Imperialism*, 17-18
60 Ibid., 35. In the first edition of *Imperialism* Hobson went so far as to argue that foreign trade overall played only a 'small part in the total income of Great Britain' (31). This contention already had been strongly criticized when first proposed by Hobson in the *Speaker* and continuing criticism led him to withdraw the argument for the second edition of *Imperialism*. There Hobson contents himself with the above claim that Britain's trade with her new colonies could be shown to be of marginal significance in boosting national income. For an interesting comment on this episode, see P.F. Clarke, *Liberals and Social Democrats*, 94-9, although, by downplaying the underconsumptionist content of Hobson's article, 'Free Trade and Foreign Policy,' Clarke overstates the shift in emphasis to be found in *Imperialism*, resulting from Hobson retracting his statement on Britain's foreign trade figures.
61 *Imperialism*, 38
62 Ibid., 38-9

appeared at first sight. Imperialism, though 'irrational from the standpoint of the whole nation, [was] rational enough from the standpoint of certain classes in the nation':

Certain definite business and professional interests feeding upon imperialistic expenditures, are ... set up in opposition to the common good, and, instinctively feeling their way to one another, are found united in strong sympathy to support every new imperialist exploit.[63]

In more recent terminology, these 'business and professional interests' constituted a military-industrial complex, operating on two levels of complicity. The inner core of this complex was made up of the military, who were 'imperialist by conviction'; certain 'big firms' engaged in supplying the military with armaments, transport, food, and clothing, etc.; the 'great manufacturers for export' who profited from 'supplying the real or artificial wants' of the newly annexed territories; and finally, the colonial civil service, for the 'colonies remain what James Mill cynically described them as being, "a vast system of outdoor relief for the upper classes." '[64]

Encircling this inner core of interests was an outer complex made up of financiers and investors. Of these two elements, it was the financier who functioned as the 'governor of the imperial engine,'[65] collecting the bits of surplus capital accumulated by the 'rank and file of the investors' and directing it abroad. In 'large measure' the investors were the 'cat'spaws of the great financial houses.'[66]

63 Ibid., 47-8
64 Ibid., 49-51
65 Ibid., 59
66 Ibid., 56. Much later in *Imperialism*, Hobson suggests that not only is the small investor heavily dependent on the activities of the financier for finding outlets for his surplus capital but that their interests are not necessarily in accord: '[The] forces of international finance ... are commonly described as capitalistic, but the gravest danger arises not from genuine industrial investments in foreign lands, but from the handling of stocks and shares based on those investments by financiers. Those who own a genuine stake in the natural sources or the industry of a foreign land at least have some substantial interest in the peace and good government of that land; but the stock speculator has no such stake: his interest lies in the oscillations of paper values, which require fluctuation and insecurity of political conditions as their instrument.' Ibid., 359. Hobson left this comment as a pointer to the future. For an interesting account of how that future turned out, see G. Arrighi, *The Geometry of Imperialism* (1978). Basically Arrighi claims that in the contest between industrial capital and money capital it was the former that ultimately gained control, so that international corporations came to replace the banks as the dominant instruments of imperialism.

These great businesses – banking, broking, bill discounting, loan floating, company promoting – form the central ganglion of international capitalism. United by the strongest bonds of organisation ... situated in the very heart of the business capital of every state ... they are in a unique position to manipulate the policy of nations. ... [Their] wealth, ... the scale of their operations, their cosmopolitan organisation make them the prime determinants of imperial policy.[67]

Hobson was convinced that this ganglion of interests was 'extremely influential and able to make a definite impression on politics.'[68] In fact, their political impact was decidedly greater than their economic importance to the nation warranted, because they were able to subserve other interests to their own. The details of this argument will be given shortly. For the moment, it is important to keep to the forefront Hobson's general contention regarding the disproportionate political influence of the imperialists in order to assess certain criticisms of his theory of economic imperialism.

It has been pointed out by D.K. Fieldhouse, for example, that although *Imperialism* contains many statistics, it does not give the figures for capital exported by Britain to other advanced industrial nations, or compare these figures with those indicating the amount of capital invested in the new territories. In Fieldhouse's opinion, this comparison would have been the undoing of Hobson's thesis. Fieldhouse's critique has been sufficiently influential to warrant detailed citation:

[The] most important fact that emerges from the work of Paish, Cairncross and Nurkse is that Hobson was entirely wrong in assuming that any large proportion of British overseas investment went to those undeveloped parts of Africa and Asia, which were annexed during the 'imperialist' grab after 1870. ... The figures published by Paish in 1911 demonstrate this conclusively. The bulk of investment then lay in the

---

67 *Imperialism*, 56-7, 59. Hobson's interesting comment as to the 'cosmopolitan' or supranational character of high finance unfortunately is not further developed in *Imperialism*. This is another of those occasions where Hobson, rather than providing a structural account of this internationalism, is content to leave the analysis at the level of a racist aside: 'business capital [is] ... controlled, so far as Europe is concerned, chiefly by men of a single and peculiar race, who have behind them many centuries of financial experience ... Does any one seriously suppose that a great war could be undertaken by any European State, or a great State loan subscribed, if the house of Rothschild and its connections set their face against it?' Ibid., 57

68 Ibid., 49

United States, £688m., South America, £587m., Canada, £372m., Aus-
tralasia, £380m., India and Ceylon, £365m., and South Africa, £351m. By
contrast, West Africa had received only £29m., the Straits and Malay
States, £22m., and the remaining British possessions, £33m. These last
were, of course, by no means negligible amounts and indicate clearly that
in some at least of the tropical dependencies which had been recently
acquired, British finance was finding scope for profit and investment. But
this does not make Hobson's thesis any more valid. The sums invested in
these tropical areas, whether newly annexed or not, were quite marginal
to the total overseas investment, and continued to be relatively small in
the years immediately before 1911. Hence, to maintain that Britain had
found it necessary to acquire these territories because of an urgent need
for new fields of investment is simply unrealistic: and, with the rejection
of this hypothesis, so ingeniously conjured up by Hobson, the whole basis
of his theory that 'imperialism' was the product of economic necessity collapses.[69]

Fieldhouse suggests, in effect, that the state could largely ignore the
demands of those capitalists with 'marginal' investments in the tropics,
because the majority of investors had interests elsewhere. The state, therefore, was free to seek its own 'independent' goals within the new territories.
Consequently, Fieldhouse proposes that the new empire was built upon
political rather than economic considerations.

However, this refutation of Hobson's position is not as solid as it may first
appear. Fieldhouse incorrectly assumes that it is necessary to show that a high
proportion of British capital went to the new territories if Hobson's thesis is to
be validated. But this is surely not so. Hobson was not trying to prove that all
capitalists were imperialists bent on a policy of foreign annexation. If this had
been the case, then it would have been reasonable to expect a high level of
capital investment in these areas. In fact, as already noted, only those who
belonged to the 'military industrial complex' were directly implicated by
Hobson in the economics of the new imperialism. In this light the real issue
would seem to be whether Hobson was correct in assuming that this select
group had sufficient power to employ the 'public purse and the public force
to extend the field of their private investments and to safeguard ... their

69 'Imperialism: A Historiographical Review' (1961), in K. Boulding and T. Mukerjee, eds.,
   Economic Imperialism (1972), 110-11. See also A.J.P. Taylor, 'Economic Imperialism'
   (1952) in *Essays in English History* (1972), for an earlier exposition of this critique.

existing investments'[70] – i.e., the £84m. mentioned by Fieldhouse. But Fieldhouse does not touch on this subject. As it stands his argument does nothing to refute Hobson's position. Fieldhouse's discovery that the majority of investors sunk their surplus capital into the more familiar markets of America and Europe does not diminish the significance of the smaller amount invested in Africa and Asia, but instead may be seen as throwing a spotlight on the military industrial complex that Hobson had already perceived lurking in the shadows and its power to generate a pushful foreign policy.

Support for this defence of Hobson's analysis also might be taken from one of his later works, *An Economic Interpretation of Investment* (1911). What is remarkable about this book is that it contains a lengthy section on 'The Distribution of Foreign Investments' based almost entirely on the very tabulations, made by Paish, which Fieldhouse argues damns Hobson's thesis. Clearly, Hobson viewed Paish's findings as not incompatible with his own, and in one respect even directly supportive since they revealed a tendency for British investments to push on to new markets, even though the absolute level of investment in the 'older' countries remained much higher. In Hobson's words, the statistics showed that:

the general tendency has been in recent years for England to go further afield for her foreign investments and to spread her holdings over a large number of geographic areas. Both relatively and in some cases absolutely, she has reduced her holdings of securities in the older, more developed, countries, where capital is available largely from domestic sources and where interest is low.[71]

There was little or nothing, then, in Paish's figures to prove Hobson's theory of economic imperialism wrong for its times.

70 *Imperialism*, 54. This argument is also made by Porter, although he goes on to suggest that Hobson made a logical error in assuming that imperialism had to be a rational, profitable enterprise for someone – namely his economic clique, and, also, in assuming that 'only self-interest which was accurately assessed had any great impact on politics.' These comments suggest strong reasons why Hobson himself did not feel obliged to undertake the empirical study suggested above. But why such assumptions constitute logical errors is none too clear. What Porter seems to present are alternative assumptions: viz., that man is moved mainly by sentiment and that imperialism was based on an 'uncalculating' fear of foreign advantage, not logical corrections. Indeed, Porter himself admits that Hobson was consistent in the pursuit of his logic – even 'rigidly' so. See *Critics of Empire*, chap. 7.

71 *An Economic Interpretation of Investment*, 73

4 THE RELATION BETWEEN HOBSON'S
AND LENIN'S THEORIES OF IMPERIALISM

Although there was little contemporary evidence to disprove Hobson's thesis, it is important to realize that Hobson himself did not consider that capitalism forever must be held in the grip of imperialists; imperialism was not the final irreversible stage of capitalism. Providing the domestic base of capitalism was properly reformed, capitalists for the most part would be content to stay at home:

If the apportionment of income were such as to evoke no excessive saving, full constant employment for capital and labour would be furnished at home. This, of course, does not imply that there would be no foreign trade ... [but now the incentive would be] the pressure of the consumer anxious to buy abroad what he could not buy at home, not the blind eagerness of the producer to use every force or trick of trade or politics to find markets for his 'surplus goods'. ... Whatever is produced in England can be consumed in England, provided that income ... is properly distributed.[72]

As is well known, it was this conclusion that raised the ire of Lenin and marked the most obvious difference in their treatment of the issue of imperialism. Thus, in his pamphlet *Imperialism: The Highest Stage of Capitalism* (1917), Lenin acidly commented that 'if capitalism ... could raise the living standards of the masses ... there could be no question of a surplus of capital. ... But if capitalism did these things it would not be capitalism.'[73]

Yet Lenin also admitted an indebtedness to Hobson's study *Imperialism* in preparing his own analysis, stating that he gave Hobson's book 'all the care ... that work deserves.'[74] Moreover, even a cursory glance at Lenin's essay would reveal that it had many features in common with Hobson's: it also stresses the centralization of capital, the emergence of monopolies and the need to export surplus capital, the strengthening of the links between finance and industrial capital, the emergence of competing empires, and the development of a labour aristocracy. In some important regards, Lenin sharpened elements of Hobson's study, for example, by giving a greater prominence to the role of monopolies and making this the defining feature

---

72 *Imperialism*, 87-8
73 723-4
74 Ibid., 677. It is noteworthy that the only work in which Hobson comments on Lenin's *Imperialism* is *Veblen* (1936), 139, and there he is totally self-effacing.

of a new stage of capitalism, and by subsuming the competition of empires under a 'law of uneven development,' but overall the contours of their arguments appear very similar.

Despite Lenin's explicit acknowledgement of Hobson's contribution to his own study of imperialism and the apparent affinity of their arguments, several commentators have sought to minimize Hobson's influence on Lenin: the divergence of their conclusions, so it is argued, seems necessarily to imply important theoretical differences. B. Sutcliffe, for example, has suggested that Lenin's indebtedness to Hobson was merely in the area of facts and figures and consequently 'to speak of a "Hobson-Lenin theory"' greatly exaggerates 'the theoretical proximity of the two.'[75] The exaggeration, however, would seem to be Sutcliffe's, for while it is true that in the opening paragraph of his pamphlet Lenin does remark on Hobson's 'very good and comprehensive *description* of the principal specific economic and political features of imperialism,' elsewhere in the text Lenin makes it clear that Hobson's identification of these specific features of imperialism also constituted an important *theoretical* advance:

Kautsky, while claiming that he continues to advocate Marxism, as a matter of fact takes a step backward compared with the *social-liberal* Hobson, who *more correctly* takes into account two 'historically concrete' (Kautsky's definition is a mockery of historical concreteness) features of modern imperialism: (1) the competition between *several* imperialisms, and (2) the predominance of the financier over the merchant.[76]

As Giovanni Arrighi has commented, this passage demonstrates that 'Lenin shared not just a few isolated hypotheses, but the very mode in which Hobson had outlined his *diagnosis* of imperialism.'[77]

An alternate and perhaps more interesting attempt to separate the theories of Lenin and Hobson has been made by James O'Connor. O'Connor grants that 'Lenin agreed with Hobson that the prime cause of capital exports was the vast increase in the supply of capital in the metropolitan countries' and that, like Hobson, Lenin linked 'foreign investments with the acquisition of colonies,' but, nevertheless, Lenin's theory is distinct because he explained the 'cause of surplus capital' differently from Hobson. Hobson's analysis was underconsumptionist, whereas Lenin argued, according to O'Connor, that

---

75 'Conclusion' in Owen and Sutcliffe, eds., *Studies in the Theories of Imperialism*, 315
76 *Imperialism*, 684 (emphasis added), 748
77 *The Geometry of Imperialism*, 24

surplus capital was generated by the 'tendency of the rate of profit to fall' with increases in the 'organic composition of capital.'[78] This theory depicts the crises of capitalism as arising, not from the difficulties of *realizing* profits in an impoverished market, but from the increasing difficulty of *creating* profits in highly capitalized industries, where the source of surplus value, labour, is more and more displaced by machinery – hence the pressure to export capital to underdeveloped countries where the organic composition of capital is lower.

The problem with O'Connor's thesis is that there is little direct evidence for it in Lenin's *Imperialism*. It would seem clear from some of Lenin's other works that he did endorse this Marxian law of economics[79] and that he was critical of underconsumption theory. On this latter score, his disagreement with the Narodniks is well known.[80] It is also significant, though perhaps less well known, that in an early, brief review of Hobson's *The Evolution of Modern Capitalism*, Lenin criticized the chapter dealing with underconsumption as the 'weakest' part of the book.[81] But at best these observations might make it plausible to assume that the theory of the 'rising organic composition of capital' is implicit in Lenin's analysis of imperialism. The fact remains, however, that Lenin's *explicit* statements connecting the centralization of industry and the export of surplus capital are very Hobsonian:

On the threshhold of the twentieth century we see the formation of a new type of monopoly: firstly, monopolist associations of capitalists in all characteristically developed countries; secondly, the monopolistic position of a very few rich countries, in which the accumulation of capital has reached gigantic proportions. An enormous 'surplus of capital' has arisen in advanced countries. ... The need to export capital arises from the fact that in a few countries capitalism has become 'overripe' and (owing to the backward state of agriculture *and the poverty of the masses*) capital cannot find a field of profitable investment.[82]

78 'The Meaning of Economic Imperialism' in R.I. Rhodes, ed., *Imperialism and Underdevelopment* (1970), 109
79 See, for example, Lenin's essay 'Karl Marx' (1915) in *Selected Works* (New World ed., 1967).
80 See Lenin, *The Development of Capitalism in Russia* (1899).
81 'Hobson's Analysis of Capitalism' (1898) in H. Pollitt, ed., *Lenin on Britain* (1934)
82 Lenin, *Imperialism* 723-4 (emphasis added). It is noteworthy that O'Connor does not directly refer to Lenin's text in support of his interpretation. Instead he footnotes his remarks as follows: 'In the following paragraph we will rely on Lenin's theory of the causes of imperialist expansion, but also on Maurice Dobbs' and John Strachey's readings of Lenin.' O'Connor, 'The Meaning of Economic Imperialism,' 145, n. 12

The relation between Hobson's and Lenin's theory of imperialism, then, would seem to be a close one. Although it might be argued that Lenin's reliance on Hobson was somewhat incautious, given the very different conclusions Hobson had reached on the basis of his theory, there seems to be little warrant for pressing this difference to the point of insisting that Lenin cannot be taken at his own word.[83]

5 THE NON-ECONOMIC FOUNDATIONS OF IMPERIALISM: THE FORCES OF IRRATIONALISM

In making the capitalist-imperialist forces the pivot of financial policy, I do not mean that other forces, industrial, political and moral, have no independent aims and influences, but simply that the former group must be regarded as the true determinant in the interpretation of actual policy. *Imperialism*, 96

Hobson's was not an economic theory of imperialism, if this is understood to mean that the interests promoting imperialism were those that belonged only to the spheres of trade, industry, or investment.[84] Hobson did contend that economic factors were of primary importance in analysing imperialism, but he did not discount the play of other forces as mere epiphenomena. Non-economic factors had an efficacy sufficient to warrant separate study. In *Imperialism*, Hobson attempted to explain the relationship between economic and non-economic forces of imperialism as follows:

In view of the part which the non-economic factors of patriotism, adventure, military enterprise political ambition, and philanthropy play in imperial expansion, it may appear to impute to financiers so much power is to take a too narrowly economic view of history. And it is true that the motor-power of Imperialism is not chiefly financial: finance is rather the governor of the imperial engine, directing the energy and determining its work: it does not constitute the fuel of the engine, nor does it directly generate the power. Finance manipulates the patriotic forces which politicians, soldiers, philanthropists, and traders generate; the enthusiasm for

83 Lenin's lack of care in this regard might be explained by the fact that his pamphlet was written in a hurry and under difficult circumstances. See Lenin's 'Preface,' 26 April 1917. On the other hand, there is a letter by Lenin, dated 1904, in which he mentions that he is translating Hobson's *Imperialism*. This would seem to provide plenty of time for reflection. See E. Hill and D. Mudie, eds., *The Letters of Lenin* (1937), 208.

84 This is the definition of economic imperialism given by R. Koebner in Boulding and Mukerjee, eds., *Economic Imperialism*, 71.

expansion which issues from these sources, though strong and genuine, is irregular and blind; the financial interest has those qualities which are needed to set Imperialism to work ... the final determination rests with the financial power.[85]

It has been said that this passage contains a bewildering mixture of metaphors,[86] and this may account for the fact that, although roughly two-thirds of *Imperialism* deals with non-economic determinants, Hobson's theory is still frequently labelled 'economic reductionist.'[87]

Some clarification of Hobson's meaning is to be found in one of the 'sister-works' to *Imperialism*, entitled *The Psychology of Jingoism*, published in 1901. In this work Hobson provides his fullest account of the non-economic sentiments and motives that supported imperialism. Although *The Psychology of Jingoism* never achieved the notoriety of *Imperialism*, some bold claims have been made as to its merit. Caroline Playne, for instance, called it a 'classic on the subject of group neurosis,' and Harvey Mitchell has suggested that Hobson's 'verbal images and ideas provide a striking anticipation of Freud's' and, further, that an examination of Hobson's argument makes it 'evident that to him should go part of the credit traditionally claimed for Schumpeter, for having advanced the theory that imperialist drives are motivated by irrational or non-rational motives.'[88]

This mention of Schumpeter is revealing, because Schumpeter's analysis of imperialism is often relied upon by those critics who wish to provide an antidote to theories of economic imperialism, Hobson's included. It is therefore worthwhile to contrast Hobson and Schumpeter's analysis of the forces of irrationalism. Schumpeter, in his essay *Imperialism and Social Classes*, argued that capitalism and imperialism are antithetic. Imperialism was 'atavistic in character,' derived from a 'purely instinctual inclination towards war and conquest.'[89] This element of irrationality was a residue left over from more savage times. In contrast, the pursuit of material wealth under conditions of a market economy required that the capitalists 'democratized, indi-

---

85 *Imperialism*, 59
86 E.M. Winslow, *The Pattern of Imperialism* (1948), 98
87 See, for example, the essays by Fieldhouse, Koebner, and Lange, in Boulding and Mukerjee, eds., *Economic Imperialism*.
88 Playne, *The Pre-War Mind in Britain*, 1928, 70; Mitchell, 'Hobson Revisited,' *Journal of the History of Ideas*, vol. 26 (1965), 405, 407. The affinity between Hobson and Schumpeter's views on imperialism was first suggested by Winslow, *The Pattern of Imperialism*, 103.
89 Schumpeter, *Imperialism and Social Classes* (1919; Blackwell, 1951), 84, 83

vidualized, and rationalized,' their environment. Schumpeter, therefore, maintained that a 'purely capitalist world [could] offer no fertile soil to imperialist impulses.' The rational capitalist and the rational worker were both free traders. Only 'export-dependent monopolists' were prone to utilize lingering passions of violence to further their material interests. But these monopolists could not be considered genuine capitalists; they were themselves remnants of an earlier period of mercantilism. There was, in Schumpeter's opinion, no reason to suppose that monopolies, and therefore imperialist policies, 'evolved by the inner logic of capitalism itself.'[90]

Hobson would have agreed, of course, that the chief proponents of imperialism were the monopolists and their financiers. And he was no less impressed than Schumpeter with the non-rational passions and sentiments that fuelled the imperialist drive. But Hobson's analysis differed from Schumpeter's in two important respects. First, he tied imperialism into the 'inner logic' of capitalism by linking it to his discussion of advanced capitalism's crises of underconsumption. Consequently, whereas Schumpeter argued that if rid of imperialist-protectionist policies capitalism would become 'pure' and competitive, Hobson argued that it would go into recession, unless 'saved' by social reforms. Second, and more relevant for present purposes, Hobson argued that the conditions of life under capitalism did not suppress but promoted this primitivism:

That inverted patriotism whereby love of one's own nation is transformed into the hatred of another nation, and the fierce craving to destroy the individual member of that other nation, is no new thing. ... The quick ebullition of national hate termed Jingoism is a particular form of this primitive passion, modified and *intensified by certain conditions of modern civilisation.*[91]

Thus, as Mitchell has commented, Hobson and Schumpeter part company not over the issue of atavism, but with regard to their 'differing conceptions of the value system of capitalist culture.'[92]

According to Hobson, capitalism had perpetuated certain unsavory primitive instincts by creating conditions conducive to the excitation of a 'mob mind.' Hobson took his cue here from Gustave Le Bon's study *The Crowd*, published in 1895. Le Bon had shown to Hobson's satisfaction that a mob

90 Ibid., 88-9, 90, 111-17, 128
91 *The Psychology of Jingoism* (1901), 1-2 (emphasis added)
92 'Hobson Revisited,' 407

exhibited a 'character and conduct which is lower, intellectually and morally, than the character and conduct of its average member.'[93] Hobson did not agree with Le Bon that this was necessarily the case, but he considered this 'hypothesis of reversion to a savage type of nature' to be 'distinctly profitable' in the study of jingoism.[94] The mind of the jingo, like that of the savage, was credulous, brutal, and vainglorious.

Where Schumpeter saw rationality, Hobson detected new forces at work within capitalism that perpetuated credulity and distinguished 'present-day Jingoism, from the national war-spirit in earlier times.' The rapidity and quantity of information, which new technology in transport and communications made possible, was in danger, according to Hobson, of overwhelming the average person's ratiocinative processes, for it made him susceptible to the 'direct influence of a thousand times as many other persons as were their ancestors before the age of steam and electricity.' Here the medium truly was the message, for such an outpouring of opinions constituted bombardment. Moreover, Hobson suggested that 'the appearance of hard truth imparted by the mechanical rigidity of print' possessed a 'degree of credit' denied to the spoken word of past ages. It was not surprising, therefore, that the untrained minds of the masses found it difficult to sift and weigh the reports they received. They remained credulous, willing to 'believe upon no evidence or insufficient evidence.' Opinions took root merely from the fact of their constant repetition, and public opinion was formed on 'precisely the same sort of evidence' as was the belief that 'Colmans is the best mustard or Branson's extract of coffee is perfection.'[95]

The average man in advanced industrial countries was not only bombarded with opinions, he also lived in a new environment that was not conducive to calm deliberation but instead excited feelings of neurosis and instability. Overcrowding in urban centres, in Hobson's opinion, was likely to 'destroy strong individuality of thought and desire' (characteristics upon which Schumpeter had placed great emphasis):

93 *The Psychology of Jingoism*, 17. Hobson rejected the determination of Le Bon's thesis by cautioning that it was not necessary to 'accept the view that the standard feeling and reason of the crowd is always lower than that of its individual members.' There was 'some evidence,' Hobson suggested, 'to indicate that it may sometimes be higher.' Much would depend on the 'character and motive of the suggestion,' and on the 'circumstances' of the crowd (20). This proviso is significant, for in other works Hobson emphasizes the importance of group action as a means of generating social sympathy and a 'general will.'

94 Ibid., 20

95 Ibid., 6, 10, 20, 28

The crowding of large masses of work-people in industrial operations regulated by mechanical routine, an even more injurious congestion in home life, the constant attrition of a superficial intercourse in work or leisure with great numbers of persons subject to the same environment – these conditions are apt to destroy or impair independence of character, without substituting any sound rational sociality such as may arise in a city which has come into being primarily for good life not cheap work.[96]

Hobson thus saw a strong correlation between the emergence of a 'mob mind,' as described by Le Bon, and industrial urbanization.

Hobson also detected within modern jingoism the remnants of a primitive 'blood lust,' but again, unlike Schumpeter, who saw the mission of capitalism as pacific, Hobson claimed that, even though capitalism had limited 'literal modes' of venting these brutal passions, the turning of violence into a specialism exercised by professional soldiers and police, had been accompanied by the diversion of the pugnacity of the rest of the population into channels of spectatorial participation. The chief culprits in this matter were the new 'cheap dailies,' whose proprietors viewed news reporting above all else as a business and appealed to their readers' crudest instincts in order to expand circulation. The harm done by the cheap 'capitalist' press was enhanced, in Hobson's opinion, by the fact that the 'vicarious cruelty' they promoted appeared especially hard to contain:

The modern newspaper is a Roman arena, a Spanish bull-ring and an English prize-fight rolled into one. The popularisation of the power to read has made the press the chief instrument of brutality. ... The businessman, the weaver, the clerk, the clergyman, the shop assistant, can no longer satisfy these savage cravings, either in personal activity or in direct spectacular display; but the art of reading print enables them to indulge *ad libitum* in ghoulish gloating over scenes of human suffering, outrage and destruction.[97]

It was possible, then, that modern wars and skirmishes actually received *more* public support than in the past, given these new conditions of spectator participation. In this light Hobson concluded that jingoism was essentially the product of 'civilised communities.' It represented the 'passion of the backer nor the fighter.'[98]

96 Ibid., 7
97 Ibid., 29
98 Ibid., 12

162 New Liberalism

Other elements of irrationality to be found amongst the supports of imperialism were discussed by Hobson without any mention of specific conditions
of modern life that enhanced their prevalence, but neither did he suggest
that they were incompatible with a capitalist milieu. Vainglory, for example,
was a primitive passion which, according to Hobson, continued to operate
vigorously in the mentality of the imperialist. It was an ego defence, which
protected the imperialist from the reality of disconcerting facts. 'Confront a
child or savage with a plain fact or figure,' Hobson wrote, 'and he will betray
a most extraordinary cunning in avoiding it, so as to preserve an illusion
which pampers that pride of personality which is the root of falsehood. So
with a people which falls back on its barbaric nature.' It should be noted that
Hobson believed that this capacity for self-deception was not the prerogative
of any class or group of men in particular: both the manipulators and the
manipulated, the educated and the ignorant, were the prey of their own
'noble lies.'[99] It was this capacity for self-deceit that enabled 'Christians in
khaki' to turn imperialist adventures into 'holy wars'; politicians to speak of
the empire as the 'white man's burden,' and businessmen to think of imperialist trade as a 'civilising mission.'

But not only was the imperialist's vision distorted, it was also myopic. This
short-sightedness, in Hobson's opinion, was evident in the jingo's demand
for punitive 'peace' settlements with his defeated enemies. The jingo's personality was too impatient to agree to reasoned conciliation which would
consider the long-term effects of any peace treaty made. He demanded
immediate gratification of his desires, as did infants and savages. In Hobson's words, 'a jingo-ridden people looks neither before nor after, but lives
in and for the present alone, like other brutes. Here is the quintessence of
savagery, a complete absorption in the present details of a sanguinary struggle, inhibiting the mental faculties of [sympathetic] imagination and fore-
thought which are the only safeguards of policy.'[100]

Hobson's comments on the irrational supports of imperialism, although
sometimes quite impressionistic, none the less would seem to refute any
attempt to characterize his theory as 'economic reductionism.' Jingoism was
a powerful force in human affairs, and was constantly being nourished by the
environment of advanced capitalism. It is, then, no refutation of Hobson's
thesis to say, as does Fieldhouse, for example, that 'imperialism owed its
popular appeal not to the sinister influence of capitalists, but to its inherent
attractions for the masses.'[101] Hobson was quite aware of this darker side of

99 Ibid., 63-4, 21
100 Ibid., 68, 78
101 D.K. Fieldhouse, 'Imperialism: An Historiographical Revision,' 123

public sentiment and he did not attempt to dismiss its significance by pretending that jingoism was the fabrication of a small economic clique. Nor is it a refutation of Hobson's thesis to point to cases, as does Landes, where an act of imperialism seems to have been motivated primarily by political, military, or some other 'non-economic' consideration.[102] Hobson did not claim that an 'economic' interest was a *necessary* feature of imperialism, since he was aware that, when this motive was absent, others like pugnacity (national security) might take its place. What he did maintain was that *when* economic interests were involved – and given the underconsumption crises of capitalism, he did anticipate their frequent involvement – a well-organized clique of financiers would experience little difficulty in manipulating the various 'non-economic' forces so as to tailor events to their private advantage.

Apparently 'bewildered' by Hobson's explanation of the interplay between economic and non-economic determinants of imperialism, Hobson's critics seem to have failed to appreciate the important distinction he drew between the volume and intensity of motives supporting imperialism and their management and direction. The non-rational motives behind imperial expansion, as he described them in *The Psychology of Jingoism*, were by their very nature blind, objectless, fitful passions. It seems reasonable, therefore, for Hobson to suppose that this atavism was well suited to direction from elsewhere. More contentious, no doubt, was his insistence that it was the financier and the cartel organizer, rather than, say, the politician or the military commander, who were in the best position to direct these forces when it suited them and to resist when it did not. But obviously in order successfully to challenge this position, it would be necessary to indicate a good deal more than the fact that non-economic considerations also entered into the imperial calculus. For Hobson's claim was not that all interests in imperialism could be reduced to economic interests, but only that it was the financier who had the last say.

The financial interest has those qualities of concentration and clear-sighted calculation which are needed to set imperialism to work. An ambitious statesman, a frontier soldier, an overzealous missionary ... may suggest *or even initiate* a step of imperial expansion [and] may assist in educating public opinion to the urgent need of some fresh advance, but the final determination rests with the financial power.[103]

---

102 D. Landes, 'The Nature of Economic Imperialism,' in Boulding and Mukerjee, eds., *Economic Imperialism*, 125-41
103 *Imperialism*, 59 (emphasis added)

Or as Hobson put it elsewhere in more philosophic terms:

Of the driving forces in history but a very small proportion enter the restricted area of clear consciousness and are fully recognised as motives. But when we analyse the actual path taken by a 'movement' and find that in all its turns it subserves the actual interests of certain groups or classes of men, we are justified in concluding that these interests constitute the real motive of the movement.[104]

This, then, is what Hobson meant by his theory of the economic determination of imperialism. It was determinist in *the last instance*. And like another famous economist, Hobson had some grounds to complain that all he intended to say was that economics was the 'ultimate determining element' and that 'if somebody twist this into saying that economics is the only determining one, he transforms that proposition into a meaningless, abstract, senseless phrase.'[105]

6 HOBSON'S INTERNATIONAL REFORM PROGRAM: THE MANDATE SYSTEM

Unless we are prepared ... to insist that the unchecked self-assertion of each nation, following the line of its own private interest, is the best guarantee of the general progress of humanity, we must set up, as a supreme standard of moral appeal, some conception of the welfare of humanity regarded as an organic unity. *Imperialism*, 233

104 *International Trade* (1904), 181-2. See also *Free Thought in the Social Sciences* (1926), 193. N.B. T. Lloyd, in a careful study of the motivations behind British imperial expansion in Africa at the turn of the century, has given cautious support to Hobson's thesis, as interpreted above. He shows, for example, that 'a great deal of Africa' was occupied by chartered businesses who were confident that they could manipulate the British government 'to protect their persons and properties.' Moreover, Lloyd points out that when businessmen did not care to enter an area, the government found it very hard 'to gain a foothold.' Lloyd concludes that this is roughly what Hobson had in mind when he said finance was the 'governor of the machine.' See Lloyd, 'Africa and Hobson's Imperialism,' *Past and Present*, no. 55 (1972).
105 F. Engels, in a letter to J. Bloch, Sept. 1890, in R. Tucker, ed., *The Marx-Engels Reader* (1972), 640-2. It is interesting in this regard that in a review of G.D.H. Cole's book, *What Marx Really Meant*, Hobson suggested that what Marx meant by the 'economic determination of history' was not 'the denial of non-economic forces, but ... the utilisation of these factors by the under-drive of the economic forces.' This is essentially Hobson's own position, as described above. See *Political Quarterly*, vol. V, no. 3 (1934), 453.

Hobson viewed imperialism as a special outgrowth of domestic under-consumption, and in the main his proposals for reform were identical with his general treatment of this problem. Indeed, one of the primary objects of *Imperialism* was to persuade 'the minority who are content neither to float along the tide of political opportunism, nor submit to the shove of some blind destiny,' that the imperialist solution to underconsumption was too costly and that his own program of domestic reforms designed to raise the purchasing power of consumers would solve the problem on a cheaper basis and with far less risk.[106]

Hobson, however, did not consider international conflict to be a mere reflex of the contradictions of capitalism. He did not make the mistake of many other social critics[107] and assume that, since capitalist states cause imperialism, the reform of capitalism would *automatically* ensure international harmony. The causal analysis could not be simply reversed: the domestic crises of capitalism were only one, albeit essential, component of the problem of international relations. The need to establish a genuine form of international regulation was the other major problem facing reformers.

Of particular interest in this regard is Hobson's outline for a system of 'mandated territories' designed to guard undeveloped countries from unwarranted interference by other more advanced industrial nations, yet at the same time avoid leaving these countries isolated in a sea of backwardness. According to Hobson's colleague H.N. Brailsford, *Imperialism* contained the 'first sketch of the Mandate Idea,' later to be incorporated in the Covenant of

106 *Imperialism*, v Presumably a wider audience was precluded by the deep wells of irrationalism Hobson had uncovered. It also should be noted that *Imperialism* contains only a minimum statement of the reforms needed. For more radical critics, like John Strachey, this was the major flaw of the book: 'Mr. Hobson's book marks the highest point of development ever reached by liberal thought in Britain. ... The weak side of [the] book is its failure to suggest any adequate way of arresting the drive towards inter-Imperial war, which he diagnoses so well ... Hobson's decisive chapter "The Economic Taproot" ... staggers the contemporary reader. For it fails so strangely to advocate the one possible remedy for the social disease which has been so well diagnosed, namely the public ownership of the means of production. So near did British Liberal thought, at its culminating point, approach the Marxist analysis, and so far away did it remain from realising the remedy.' *What Are We to Do?* (1938), 87-8. A similar lament can be found in H. Magdoff, *The Age of Imperialism* (1969), 23-4. However, as will become evident later, *Imperialism* is not representative of Hobson's full domestic reform program which, as outlined in other and *earlier* works, does contain proposals for the public ownership of monopolies.

107 Cf. Kenneth Waltz, *Man, the State and War* (1965), esp. chaps. IV and V. It should be noted, however, that Waltz is not persuaded that Hobson did avoid the mistakes of these other social critics.

the League of Nations, albeit in a different and 'very faulty shape.'[108] In this light, Adam Ulam's comment that Hobson came 'perilously close to recommending that the non-European areas be allowed to stew in their own juice,' is altogether curious.[109]

Hobson was not in principle opposed to advanced industrial nations exporting capital to the third world, but he insisted that the validity of this trade must be based on 'some conception of the welfare of humanity regarded as an organic unity.'[110] Making industrial nations susceptible to this 'moral appeal' presupposed the abatement of the imperial drive through domestic reforms designed to replenish domestic consumption. But granted this, Hobson put the argument in favour of capital exports in surprisingly forceful terms:

There is nothing unworthy, quite the contrary, in the notion that nations which, through a more stimulative environment, have advanced further in certain arts of industry, politics, or morals, should communicate these to nations which from their circumstances were more backward, so as to aid them in developing alike the material resources of their land and the human resources of their people. Nor is it clear that in this work some ... compulsion is wholly illegitimate. Force itself is no remedy, coercion is not education, but it may be the prior condition to the operation of educative forces.[111]

It was Hobson's contention that it was the height of international irresponsibility to allow world resources to lie fallow or go to waste while people remained in need. The question was not so much one of the right of interference, for there 'could no more be absolute nationalism in the society of nations, than absolute individualism in the single nation,' but rather one of 'safeguards, of motives, and of methods.'[112] Elsewhere Hobson explained this parallel between the nation and the individual in more detail:

If an individual member of society, owning land, neglects to develop its natural resources or so uses it to make a public nuisance, or refuses permission to the public to utilise it for fair compensation, it is admitted that society has a right ... to interfere ... on the ground that certain exercises of

108 *The Life-Work of J.A. Hobson* (1948), 25
109 *Lenin and the Bolsheviks* (1969), 405
110 *Imperialism*, 233
111 Ibid., 228-9
112 Ibid., 225, 229

these rights [of individual property] are not self-regarding actions, but are social wrongs. In similar fashion ... the sacred rights of nationality ought not to protect [a country] from coercion imposed on behalf of the general good of nations. ... With the general principle which underlies this argument no one but an individualist of the old school can quarrel.[113]

Nationalism, then, could easily turn into an 'injurious assertion of individuality.' But Hobson had no intention of allowing this argument to become a pretext for imperialism, under the guise of international guardianship. Consequently he stipulated that such interference was permissible, only provided that three conditions were met.

[First], the government of a lower race must be directed primarily to secure the safety and progress of the civilisation of the world, and not the special interest of the interfering nation. [Second], such interference must be attended by an improvement and elevation of the character of the people who are brought under this control. [Third], the determination of the two preceding conditions must not be left to the arbitrary will or judgment of the interfering nation, but must proceed from some organised representation of civilized humanity.[114]

This represents the core of Hobson's mandate system. The first principle requires no further commentary, since it merely reiterates Hobson's condemnation of imperialist economics. The two other principles, however, warrant separate consideration.

Hobson's second principle implied that he would countenance no argument for interference based on premises drawn from 'Social Darwinist' notions about the right of the fittest or strongest nations to absorb the weak, as part of the struggle for the progress of humanity. Hobson's objection to this biological defence of imperialism was two-fold. First, he argued that the Social Darwinists were at fault in abstractly or blindly modelling their social theory upon observations drawn exclusively from the study of the natural world. As a consequence they failed to perceive significant differences between the two realms:

The validity of the whole argument from natural history is contestable. As man grows in civilisation, i.e., in the art of applying reason to the adjust-

113 'Socialistic Imperialism,' *International Journal of Ethics*, vol. XII (1900-2), 44
114 *Imperialism*, 231, 232

ment of his relations with his physical and social environment, he obtains a corresponding power to extricate himself from the necessity which dominates the lower animal world.[115]

The struggle for survival did not have the compelling force that Social Darwinists ascribed to it. Man could increasingly establish his own standards of fitness. Thus, what seemed an inevitable drive to war and expansion could be avoided by 'a progressive mitigation of the law of diminishing returns' and by 'limiting the rate of growth of population' – the two key elements in the Social Darwinist doctrine. Hobson perceived that there were opportunities in 'rational' economies to 'employ both methods.' In this light the Social Darwinists' craven attitude before the 'laws of nature' merely marked his fear of freedom, and his need for 'dogmatic supports of conduct.'[116]

Hobson's other major objection to the Social Darwinist argument for imperialism was that it failed to appreciate the importance of co-operation in the evolutionary process. Co-operation made the evolutionary process progressive by eliminating wasteful elements of competition. It thus allowed the struggle to shift to 'higher planes' than that of 'bare animal existence,' and the standard of fitness changed accordingly. An individual's 'skill, knowledge, character' and even his 'service to his fellow-men' became the new tests of fitness. But Social Darwinists were blind to this element of progression in history and hence continued to insist upon retaining 'the older, cruder, irrational method of securing progress, the primitive struggle for existence.' The fallacy of their doctrine, however, was clearly exposed by the logic of their own reasoning, when they argued, as they invariably did when discussing imperialism, that the unit of this struggle was the nation-state. 'If it is profitable and consistent with progress,' Hobson asked, 'to put down the primitive struggle for life' among individuals, families and tribes, and to 'enlarge the area of social internal peace until it covers a whole nation,' then was it not possible to 'extend the same mode of progress to a federation of European States, and finally to a world-federation?'[117] Hobson found nothing in the logic of the Social Darwinist argument to deny this proposition,

115 Ibid., 176
116 Ibid., 'Mr. Kidd's "Social Evolution,"' *American Journal of Sociology*, vol. 1 (1895), 312, cited in R. Hofstadter, *Social Darwinism in American Thought* (1968), 101. It might be noted that Hobson did not include Herbert Spencer among those Social Darwinists advocating imperialism. His main targets of attack were B. Kidd, K. Pearson and Professor Giddings. Spencer objected to imperialism on the grounds of cost – much like Hobson! Cf. J. Peel, *Herbert Spencer* (1971), 232-5.
117 *Imperialism*, 172, 164

except prejudice. Social Darwinism, then, provided a poor pretext for armed combat with native peoples.

In opposition to the Social Darwinists, Hobson insisted that the mandate should be exercised to ensure the elevation of 'weak varieties' not their subjugation. On this basis he presented a lengthy and vigorous condemnation of the methods used by European traders to indenture native labour and repeated his argument, already noted, that a 'sane' method of civilizing the lower races would involve a gradual process of re-education, by acquainting them with 'new wholesome wants' and 'new industrial methods applicable to work in their own industries,' whilst preserving 'as far as possible the continuity of the old tribal life and institutions.'[118] Such regard for native welfare and subject cultures clearly distances Hobson's approach from that of the Social Darwinists.

Similarly, Hobson argued that, unlike the Social Darwinists who accepted the wasteful methods of nature 'requiring innumerable individuals to be born in order that they may struggle and perish,' rational humanity would 'economise and humanise the struggle by substituting a rational, social test for parenthood.'[119]

Having distinguished the exercise of the mandate in this fashion, Hobson was nevertheless disconcertingly vague about the details of these two proposals. For example, he provided no standard of fitness for his 'test of parenthood,' and did not directly confront the question whether this test is to be forcibly imposed if voluntary restraint fails. With regard to the process of industrialization, as previously noted, Hobson does allow for the forcible industrialization of a country should its native population prove immune to the appeals of the mandatory, and he is aware that this can lead to abuses. However, the principle of equity to which he appeals in the following statement is, perhaps, not as self-evident as he assumed:

To step in and utilise natural resources which are left undeveloped is one thing, to compel the inhabitants to develop them is another. The former is easily justified, involving the application on a wider scale of a principle whose equity, as well as expediency, is recognised and enforced in most civilised nations. The other interference whereby men who prefer to live on a low standard of life with little labour shall be forced to harder or more continuous labour, is far more difficult of justification.[120]

118 Ibid., 279
119 Ibid., 163
120 Ibid., 228

This passage indicates the importance in Hobson's mind of the rider 'to civilisation' in his discussion of cultural relativism, described earlier. Paths leading in other directions were to be ignored.

Hobson's second mandate principle also brought him into conflict with certain socialists, including important members of the Fabian Society. Initially, the Fabians were taken by surprise with the fuss caused in radical circles by Britain's pressuring of the Boers, and it was not until the actual outbreak of war that they took formal notice of the issue. When they did, there resulted a minor split in the society, with eighteen or so of its members preferring to hand in their resignations rather than accept the majority view that the society should reserve judgement about the war. Shortly after the 'pro-Boers' had quit the society, George Bernard Shaw wrote a short pamphlet, *Fabianism and the Empire*, in which he sought to clarify the majority position on imperialism.

Broadly speaking, Shaw argued that imperialism was acceptable to Fabians provided that two criteria were satisfied: first, that the imperialist state be of a higher type of civilization than the state it was about to absorb; second, that the imperialist state conduct its economic affairs with a view to the interests of the rest of the world, and not merely with a concern for its own coffers.[121] Both these arguments, in Hobson's opinion, were defective and in *Imperialism* and a contemporaneous article 'Socialistic Imperialism' he took the Fabians to task both for their élitist attitude towards indigenous cultures and the oppressive nature of their economic criterion.

The focus of Hobson's criticism was the issue of nationalism:

The presumption must always hold that a nation in being is better adapted to its territorial environment than any other nation seeking to subjugate it, and should be left free to utilise its land and grow its own political institutions.[122]

This presumption was not allowed in the Fabian argument. Consequently, although Hobson and Shaw talk in very similar language about nations having no absolute right to do as they please with their resources, to the point even of accepting the same analogy between nations and landlords to support their case, none the less the starting points of their analyses are very different. Whereas Shaw confidently dismisses arguments against the absorption of nations within empires as mere 'romantic nationalism,' and allows

121 Shaw, *Fabianism and Empire* (1900), 44-6
122 'Socialistic Imperialism,' 57

only for a certain devolution of power within empires to accommodate national groupings, Hobson is altogether more hesitant. Hobson insists that even where it can be shown that a just cause exists for interference, such cause would not legitimate the absorption of one state by another:

Either a nation, such as the Transvaal or China, is growing a radically different civilisation with different sorts of government from ours, or else such a nation is backward in the same course of civilisation. In the one case it is impossible for us to civilise it, in the other, 'forcing' the pace is unwise and ultimately defeats its end by substituting artificial for natural progress.[123]

The Fabians thus failed to appreciate both the positive and the negative aspects of nationalism: its serviceability as an 'instrument of social growth' and its resistant powers. In this latter regard Hobson once more repeated his warning about the 'dangerous fallacy' that there was a common brand of civilization capable of being imposed on divergent peoples.

Further, Hobson argued that to justify the occupation of lesser nations on the grounds of 'world interests' alone, though perhaps an advance on Social Darwinist attitudes, nevertheless was an example of oppressive collectivism. Such a position was to be condemned on the grounds that 'the maxim which recognises the individual as an end, and requires State government to justify itself by showing that the coercion it exercises does in reality enlarge the liberty of those whom it restrains, is also applicable to the larger society of nations.'[124] The Fabian position thus fell short of Hobson's mandate that the interference must directly benefit the subject peoples.

Finally, Hobson's different perspective on nationalism led him to criticize the Fabians' understanding of internationalism as something that could be built by vanguard states from the top down:

To imagine that the cause of an ideal internationalism can be promoted by breaking down the forms of nationalism and seeking to destroy its spirit ... is wholly to misunderstand the social problem. *Internationalism is not the negation but the expansion of the national spirit.* ... This is no idle speculation but verifiable hypothesis. Those best acquainted with the spirit and temper of citizens of small states like Switzerland and Denmark will testify that life in these small democratic states, while stimulating an intense love of

123 Ibid., 57-8
124 *Imperialism*, 235

country, equally favours a tolerance of foreigners, a sympathetic interest in their affairs, and a desire to be on friendly terms. ... The forcible breaking down of small national boundaries ... [inevitably] retards the process of world civilisation.[125]

National self-respect was a prerequisite for respecting other nations. It followed that the Fabians' hostility towards nationalism and their exclusive concern for the 'world's interests' meant they were unduly forcing the pace of internationalism; Fabians, of all people, were in danger of moving too fast!

Hobson's third mandate principle is discussed below, in the wider context of his criticism of the League of Nations.

7 A LEAGUE OF NATIONS

In *Imperialism*, Hobson had intimated that the determination and supervision of access to the resources of undeveloped countries should be the concern of some 'organised representation of civilised humanity.' However, the details of this organisation were not sketched for over a decade. In the first year of the First World War, Hobson was invited to join the Bryce Committee (named after its most prestigious member, Lord Bryce), which had as its aim the drawing up of proposals for a League of Nations.[126] Service on this influential committee provided Hobson with a stimulating environment in which to study more closely the problems of instituting world government. Hobson, along with Bryce, G. Lowes Dickinson (the founder member), Graham Wallas, A. Ponsonby, and others, signed the Committee's first report. But he also published an independent assessment, entitled *Towards International Government* (1915), which, while it reflected the broad aims of the committee – especially its recommendation to limit the sovereignty of nations in international affairs – also constituted a dissenting opinion. Hobson's excuse for writing it was that the Bryce scheme 'did not take adequate account of the economic inequality of nations in regard to the resources of the country or colonies under their control, as a source of discord and strife.'[127] This raised once more the question of Mandates.

125 'Socialistic Imperialism,' 56
126 The Bryce Committee had an important part in influencing the foreign policy of the Labour party and helped shape the Covenant of the League of Nations. President Wilson is believed to have been personally influenced by the Committee's proposals. C.A. Cline, *Recruits to Labour, 1914-1931* (1963), 16
127 *Confessions* (1938), 109

Hobson began by confessing that it was difficult 'to pre-figure an international Government' that could be trusted 'not to abuse the tutelage over 'lower' or 'backward' peoples. ... Could the white nations of the earth thus banded together be entrusted with the fate of their coloured fellow beings?'[128] Hobson was not certain of the answer, but he suggested that a number of safeguards were available. These recommendations may be usefully examined in the light of Hobson's subsequent criticism of the actual system of mandates set up under Article 22 of the Covenant of the League of Nations in 1919. In this way it is possible to gauge the radicalism of Hobson's proposals.[129]

The opening chapter of *Towards International Government* contains a plea that the future league should be inspired by thoughts more noble than merely settling accounts with German militarism. To this end Hobson proposed that all states, no matter what their part in the war, should be included in the new organization. Likewise, the protectorates and dependencies of every nation should come under the supervision of the international government. The actual League of Nations, however, had failed miserably on this count. Its war origins, as Hobson explained in *Problems of a New World*, had been allowed to impair its functions, making it an instrument of a dictated peace settlement. Thus it incorporated 'the principle not of equal justice, but of force in its very origin' and this, in Hobson's opinion, helped vitiate its mandate system. 'If this League,' Hobson asked, 'were really designed, as its advocates pretend, to be a genuinely international instrument, why should this mandatory principle be confined expressly in its application to "those colonies and territories which, as a consequence of the last war, have ceased to be under the sovereignty of the states which formerly governed them"?'[130] Such an arrangement smacked of a division of spoils.

The second major failing of the League's mandate system was that it lacked teeth. Hobson claimed that the insincerity of the super-powers was

---

128 *Towards International Government*, 145

129 Hobson's fullest account of the defects of the League of Nations is found in *Problems of a New World*, part v, chap. ii. This book was also the subject of an interesting report published by the Australian League of Nations Union in the early 1920s. The report concluded that, whilst there was substance to Hobson's criticisms, overall he had been too hasty in condemning the League. See *The League and Its Critics: A Report to the Council of the Australian League of Nations Union* [NSW Branch].

130 *Problems of a New World*, 230. Virginia Woolf relates that this was the subject of a 'great row' within the League of Nations Society (a sister organization of the Bryce Committee) and that Hobson was instrumental in defeating a motion by H.G. Wells to exclude Germany from the proposed League. Cf. A.D. Bell, ed., *The Diary of Virginia Woolf 1915-1919* (1977), vol. 1, 157.

revealed by the fact that they proposed that 'the vital interests of the mandated populations' could be protected by means of 'annual reports, or appeals to a Council ... which has no means of enforcing any judgment it may form.' Hobson insisted that the Council's powers of enforcement should not rest on moral guardianship alone. Instead of awaiting an annual report from the caretaker nation, the Council should have been entrusted with the power to initiate its own independent reports and to maintain sufficient agents in the field to effect constant supervision of the operations of the mandate.[131] But, most strikingly, Hobson also proposed that the authority of the League should rest on force. In his own blueprint for world government, he had argued that it was essential for the League to be backed by a pledge from the members 'to bring concerted pressure, by armed force if necessary, upon any signatory power which declined to fulfil its treaty obligation.'[132] In seeking to provide effective sanctions for his system of mandates, Hobson clearly was not the pacifist Lenin had made him out to be.[133]

Hobson's third indictment of the League's system of mandates was that it provided only a weak and limited commitment to free trade. Only the mandates in central Africa were protected by an 'open door' policy (Article 22, sec. 5) and even then, as Hobson pointed out, the provision was confined to other members of the League. In Hobson's opinion there was little in the Covenant to prevent industrial nations from encircling their mandate territories with protective tariffs, thereby providing themselves with privileged access to raw materials, cheap labour, and so on.[134] In *Towards International*

---

131 *Problems of a New World*, 232, 229
132 *Towards International Government*, 76. See also 'Is Force Necessary to Government?' *Hibbert Journal*, vol. 33, no. 31, (1934-5).
133 *Imperialism*, 684
134 This was an oft-repeated warning of Hobson's. Cf. *Imperialism*, 64-70, and *The New Protectionism*. This latter work should be read in conjunction with *Towards International Government*. Aside from its tendency to engender retaliation and hostility between nations, protectionism was attacked on the grounds of its inefficiency. It interfered with the international division of labour and the economies of scale derived from the specialization of tasks based on natural comparative advantage. Hobson did allow that in conditions of world-wide overproduction it might prosper one nation to keep out the goods of another, since this would enable these goods to be produced at home by utilizing idle factors. In these circumstances, protection would not involve the withdrawal of 'scarce' resources from naturally more efficient fields of employment. To this extent the classical criticism of protectionism was invalid. (The classical economists, of course, had no appreciation of the problems of overproduction.) Cf. *The Physiology of Industry*, ix; and *Property and Improperty* (1937), 124-6. None the less, Hobson considered tariffs, etc., to be too crude an instrument to be used effectively during periods of economic

Government, Hobson had warned that protectionism was a natural accompaniment of imperialism and that a failure clearly to repudiate such policies would mean that any future League of Nations would be of little use in preventing the re-emergence of that same sense of jealousy and covetousness between nations that had helped precipitate the Great War.

But even had the League's mandate system been universal, efficacious, and part of a general policy of free trade Hobson would not have been content. For he considered that ultimately the problem of ensuring an impartial administration of the mandates could be solved only by encouraging the growth of what he termed an 'international mind.' And for this the actual League of Nations was an imperfect instrument.

Hobson granted that some identification with international causes would result from the setting up of a permanent institution of international co-operation, but he insisted that more was required.[135] Thus he proposed that diplomats of the 'old school' be excluded from service in international organizations: they had too long pleaded the cause of state sovereignty. These diplomats were to be replaced by sagacious, broad-minded men of cosmopolitan outlook, drawn from a wide variety of backgrounds. Where possible (Hobson was not very specific), these men were to be elected by the general public of the constituent nations. Hobson clearly hoped that popular election combined with a policy of open diplomacy would prove to be a mix of responsibility and education sufficient to undo the sense of credulity in the masses which he had earlier analysed to be a source of imperialism.[136] In these aspects, the actual League had proven to be a sham. It did not help generate an 'international mind,' because it maintained the nation-state as its ultimate unit and the servants of the state as its personnel. 'Interests of state' were likely to thwart or bias its rulings, not only on the issue of mandates, but in general. Hobson predicted that 'this perversion of [the] ... great ideal of a League of Nations into a present instrument for autocratic and imperialistic government will rank in history as a treason to humanity.'[137]

---

crisis. More important, he thought that in the long run protectionism tended to aggravate the maldistribution of income in society (the real cause of overproduction) by pumping monies into the hands of big business. See *Canada To-day* (1906), 47; *International Trade* (1904), chap. XI, and 'Protection as a Working-Class Policy,' in H.W. Massingham, ed., *Labour and Protection* (1903).

135 *Towards International Government*, 196
136 Ibid., 65, 205
137 *Problems of a New World*, 233

8 A NOTE ON FREE-TRADE IMPERIALISM

Modern internationalists are no longer mere non-interventionists. *Richard Cobden*, 406

It has been suggested by Semmel, Fieldhouse, Robinson, Gallagher, and other advocates of the idea of 'free-trade imperialism' that Hobson was incorrect to argue that imperialism is incompatible with free trade.[138] Semmel, for instance, has formulated the charge as follows:

Hobson [was] convinced ... that the principles of free trade economics ... left no room for imperialism, that in a world where free trade prevailed, all trade would be regulated by *impartial economic law*. ... The same men whom ... Hobson ... regarded as the spokesmen of this anti-imperialism [e.g., Cobden, Molesworth, and Wakefield], because they were the leaders of those groups who wished to dismantle the old colonial system of mercantilism, were also the spokesmen ... of a new free trade imperialism, which they held would prove more effective and profitable.[139]

Semmel thus presents Hobson in a curious light: he appears as a harsh critic of *laissez-faire* in the domestic economy but a friend of non-interventionism, or free trade, in international affairs. But Hobson's support for a system of mandates suggests that Semmel's contrast is too stark. Hobson did not automatically associate free trade with anti-imperialism. If he had done so, then his system of mandates, which was to operate within a general policy of free trade, would have been superfluous. To put the matter positively, Hobson believed that the interests of undeveloped countries still required safeguarding, even granted the existence of an unrestricted international market. Free trade, in its proper context, might help pacify foreign relations, but it was no panacea automatically guaranteeing 'impartial law.'

Free Trade is indeed the nucleus of the larger constructive economic internationalism, but it needs a conversion from the negative conception of *laissez-faire* ... to a positive constructive one. ... This fuller doctrine of ... equality of economic opportunity, cannot, however, be applied without definite co-operative action on the part of nations.[140]

138 A useful compendium of the writings of Gallagher and Robinson on free-trade imperialism and the replies of their critics is to be found in Wm. Roger Louis, *Imperialism: The Robinson Gallagher Controversy* (1976).
139 B. Semmel. *The Rise of Free Trade Imperialism* (1970), 4, 3 (emphasis added)
140 *The New Protectionism*, 121-2

And elsewhere he noted that:

An agreement of the Powers to proceed no farther with the policy of the political absorption of backward countries, and with the political assistance hitherto given to private businesses for purposes of trade and finance, could furnish no possible basis for a pacific future. ... Such a policy of naked *laissez-faire* is quite inadmissible. A deliberate acceptance of the theory that bands of armed buccaneers calling themselves traders are free to rob defenseless savages ... is inconceivable. Such *laissez-faire* would soon convert any rich unabsorbed corner of the world into a Congo, a San Thomé, or a Putumayo. ... The mere abstinence from political intervention on the part of civilised states would plunge every unappropriated country into sheer anarchy.[141]

It would seem, then, that Hobson was quite aware that imperialism could operate within a free-trade environment.

It is perhaps to be regretted that Hobson did not closely examine the reality of the anti-imperialist-mercantilist claims of Cobden and others, for this might have provided his analysis of the emergence of imperialism with a certain continuity, linking both informal and formal empire-building under the same rubric.[142] But whatever the merits of this suggestion, it remains evident that Hobson was not committed to a servile reliance on the principle of free trade automatically to guarantee the general interest of the community of nations against imperialism.

141 'The Open Door,' in C. Roden Buxton, *Towards a Lasting Settlement* (1915), 103-4. See also *Imperialism*, 292, where Hobson quotes approvingly a statement by M. Martin, showing how '*under the pretense of Free Trade*,' England 'compelled the Hindus to receive the products of the steam-looms of Lancashire ... at mere nominal duties,' thereby helping to destroy India's own weaving industry (emphasis added). Hobson discussed the general tie between Britain's advocacy of free trade and its privileged position as the most industrialized nation in the world in *From Capitalism to Socialism* (1932), 11-13.
142 T. Kemp, for example, suggests that Hobson's 'main weakness was his tendency to "confine the term imperialism to relations between advanced countries and their subject territories – so that he misses the significance of "informal empire" based almost exclusively on investment links.' Kemp, *Theories of Imperialism* (1967), 29. However, it might be pointed out that, given the historical circumstances in which Hobson was writing, his concentration on formal empire was only to be expected. Moreover, there is a suggestion of the possibilities of an 'informal empire' in Hobson's discussion of the Monroe Doctrine. See *An Economic Interpretation of Investment*, 114.

6

The Foundations of a Welfare State

1 INTRODUCTION

Hobson's examination of the political and philosophical tenets of liberalism is best considered an outgrowth of his studies in economics. The key elements in Hobson's critique of classical economics were, first, his rejection of the 'individualist notion of production,' and, second, his criticism of the economists' 'separatist treatment' of social phenomena, or methodological individualism. Recast in political terms, the first of these criticisms led Hobson to question the liberal doctrine of self-reliance, especially the way in which this notion had come to be associated with the principle of *laissez-faire* in the works, for example, of such varied thinkers as Cobden, Smiles, Acton, and Spencer. Self-reliance or autonomy, in Hobson's opinion, had to be built upon a foundation of social co-operation – the support of the polis – not in opposition to it.

By Hobson's day this debate had already crystallized around the notions of positive and negative freedom. Negative freedom had the longer ancestry within the liberal school of thought, the concept taking on a meaning, as Hobson explained, closely identified with the early liberal struggle against feudal institutions:

The removal of a number of restraints and disqualifications, legal, political, religious, economic, the remnants of a feudal aristocratic order, which hampered the freedom of large classes of people, necessarily took precedence in the early half of the last century. Full civil rights for Roman Catholics and dissenters, freedom of contract and of combination, repeal of the Law of Settlement and of other restraints on the mobility of labour, removal of the taxes upon food and knowledge, the widening of the franchise, increased liberty of local self government – such were the reforms which occupied the field of domestic politics, all making for the greater liberty of large numbers of inhabitants. ... [For] our nineteenth-century Liberals ... 'liberty' meant primarily the removal of legal and political restraints.[1]

Hobson did not deny, of course, the worthiness of these reforms. Nevertheless, he considered the notion of negative liberty defective. Negative liberty could leave the individual inviolable yet inert, free from the interference of others, yet unable to achieve his own objectives. 'Liberty,' Hobson insisted, 'means more than the removal of restraints and prohibitions: it means positive access to opportunities for a fuller life and a richer personality.' And while it was not entirely true that early liberals had ignored these 'positive needs,' they had failed to grasp the consequences of advocating negative liberty in a capitalist society, where economic inequality prevented most of the population from actively utilizing the new areas of freedom that had been marked out by liberal reformers. In these circumstances, negative liberty took on 'so entirely the petit-bourgeois ... conception of the desirable state of things' that in practice it meant little more than 'relief from the oppression of the seigneur' and permission for some people 'to make as much money as [they] can. ... '[2] As will be seen, Hobson's solution to this problem was the advocacy of a welfare state, based not only on the principle of positive liberty (suitably revamped), but also on his own special doctrine of public proprietary rights.

Hobson's second major critique of classical economics, namely, its methodological individualism, when transcribed from economics to politics, led him to criticize the liberal image of a citizen as a discrete individual forever wary of the intrusion of other citizens in his affairs. Hobson countered this individualistic portrayal of political life with the claim that there existed in society a 'group mind' or 'social will,' different from the sum of individual wills. On this basis he criticized orthodox liberalism for minimizing man's sense of community and attacked liberal society for perpetuating irrationality in politics.

Hobson's assessment of *laissez-faire* liberalism and his advocacy of a welfare state is the primary concern of the present chapter; his analysis of the social will is discussed mainly in chapter 7. In both cases it seems clear that Hobson took his views from his study of liberal economics and simply

1 *Democracy and a Changing Civilisation* (1934), 22-3
2 Ibid., 23, 24

applied them to politics, since his discussion of particular philosophers is minimal. However, despite what may be considered Hobson's lack of interest in political philosophy *per se*, his appreciation that economics and politics could not be properly studied separate from one another, and his consequent overstepping of the boundaries, resulted in a number of valuable contributions to the study of political economy.

2 LAISSEZ-FAIRE LIBERALISM AND THE DISCREDITED STATE

The negative conception of Liberalism, as a definite mission for the removal of certain shackles upon personal liberty, is not merely philosophically defective, but historically false. ... Liberals ... never committed themselves to the theory or the policy of this narrow *laissez-faire* individualism. ... But it is true that they tended to lay an excessive emphasis upon the aspect of liberty which consists in the absence of restraint, as compared with the other aspect which consists in the presence of opportunity; and it is this tendency, still lingering in the mind of the Liberal Party, that today checks its energy and blurs its vision. *The Crisis of Liberalism*, 92-3

Hobson's economic analysis had provided a profound repudiation of the operation of natural, harmonious laws in the market. And with this repudiation went the major justification which liberals had used to minimize the role of the state in social life. Moreover, Hobson's analysis had revealed that within the 'ring' which liberals kept free from the encroachments of the state, there existed 'many modes of human oppression' each creating 'social diseases' more worrisome and debilitating than those which originally made liberals suspicious of the state and its fetters.[3] As one scholar has commented, this kind of consideration required that liberal theory be 'extended to considering the relation of legal coercion to the effective though non-legal coercion that would exist if the state abstained from acting.'[4] Hobson's own conclusion was that the discredit liberals had traditionally heaped upon the state had to be removed, so that the state could perform a more positive function in promoting social welfare:

Though Liberals must ever insist that each enlargement of the authority and functions of the State must justify itself as an enlargement of personal liberty, interfering with individuals only in order to set free new and larger opportunities, there need remain in Liberalism no relics of that positive

3 *Richard Cobden* (1919), 21-2
4 G. Sabine, *A History of Political Theory* (4th ed., 1973), 644

hostility to public methods of cooperation which crippled the old Radicalism.[5]

This naturally gave rise to the question whether the Liberal party could accommodate the idea of a 'positive state.' The question was made even more urgent because newly emergent socialist parties were already beginning to taunt liberals with the accusation that their dependence on the philosophy of *laissez-faire* 'made them incapable of thinking out schemes of social reform.'[6] Hobson considered this jibe unfair. He closely examined the possibilities of liberalism disengaging itself from the *laissez-faire* ideology and found there were grounds for a *cautious* optimism.

The doctrine of *laissez-faire* had never succeeded in keeping the statute books of the nineteenth century empty. Indeed, as early as 1889, Sidney Webb thought it warranted to comment that the state 'provides for many thousands of us from birth to burial.'[7] For Hobson, the history of this legislation in matters of public health, education, and factory regulation, indicated that although such 'interferences' by the state were usually instituted by 'nominally conservative governments,' a sufficient number of liberals had supported them as to bear testimony to the failure of a system of complete *laissez-faire*, even among its advocates.[8] In Hobson's opinion this revealed a healthy 'adaptability' and 'plasticity' within liberalism, thus holding out the possibility of it incorporating a more positive role for the state in its program.[9]

Nevertheless, Hobson believed that a good deal of circumspection was required in assessing this prospect. Liberals might not have proven dogmatic advocates of *laissez-faire* in many areas of social policy, but there was one area in which they were rigid, and that was in matters economic. A typical reflection of this selectivity could be seen in the writings of Richard Cobden. On 31 July 1856, Cobden could write that he was 'not dogmatical on the Education Question,' that his 'political sympathies' were 'with the masses' and the British voluntary system of education had 'undoubtedly failed.'[10] But the very next day he could write that with regard to the subject of trade unionism, it was only 'sound and honest' to 'tell the people plainly that they are under a delusion as to their assumed power ... permanently [to] influence

5 *The Crisis of Liberalism* (1909), 94
6 M. Freeden, *The New Liberalism* (1978), 33
7 'The Basis of Socialism: Historic,' *Fabian Essays in Socialism* (1889), 79; 1962 ed.
8 *Problems of Poverty* (1891; 2nd ed., 1895), 186, 188
9 *The Crisis of Liberalism*, xii
10 *Richard Cobden*, 164

in the slightest degree by *coercion* the rate of wages. They might as well attempt to regulate the tides by force ... or subvert any other laws of nature – for wages of labour depend upon laws as unerring.'[11] Hobson could discover only one occasion during the nineteenth century when a prominent Liberal statesman had gone so far as to urge Liberals to 'apply the principles of self-government in such a manner as involved reformation in the ownership of property' and that was Gladstone, in advocating his Home Rule bill of 1886. However, on this occasion, the Liberal party deserted him and the bill was defeated.[12]

This intransigence on economic matters meant that, although liberalism was more flexible on the issue of *laissez-faire* than was commonly supposed, it was still not fully fit for the tasks of social reform that confronted it.

In Hobson's opinion, the revitalisation of liberalism depended upon liberals recognizing that social ills had a unity which disallowed any piecemeal approach to social reform. 'All the great antagonisms which loom so big as Social Problems, Luxury and Poverty, Toil and Idleness, the Individual and Society, Authority and Liberty,' were connected to the issue of the distribution of economic surplus.[13] It was necessary, therefore, to substitute an organic or programmatic approach to these problems, in place of the opportunistic 'great causes' approach of the Liberal party.[14]

Hobson's second reason for guarded optimism in reviewing the reforming capabilities of liberalism was based on the observation that there already existed within the movement several brands of thought which attempted to show that a belief in *laissez-faire* was not integral to liberal philosophy. The two most notable examples were the works of J.S. Mill and the liberal idealists, Thomas Hill Green and Bernard Bosanquet. In neither case did Hobson consider these philosophical reformulations of liberalism entirely satisfactory, but they were a marked improvement on the extreme *laissez-faire* position.

3 HOBSON AND J.S. MILL

In passing comment on a work by Harriet Martineau, Mill observed that the 'system of *laissez-faire*' could be 'reduced to an absurdity' if the principle were insisted upon dogmatically and carried out 'to all its consequences.'[15]

11 Ibid., 166
12 *The Crisis of Liberalism*, vii
13 *Work and Wealth* (1914), 189
14 *The Crisis of Liberalism*, xi
15 Cited in Pedro Schwartz, *The New Political Economy of J.S. Mill* (1972), 109-10

This was written not long after Mill had emerged from his mental crisis of 1826 and was seeking guidance from schools of thought other than Benthamism. It was during this period that Mill came under the influence of the Saint Simonians and, in turn, formulated the bulk of his criticisms of *laissez-faire* – although this was always done in the spirit of one who never doubted that the burden of proof fell on those advocating state intervention, not those resisting it: *laissez-faire* remained the general rule.

In line with the Saint Simonian view of history, Mill argued in *The Principles of Political Economy* (1848) that the principle of *laissez-faire* was not universally valid, as many liberals held, but should be applied relative to time and place. Mill argued, for example, that the system of economic distribution could be modified according to human will and the level of industrial advancement, and consequently that the state could take action to redistribute income so as to brighten the 'Probable Futurity of the Labouring Classes.'[16] Further, Mill devoted a chapter of *The Principles of Political Economy* to discussing the 'Grounds and Limits of the Laissez-faire or Non-Interference Principle.' He suggested that various drawbacks in the system of self-interest required that the state take measures to regulate the ad hoc arrangements of private charities, and supervise the activities of large companies where shareholders meetings were ineffectual in combatting managerial bureaucracy. Mill also argued that the state had an obligation to enforce contracts where joint action was necessary for success, but where such concert could only be attained with the backing of the law. The example he gave was the demand of workers for a reduction in their hours of labour. Such a policy would be collectively beneficial 'but the immediate interest of every individual would lie in violating it.'[17] Finally, Mill advocated the state supervision of family relationships and compulsory education,[18] on the grounds that these were cases where state action was required to take care of those who were not capable of judging their own best interest.

Hobson was appreciative of the extent to which, as he put it, Mill, 'starting as a rigid theoretic individualist, with a conception of the State as narrow as that of Spencer, ... came ... to so passionate a realisation of the need of social reconstruction as to accept and apply to himself the name Socialist.'[19] And it is noteworthy that in this regard Hobson defended Mill even against the attacks of Ruskin, who continued to view Mill as an advocate of the empty

16 J.S. Mill, *Principles of Political Economy* (1848; Longmans 1909), Book IV, Chapter VII
17 Ibid., 582
18 Mill insisted, of course, that although the state was to enforce a system of universal education, that system was to be a mixed one, including both private and public schools.
19 'John Stuart Mill,' *The Speaker* (26 May 1906), 178

liberty of *laissez-faire*.[20] Mills' socialism, Hobson explained, was that of the 'co-operator rather than of the politician,' for his 'hatred of bureaucracy remained,' as did his desire 'to limit government as far as possible,'[21] nevertheless his exceptions to the rule of *laissez-faire* were capable of more vigorous application. In particular Hobson embellished Mill's principle of 'public goods,' as it has come to be known,[22] so as to envisage a wider range of instances where state intervention was required in order to give effect to the joint decisions of individuals.[23]

The main focus of Hobson's critique, however, was Mill's later attempt, in *On Liberty*, to provide a framework in which to make the 'fitting adjustment between individual and social control.'[24] This work was written primarily under the influence of de Tocqueville rather than Saint Simon, and represents something of a retreat from Mill's earlier critique of *laissez-faire*.

One important aim of *On Liberty*, according to Mill, was to 'point out to those who do not desire liberty, and would not avail themselves of it, that they may be in some intelligible manner rewarded for allowing other people to make use of it without hindrance.'[25] Most of chapter III of *On Liberty* is taken up with showing that individual liberty has social utility; it was one of the 'permanent conditions' of a healthy progressive society and thus served the public good.

This utilitarian argument, however, was not entirely satisfactory to Mill. Perhaps society would be too hasty in judging the social utility of the thoughts and actions of individuals. Consequently, Mill developed a second line of argument based on a distinction between self- and other-regarding acts. Society had a right to intervene to prevent actions which caused harm to others, but when the individual's conduct 'neither violates any specific duty to the public, nor occasions perceptible hurt to any assignable individual except himself,' then, claimed Mill, 'the inconvenience is one which society can afford to bear, for the sake of the greater good of human freedom.'[26]

It was this line of argument to which Hobson objected. Mill never appreciated, as did 'many of his readers,' the 'difficulties involved in his sharp distinction between "self-regarding" and "other-regarding" activities.'[27]

20 *John Ruskin* (1898), 190
21 'John Stuart Mill,' 178
22 On the doctrine of 'public goods,' see Brian Barry, *Sociologists, Economists and Democracy* (1970). It should be noted that Mill's doctrine of 'public goods' finds an earlier expression in the works of Adam Smith.
23 Cf. *John Ruskin*, 197f.
24 *On Liberty* (1859; The Liberal Arts Press, 1956), 8
25 Ibid., 78
26 Ibid., 100
27 'John Stuart Mill,' 178

Hobson gave little credence to this distinction: It did not accord with his own concept of an organic society:

If [an individual] ... is living as a member of a society, since he is an organic being in an organic society, no action of his can be considered purely self regarding or wholly void of social import. Some individual actions may be so indirect, so slight, or so incalculable in their social effects, that we speak of them and treat them as 'self regarding,' and hold it foolish for society ... to interfere with individual liberty with respect to them. But such 'individual rights' can have no ... absolute validity; for society, and not the individual, must clearly claim, in the social interest, to determine what actions fall within this 'self-regarding' class.[28]

Hobson thus used his concept of organic society to trivialize Mill's distinction between self- and other-regarding acts. According to his interpretation of Mill, the only acts for which an individual could claim personal control and responsibility – the foundation of Mill's notion of moral self-development – were those 'void of social import,' but these turned out to be acts of 'slight' or no significance. Viewed in this light, Mill's rule for demarcating a realm of private action, in which individuality was to flower, seemed quite inadequate. Hobson's critique, however, takes little account of Mill's various attempts in *On Liberty* to define 'self-regarding' more strictly as an act which does not 'harm,' 'hurt,' or 'prejudice' the 'permanent interests' of others as moral beings, rather than one that does not affect them at all.[29] This would seem to expand the scope of individual liberty, since an individual's acts might well affect other people, even in significant ways, yet not harm their interests. Hobson's interpretation of Mill, therefore, was not very rigorous, although it is also worth noting that several other New Liberals shared his opinion, including Hobhouse, Ritchie, and MacIver.[30]

Despite this dissatisfaction with Mill's approach, Hobson did appreciate the problem with which Mill was grappling. The utilitarian argument that individuals should have as much liberty as is socially expedient needed to be supplemented. Consequently, Hobson attempted to provide his own rules for establishing the minimum amount of liberty required by individuals in organic society. Since he was unable to accept the basis of Mill's attempt to fix individual rights more securely, Hobson returned to the earlier liberal

28 *The Social Problem* (1901), 88-9
29 *On Liberty*, 14
30 See L.T. Hobhouse, *Liberalism* (1911), 120; D.G. Ritchie, *The Principles of State Intervention* (1891), 11-12; R.M. MacIver, *The Modern State* (1926), 457

tradition of natural rights for his starting point. The details of Hobson's theory of natural rights are discussed later.

Hobson not only considered Mill's notion of self-regarding acts as unrealistic, but he also believed that the concept of freedom it encompassed was too negative. In *On Liberty*, Mill defined freedom as the pursuit of 'our own good in our own way.'[31] However, this was not intended as an endorsement of licentiousness, for he also held that liberty was a condition of human affairs that 'brings human beings themselves nearer to the best thing they can be.'[32] Mill's difficulty arose from those occasions when individuals were not striving to be their best but had fallen into vice and corruption. In this situation, and on the important proviso that such vices were self-regarding, Mill argued that such individuals must be allowed to continue to do as they choose, even though they were choosing badly. The single exception Mill allowed to this rule applied on those occasions when it could be ascertained with certainty that the action undertaken by the individual was not in accord with his wishes. The example Mill gave was of an individual unwittingly about to cross an unsafe bridge. To seize this individual and forcibly turn him back was legitimate as a last resort, in Mill's opinion, because 'liberty consists in doing what one desires' and this person did not desire 'to fall in the river.' The very narrow construction of this caveat becomes evident, however, when Mill cautions that 'when there is *not a certainty*, but only a danger of mischief, *no one but the person himself* can judge the sufficiency of the motive which may prompt him to incur the risk.'[33] For the state or society to meddle directly with such actions, other than by merely pointing out the harm they caused the individual, seemed to Mill to be the thin end of the wedge: society could not then be denied the right to meddle with experiments in living undertaken by its more imaginative members, whenever these seemed eccentric or unorthodox. The ruination of some men's lives was an unfortunate part of the experiment in individuality which Mill considered vital to the improvement of mankind.

For Hobson, this attitude of Mill's was indicative of his continuing commitment to the principle of *laissez-faire* and self-help: the improvement of mankind was to be measured by the diminution of the powers exercised by

31 *On Liberty*, 16
32 Ibid., 77
33 Ibid., 117 (italics added). It might be noted that Mill also refused to countenance the right of individuals to contract themselves into slavery, even though this might be considered a self-regarding action. Mill's point here, however, seems to have less to do with the certainty of the risk involved in such an undertaking than with his objection to laws that prohibit individuals from changing their minds, if just cause can be shown.

governments, no matter that some individuals hurt themselves in the process.

As the following statement suggests, Hobson judged Mill's argument that individuals should bear the costs of self-hurting actions unless it could be shown conclusively that their involvement in such actions was purely accidental, as much too stringent; and the related presumption that each individual knows his own interest best, as much too simplistic.

How far governments should go in these constructive and restrictive policies will evidently vary with the different views of the value set on individual liberty on the one hand, and of the wisdom of governments upon the other. Here Mill's distinction between self-regarding and other-regarding conduct cannot help us much. For the implied judgment that a person should be at liberty to injure himself in body or mind by any sort of foolish conduct, provided he does not injure others, has no relevance in the web of interdependencies presented by any actual society. The only absolute rule of social interference is the consideration whether such interferences conduce upon the whole, and in the long run, to enfeeble or to strengthen the will and capacity of the subjects of such interferences to realise themselves in ways serviceable to society. Here the value set upon the unique in personality will give powerful support to securing for everyone the right and opportunity to make his own mistakes and exercise his own will to correct them, provided that these mistakes and corrections are not too costly to his dependents or other members of society. But even such a principle does not carry us very far, for the social costs of such personal experiments will be assessed with wide differences by different minds. Much will depend upon the respective stress upon order and adventure. ... It is no doubt possible to conceive governments accepting the advice of able experts upon various ways of life, and enforcing ru!es of conduct ... so enabling its members to enjoy a longer and fuller life than if it left more to their private devices.[34]

It seems clear, then, that Hobson is a more consistent utilitarian than is Mill in assessing the relationship between liberty and well-being. Whereas Mill refuses to prohibit self-regarding actions that diminish an individual's happiness, Hobson believes that, although a freedom which results in self-hurt should be tolerated as a learning experience, it has no absolute value. 'I cannot accept,' Hobson writes in another of his essays, 'the view that freedom has a value independent of the use to which it is put, nor can I share [the] related assertion that "ultimately we either believe intuitively that freedom is good, or we do not." Even the satisfaction that adheres to "a sense of freedom" posits some sphere of thought or action with a content that is desirable.'[35]

Consequently, a negative attitude towards the state was unwarranted. If self-help seemed too costly as a method of progress, state assistance was equally valid. A society's worth was to be measured by the 'will and capacity of the subjects to realise themselves in ways serviceable to society.' An active government could promote this end as well as hinder it, but there was no basis for a presumption against state intervention. The state had the right to function as an

instrument for the active adaptation of the economic and moral environment to the new needs of individual and social life, by securing full opportunities for self-development and social service for all its citizens.[36]

Hobson termed the kind of freedom involved in this approach 'positive freedom.' A fully understanding of what Hobson meant by this term is best attained by examining his assessment of its use by the liberal idealists.

4 HOBSON AND THE LIBERAL IDEALISTS

The notion of positive freedom was not originated by Hobson. The concept is especially associated with the ideas of T.H. Green, at least within the liberal school of thought.[37] Hobson does not appear to have been a close student of Green's works, although in his autobiography he recalled that his liberation from 'materialistic and narrowly utilitarian' doctrines was in part the result of his imbibing the 'atmosphere of an Oxford in which Jowett, T.H. Green and Mark Pattison were leading figures.[38] Hobson's schooling in liberal idealism was to come later through his association with the London Charity Organisation Society, which was set up, according to its two leading

---

35 'Democracy, Liberty and Force,' *Hibbert Journal* (1935), vol. 34, 38
36 *The Crisis of Liberalism*, 3
37 Cf. H.J. Laski, *The Decline of Liberalism* (1940); I. Berlin, 'Two Concepts of Liberty,' in *Four Essays on Liberty* (1969); and D. Nichols, 'Positive Liberty, 1888-1914,' *American Political Science Review* (1962), 114-28.
38 *Confessions* (1938), 26

members Helen and Bernard Bosanquet, to 'apply the philosophy of T.H. Green to current problems.'[39]

Given that Hobson and the idealists shared the same general notion of freedom, it is remarkable how much more critical he was of them than he had been of J.S. Mill, whom he once described as having 'stimulated more well-directed thought in philosophy and politics than any other British thinker of his time.'[40] The reason seems to be that he considered the idealists to have a less sure grip on the demoralizing effects of capitalism than had Mill. This led Hobson to conclude that the idealists were in danger of transforming the notion of positive freedom into one of the 'tactics of Conservatism.'[41]

Green had utilised the concept of positive freedom to expose the limitations of the old liberal dictum 'only interfere to prevent interference.' The mere removal of barriers, in Green's opinion, was in itself 'no contribution to true freedom.'[42] For men to be truly free it was necessary for them, first, to possess at least the minimum amount of material wealth and life-chances required for self-realization. Second, it was necessary that the individual seek and object adequate for the realization of freedom. The infliction of self hurt through the pursuit of demeaning objects, eg. alcohol, could not be defined as an exercise of freedom in the positive sense, according to Green.[43] Finally, self-realization was to be understood as the achievement, not of the egoistic happiness espoused by utilitarians, but the development of moral excellence in common fellowship with other members of society. This was the 'idealism' which Green bequeathed to his followers at Oxford. And it was one of the duties of the state to ensure the conditions under which the realization of the moral capacity of man became a possibility. The principle of state intervention was thus admitted. In particular, Green mentioned the need for the state to supervise contracts drawn up between landlords and tenants, to regulate the work and health conditions in factories, to provide for a system of compulsory education, and to restrain the sale of liquor.[44]

39 H. and B. Bosanquet, 'Charity Organisation: A Reply to J.A. Hobson,' *Contemporary Review* (1897), 67
40 'John Stuart Mill,' 178
41 Ernest Barker, *Political Thought in England 1848-1914* (1915, rev. ed., 1947), 67
42 'Liberal Legislation and Freedom of Contract,' (1881) in R. Nettleship, ed., *Works*, vol. III, (1891), 368
43 See his *Lectures on the Principles of Political Obligation* (1911), 2.
44 'Liberal Legislation,' 371-3

However, Green also cautioned that 'there can be no freedom among men who act not willingly but under compulsion.'[45] This statement had two implications: first, it led Green to investigate those power structures in society that placed one set of men under the compulsion of another; second, it served as a warning against paternalism.

With regard to the first of these two concerns, Green asserted, in *Lectures on the Principles of Political Obligation*, that private property rights could be claimed only on the condition that 'everyone should be secured by society in the power of getting and keeping the means of realising a will.'[46] Hobson considered this an excellent starting point for evaluating the economic and political structures of capitalism. However, Green's analysis also suffered from serious weaknesses. Above all, it lacked an adequate understanding of the nature of capitalist society. He asserted, for instance, that for the most part the ills of capitalism were merely the remnants of feudal injustices; that 'capital gained by one is not taken from another'; and that there was 'nothing in the fact that labour is hired in great masses by great capitalists to prevent [the proletariat] from being small scale capitalists themselves,' etc.[47] Green's evaluation of capitalism, then, was very different from Hobson's. Hence an inevitable and marked divergence arose in their appreciation of the notion of positive freedom. As will be shown, Hobson extrapolated this concept in a much more radical fashion than did Green.

Green's jejune assessment of capitalism was shared by his followers at the Charity Organisation Society (COS). It is not surprising, therefore, that Bosanquet and the others felt confident in placing most of their stress on the second aspect of Green's analysis of property, namely that it objectified the virtues of thrift and self-reliance.

The leaders of the COS had applied Green's rationale of private property to various governmental and private schemes for assisting the poor, and reached the conclusion, in Hobson's words, that 'indiscriminate charity and wasteful doles ... sap the sense of responsibility in the individual, weaken his incentive to effective work and break up the solidarity and unity of family life.'[48] The poor needed help; thus state intervention was legitimate as a means of providing this help. But this intervention had to be properly supervised.

45 Ibid., 371
46 *Lectures on the Principles of Political Obligation*, sec. 221, 220
47 Ibid., sec. 229, 226-7; sec. 227, 229
48 *The Crisis of Liberalism*, part III, chap. III, 'The Social Philosophy of the Charity Organisation,' 195 (first published as an article in the *Contemporary Review*, 1896)

I believe [said Bosanquet] in the reality of the general will and in the consequent right and duty of civilised society to exercise initiative through the State with a view to the fullest development of the life of its members. But I am also absolutely convinced that the application of this initiative to guarantee without protest the existence of all individuals brought into being, instead of leaving the responsibility to the uttermost possible extent on the parents and the individuals themselves, is an abuse fatal to character and ultimately destructive of social life.[49]

Above all else, then, it was necessary to avoid being paternalistic towards the poor. Paternalism would destroy their chances of becoming autonomous individuals; it would frustrate the 'realising of a will.' 'The point of private property,' claimed Bosanquet, echoing Green, was that 'things should not come miraculously and be unaffected by your dealings, but you should be in contact with something which in the external world is the definite material representation of yourself.'[50] The COS viewed the existence of large numbers of 'idlers and ne'er-do-wells' in the major urban centres as confirmation of their argument. On this basis they opposed all 'non-contributory' schemes of social assistance, such as the pension scheme proposed by Charles Booth in 1891; fretted when public sympathy for the poor swelled to the point where their charitable donations became 'indiscriminate'; and were cheered by the sight of unemployed workers uprooting themselves and leaving for the colonies.[51]

Hobson considered the COS stand on state intervention as indicative of how little different the liberal idealists were in practice from the *laissez-faire* liberals who had earlier failed to cope with the 'social problem.' Hobson had little objection to the aims of the COS in providing a 'substitute for the broken personal nexus between donor and recipient,' which seemed an almost inevitable consequence of any scheme of government assistance.[52] Like most liberals, Hobson was concerned with the effects of bureaucracy. None the less, he was convinced that the preoccupation of the liberal idealists with matters of morality and thrift served to negate much of the advance they had made in perceiving the importance of material liberties for self-reali-

---

49 'Socialism and Natural Selection,' in B. Bosanquet, ed., *Aspects of the Social Problem* (1895), 290
50 Bosanquet, cited in *The Crisis of Liberalism*, 196
51 Cf. Gareth Stedman Jones, *Outcast London* (1976), esp. part III. See also Helen Bosanquet, *The Strength of the People* (1903).
52 *The Crisis of Liberalism*, 194

zation. Having come one step forward, they had then proceeded two steps back, because of their inability to analyse the structures of capitalism.

Hobson, unlike Green and his followers, had managed to generalize the theory of rent or surplus value. Whereas Green had argued that 'land-lordism' was the source of capitalism's ills, Hobson's analysis had revealed that surplus value was not something generated only in the dealings of land-lords, rather it emerged in every competitive bargain and adhered to the stronger bargainer. Consequently, those areas of economic contest which the liberal idealists viewed as being free from iniquity were exposed by Hobson as largely illusory. The possibility of genuine thrift was thus reduced, as the range of unfair bargaining expanded. Hobson was much more impressed than Green or Bosanquet with the extent to which capital in a market economy was derived from unearned income. In these circumstances, to berate the poor for their lack of thrift was grossly unrealistic.

Further, Hobson contended that the liberal idealists' inability to 'think straight against the pressure of class interests and class prejudices' was revealed not only in their treatment of poverty, but also in their treatment of riches.[53] Might not Green's 'great capitalists' be 'assailed by [the] same demoralising forces' that debilitated the poor, not because they had so little, but because they had too much?

Why do the Charity Organisation Society and their philosophers constantly denounce small gifts to the poor, and hold their peace about large gifts to the rich? We might press the application of [their] ... rule of private property a little further and ask whether the economic rent of land and certain elements in the profits of invested capital, do not come under the same category of the 'miraculous,' or, whether they are the natural results, the 'material representation' of the productive efforts of the receivers. Can anything be more miraculous than that I should wake up tomorrow and find certain shares which today are worth £100 are then risen to £105?[54]

The failure of liberal idealists to 'search into the foundations of social inequality' prevented them from recognizing that the incomes of rich property owners also contained large 'unearned elements' which, on their own view, would be no less enervating than the charity received by the poor. As used by these liberals, the notion of positive freedom seemed to have a

53 Ibid., 217
54 Ibid., 196-7

bottom limit, below which lack of material resources cramped self-realization, but no ceiling. So interpreted, positive freedom contained an apology for the rich and placed false curtailments on state action in redistributing the 'means of opportunity' in society.

It followed from these arguments that the scope of state intervention required by Hobson to remedy or compensate for market imperfections was much greater than that countenanced by the liberal idealists. In order to promote the proper use of property as a means of self-realization, it was essential that the state directly regulate all the processes by which property was accumulated.

The failure of Green and others to comprehend the realities of capitalism also resulted in them grievously misapplying individualist solutions to problems which were essentially social in origin. In the final analysis, the COS 'always or nearly always' associated the existence of poverty 'with the personal defects of the poor' and confined themselves 'wholly to facts in their bearing on individual cases.' Hobson considered that the emphasis the liberal idealists placed on temperance was revealing in this regard. They argued that, because some unemployed workers were observed drunk, while those at work were usually sober, then 'if these unemployed were put upon the same industrial and moral basis, there would be work for all.'[55] But such arguments, in Hobson's opinion, merely perpetuated the old liberal 'fallacy of composition,' failing to recognize that there were 'economic forces' which operated 'independent of individual control' and prevented individual cases of 'moral elevation' from becoming the general rule:

[They assume] what it is required to prove – viz., that there are no ... social forces which limit the number of successful rises [within and out of the lower class]. ... [They] assume that every workman can gain regularity of employment and good wages; that the quantity of 'savings' which can find safe and profitable investment is unlimited; and that all can equally secure for themselves a ... solid economic position by wise exertion of individual powers.[56]

Elsewhere, Hobson put the matter in even more trenchant terms:

The ability of one, or any, individual to get out of his class no more implies the ability of a whole class, or of any considerable proportion of a

55 Ibid., 204, 205
56 Ibid., 204-5

class, to get out of its condition than the fact that any boy in America is able to become President ... implies the ability of all the boys living at any given time to attain this position. *To impute this power to a class involves a total misunderstanding of the nature of individual and class competition in industrial society.*[57]

In Hobson's opinion, the state had to do more than help individuals 'back on their feet'; it had to abolish or mitigate the socio-economic conditions which kept those feet running on a treadmill.

Unable to appreciate the structural causes of unemployment, it was not surprising, in Hobson's opinion, to see the liberal idealist's continuing to preach the virtues of self-help as a prerequisite for social change, especially in a social atmosphere they now believed to be warmed by the presence of a concerned COS delegate, carrying his or her little black book, in which was recorded the merit points of the recipient of state relief, as an encouragement to further effort. Hobson believed this attitude towards the poor reflected a monistic and shallow psychology, which naively assumed that the individual spirit or moral will could become energized largely separate from its material surroundings. It followed that, although liberal idealist arguments made greater state intervention permissible, it was not encouraged. Emphasis, instead, was placed upon voluntary action, while state intervention was viewed as a course of last resort. This was the interpretation Hobson placed on Bosanquet's dictum that 'in social reform ... character is the condition of conditions.' As Hobson pointed out, this was merely the obverse of the 'less thoughtful section of Social Democrats' who claimed that spirit was mere epiphenomena and social environment was the 'condition of conditions.' In Hobson's estimation, both were wrong:

Neither individual character nor environment is the 'condition of conditions.' The true principle which should replace these half-falsehoods is a recognition of the interdependence ... of individual ... and social character as expressed in social environment.[58]

Without taking proper regard of the impress of environment on the 'will' and thus insisting that 'the moral elevation of the masses must precede in point of time all successful reforms of environment,' the liberal idealists

---

57 *The Social Problem*, 84 (emphasis added). It might be noted here that in this passage Hobson was criticizing the philanthropic approach to poverty in general and not just the COS.

58 *The Crisis of Liberalism*, 206-7

were likely to 'block the work of practical reformers.' Their perspective ignored those environmental conditions which prevented the birth of that energy so anxiously awaited by the COS. It was impossible to sustain the will to achieve in the face of continuously discomfirming evidence. Hobson did agree that each reform of social conditions would be effectual only if it succeeded in elevating character. But he viewed this as an argument for gradual reform done in such a way as to involve and educate those who needed help (something which 'crude socialists' were prone to forget in their hurry to carry out reforms from above); it did not detract from the fact that 'in the education of a class ... the historic priority must be given to the *corpus sanum*, the material physical environment.' Thus there were circumstances in which state intervention was appropriate as a course of first rather than last resort. Once again Hobson attributed this defect in the liberal idealists' philosophy to their not having 'studied the industrial structure of society,' since the analysis of economic history quickly revealed that 'though moral reform may be prior "in the nature of things," economic reform is prior in time.'[59]

5 PUBLIC PROPERTY RIGHTS:
THE FOUNDATION OF A WELFARE STATE

Just as it is essential to the progress of the moral life of the individual that he shall have some 'property,' some material embodiment of his individual activity which he may use for the realisation of his rational ends in life, so the moral life of the community requires public property and public industry for its self-realisation, and the fuller the life the larger the sphere of these external activites. 'The Ethics of Industrialisation,' 104

Although Hobson believed that J.S. Mill had made some important inroads into *laissez-faire* doctrine and that the liberal idealist's concept of positive freedom could be radicalized, he was none the less convinced that these earlier frameworks were ultimately unsatisfactory and therefore could not provide a fitting ideology for social reform. Both of these attempts to recall the state for active service worked almost exclusively within the confines of private property. In this regard, there was no basis for distinguishing Mill's and Green's approaches from other individualistic doctrines

59 Ibid., 207-8. Though the Bonsanquets did attempt to rebut Hobson's charge of 'spiritual monism' their reply is not convincing. It still leaves the impression that the will must be willing before state assistance is to be considered worthwhile. Cf. H. and B. Bosanquet, 'Charity Organisation.' On the other hand, there is evidence that Green was not so 'monistic' as his followers: see 'Liberal Legislation and Freedom of Contract,' 376-7.

which left the state, in Hobson's words, to live on 'suffrance, by taxes paid grudgingly out of private purses.'[60] – though presumably Mill's and Green's citizens, being less self-absorbed, would also have been less grudging. Moreover, Hobson believed that this narrow view of the state 'resulted in an equally false and narrow conception of the meaning and the possibilities of social life.'[61] It limited both the degree and scope of state activity and left the civic spirit unnurtured.

Hobson sought to push liberalism in a new direction. He attributed the impoverished view of social life, held by other liberals, to their failure to appreciate the part played by the state in the production of wealth. It was the liberals' individualistic notion of production which kept the state at the behest of private property, thus cramping its functions. It followed that if the state was to perform a more positive role in men's lives, it needed property of its own – public property – to work with, just as Green, Bosanquet, and others had argued that an individual required private property in order to realize his full potential. By combining his theory of organic surplus value with an innovative extension of the idealist theory of objectification, Hobson believed that he could 'turn the edge of the stock arguments of the individualist school by basing the claims for social property upon the same reasoning which defends individual property.'[62] Proprietary right, not prudence or even altruism, was the key to Hobson's theory of the welfare state.

At the same time, however, it is important to stress that Hobson did not want his case against the individualist school to be read as an endorsement of state socialism. He wished to avoid the twin errors of 'statism' and 'atomism.' Hobson described the dilemma as follows:

The individualist recks nought of social work or social needs; or, if he gives some half-hearted recognition to the advantages of social cooperation, he is sure that the gains are best utilised by handing them over to the private control of the cooperating units, reserving as little as possible for social use. The socialist ... will, on the contrary, ... cavil at the allowance of private property, insisting that ... all value is social.[63]

Hobson considered that the reconciliation of these two contradictory positions was a 'most important duty of statecraft.'[64] Indeed, it was an essential

60 *Wealth and Life*, 162
61 *The Social Problem*, 149
62 Ibid., 154
63 Ibid., 155
64 *The Industrial System* (1909; 2nd ed., 1910), 230

and necessary step in the advancement of New Liberalism as a separate creed.

Hobson began by suggesting that, granted that both the individual and society contributed to the creation of economic values, as shown by his organic theory, the problem was simply one of differentiating the claims of each. Thus, instead of having somehow to synthesize the contradictory positions of the individualist and the socialist, Hobson was able to side-step this dichotomy and show that what was needed was a 'just, rational demarcation between private and public property.'[65]

In line with this argument, Hobson proposed an ingenious reformulation of the traditional liberal theory of individual natural rights, based on physiological and psychological criteria, and regarding such rights as *media axiomata*, rather than as innate rights. Moreover, he argued that once the organic concept was properly grasped it was obvious that these natural laws applied to individuals and society alike: both were vital organisms. It followed that 'every defence of individual property [was] likewise a plea for social property,' and vice versa.[66]

a / Individual Property Rights

To simplify matters at the outset, Hobson recommended that individual rights be reduced to property rights.[67] Illustrating his point with reference to the French Declaration of Rights, Hobson reasoned that 'Liberty, Property, Security and Resistance of Oppression' could be 'legitimately brought under the same head.' The right to resist oppression 'involved' the right to be secure. Similarly, the right to security was included in the right to liberty and property, 'for a breach of security is an actual or threatened assault on liberty and property.' Finally, Hobson argued that liberty and property were not separate rights, but the 'negative and positive aspects of the same right':

[Liberty] signifies the existence of a special sphere of activity, a scope of work and life, which is apportioned to the individual, and which may not

---

65 *The Social Problem*, 153
66 Ibid., 150
67 Elsewhere Hobson recognized that not all human rights (e.g., the rights of the infirm and disabled) could be founded upon proprietary rights. See his article, 'Old Age Pensions: The Responsibility of the State to the Aged Poor,' *Sociological Review* (July 1908), and *The Social Problem*, 163. Also, in *A Modern Outlook* (1910), chap. 2, 'Co-partnership in Nature,' Hobson makes the interesting observation that basing human rights on property or labour can result in an anthropocentrism that endangers mankind's relations with the natural world. Unfortunately Hobson nowhere develops this thesis.

be invaded by another. And what else is this private sphere of activity but 'property,' the *proprium* of each person – that domain in which he may freely express himself? ... This presence of opportunity for self-expression ... is the essence of 'true property' [and] though [this] does not always imply the exclusive possession of some objective good, it does imply exclusive use.[68]

In reducing individual rights to property rights, Hobson was perhaps unduly secularizing the liberal philosophy of natural rights,[69] but the advantage in making this reduction, according to Hobson, was that it made it possible to pose the problem of rights in quantitative terms:

Under conditions of actual life there is not enough [property] 'to go round.' This is the root from which the most pressing economic and social problems spring. How much shall each have? Does nature throw no light upon this question? Is there any natural basis ... for the guidance of society in determining the socially expedient 'rights of property'?[70]

Hobson credited Ruskin with being among the first to recognize that nature did provide an answer: 'Ruskin [perceived] that every great social question had one of its roots in physiology.'[71] Elaborating this thought, Hobson claimed that there existed certain laws of the physical and psychological nature of man which marked out the true limits of property in any given society.

The first natural right to private property was based on the 'physiological relation of function to nutrition.' A worker had a right to a certain amount of property in food, clothing, and shelter in order to replenish his labour-power given out in work. In this regard Hobson cited approvingly Adam Smith's statement, 'the produce of labour constitutes natural recompense.' Hobson also pointed to studies by German scientists and the observations of certain

---

68 *The Social Problem*, 96-7
69 It is worth noting that in *God and Mammon* (1931), Hobson suggests (following Tawney) that in its origin protestantism was 'not disposed to relax any of the spiritual authority exercised by ... religion over the ... economic conduct of [its] members.' Only later was 'the ethic of the calling' insensibly adapted so as to reinforce and bolster the 'acquisitive and possessive urges' of the bourgeoisie. In its original intent, religious individualism could not be closely identified with the bourgeoisie's demand for private property. *God and Mammon*, chap. III, esp. 25-31
70 *The Social Problem*, 98
71 *John Ruskin*, 155

enlightened businessmen to show that, when labour is 'sweated,' this was 'naturally attended by a ... decrement of working efficiency.'[72] Such was the sanction of natural law.

Superimposed upon this first element of private proprietory right was a second, based upon the proposition that the 'human will is part of nature and the motives which operate through it conform to natural laws.' By this somewhat obtuse statement, Hobson simply meant that personal gain was a necessary component of any individual's motive to work. The worker, therefore, had a 'natural right' to 'such portion of any extra product he may produce as is required to stimulate the necessary effort of production,' although Hobson cautioned, for reasons that soon will become apparent, that 'the property claimed by the worker in this extra-product, bears ... no fixed relation to the total value of the product.'[73] Again, natural right was backed by natural law, so that if this increment was withheld from the worker, eventually but inevitably a fall in productivity would ensue:

[In a] society where endeavours are made to infringe this right, the result is a restriction of productive energy given out. ... Man desires not only to live, but to live abundantly and for that he will undergo increased effort. But where more abundant life is not secured, nature withholds the effort; under such conditions torpor sets in, activity becomes inured to a low routine, and soon the very possibility of progress disappears by atrophy of the will and intelligence.[74]

Combining these two elements of natural proprietorship, Hobson claimed that they represented an individual's right to a 'normal standard of comfort,' providing for the 'maintenance of life' and 'provision for the progressive demands of his nature.'[75] On this basis, then, Hobson accepted the liberal tradition regarding the individual's ineradicable need for private property.

b / Public Property Rights
According to Hobson, the old liberal theory of property rights nevertheless had two major defects. First, it assumed that each individual had a natural interest in maximizing the extent of his property. Second, it assumed that all labour was individual.

72 *The Social Problem*, 99-101
73 Ibid., 103, 104
74 Ibid., 106
75 Ibid., 105

In positing that the goal of each individual producer was to maximize his possessions, early natural rights theorists had explored a number of motivations.[76] However, in what Hobson termed 'the crude current treatment of industrial economy,' these motivations had been narrowed down to two: idleness and greed. It was assumed 'an eternal law of nature that idleness and greed are the sole directing powers of industry.'[77] Man's appetitiveness compelled him to labour, but his idleness further determined that he would experience his labour as costly toil. In these circumstances, it seemed only natural to assume that each man would want to claim, to the fullest extent, the property created by his labour. Possessiveness was the individual's only source of satisfaction in his work.

The error in this theory of property rights occurred, in Hobson's opinion, because it transformed matters of historical contingency into points of general principle:

The root issue is this: Must the worker necessarily, and in all cases, find his motive to labour in the desire to possess as his 'property' the product of his labour, or may he find it in the satisfaction afforded by the process?[78]

The answer depended 'largely on the character of the process.' If the productive process was 'utterly unattractive,' then labour would be experienced as something alienating and the worker could 'only look to the property in the product for his motive.' On the other hand, if 'the process was itself desirable, a far smaller property in the product' was required:

An artist will often work for what seems to the 'business man' a totally inadequate reward. It is not true that man 'naturally' refuses effort unless he can secure a full selfish enjoyment of the product. Man is the owner of a recurrent fund of superfluous vital energy, over and above what is needed to procure the necessities of physical life, and he is willing to use this energy for pleasurable activities of self-expression, without demanding that all the matter he may inform with his superfluous energy shall be earmarked for his private property.[79]

76 In *God and Mammon* (p. 30), Hobson mentions the egalitarian doctrines of Levellers and Diggers only to dismiss their impact on the liberal tradition.
77 *The Social Problem*, 107
78 Ibid.
79 Ibid., 108

Thus, to the extent that society could enhance the attractiveness of work, it would be in a position to modify individual claims to property without contravening natural rights. This positive assessment of the productive process and its potential for curtailing possessiveness was an alternative the old school of liberalism excluded.

Hobson's second and more significant criticism of traditional liberal natural rights theory rested on his contention that society was a producer of values. On this basis, he rejected liberalism's preoccupation with the individual producer:

The community [should] refuse ... to sanction absolute property on the part of any of its members, recognising that a large proportion of the value of each individual's work is due, not to his solitary efforts, but to the assistance lent by the community.[80]

Although Hobson is not strictly accurate in ascribing a doctrine of 'absolute' property rights to early liberal theory – neither Locke nor Smith, for example, left private ownership completely unregulated – his main point was to stress that such restrictions as were imposed were done primarily for eleemosynary considerations, or to make the general system of private ownership more orderly. What early liberalism did not recognize, according to Hobson, was that the state or community had a natural claim to property, co-equal with that of individuals, based upon the social work it performed:

An economic system which so operates as to assign the great body of accumulated wealth to ... individuals, as their private property, and gives no recognition to the ... activities of the community, society as an organic whole, in the production of wealth, deprives the latter of the means to organise effectively the services which properly belong to it. The necessity of calling upon individual owners to surrender to the state out of their private property the revenue required for public services inevitably tends to restrict those services, and to prevent the development of public activities commensurate with the more enlightened interpretation of public welfare. ... [When] wealth is treated as if it were entirely the product of private personal efforts [then] the community is only dragged in at a later stage: its claims are based upon necessity, or upon eleemosynary considerations, and not upon the right to draw for the community life the income which community services have earned.[81]

Hobson believed that this failure to concede public proprietory rights was best evidenced in the liberals' attitude towards taxation. Liberals accepted taxation and other forms of public funding as necessary but regrettable and only legitimate provided the individual property owner had consented to them. Taxation, in essence, was a form of coercion to be suffered for the greater good. 'Writers to the *Times*,' Hobson observed, often opined 'upon the high rate of income-tax,' claiming that it was 'confiscatory,' though most also 'grudgingly' admitted that the state may take 'some fraction' of their income for a good cause.[82] No doubt to these liberals it sounded shocking to assert that state taxation was not necessarily an infringement upon personal liberty and property, but an exercise of natural right. However, in Hobson's opinion, liberals would have to accept this consequence of the organic nature of production, if they wished fully to accredit the principle of state intervention.

For Hobson, public property was the life-blood of the welfare state. Without this right, the state was forever in danger of being 'Sweated' out of its necessary funds. Society needed to 'realise herself by means of her property,' as did the individual. Conversely, the misappropriation of public property drained the strength and impaired the productivity of society: 'a starved society is injured just as the individual starveling is injured.'[83] Examining his own society, Hobson found that even the accoutrements of a healthy public life were absent:

It is the denial of this full property which starves our social life today. Look, for example, at the civic life of an average municipality in England, the richest country that the world has ever known. Is this civic life as strong, as rich, as it might be? ... Are its streets, its public buildings worthy of a rich and civilised community? Is it not a commonplace that these external embodiments of our civic life are, in every quality of excellence, inferior beyond all comparison with the attainments of most of the great cities of antiquity, the private wealth of whose citizens was not one hundredth part as great as ours?

81 *Wealth and Life*, 161-2
82 *Property and Impropery* (1937), 68. On early liberal views towards taxation, see Peter
    Manicas, *The Death of the State* (1974), 232-5.
83 *The Social Problem*, 151

Or, turning to ... the State – do we not find its services everywhere crippled by lack of property? The miserably penurious provision for ... public education ... is one crucial instance ... [the lack of] monetary aid for the aged poor ... [is another]. Yet these instances refer to the prime necessities of a healthy stable society.[84]

Moreover, if the state's maintenance costs were scarcely being met, then it was hardly surprising that no social property was 'accumulated to work out the progressive character of society, which should seek constantly to develop and satisfy higher and more complex needs of life.'[85]

Thus having found a basis for establishing public natural rights alongside those traditionally claimed by individuals, Hobson next turned to the task of redressing the balance between private affluence and public squalor.

6 THE MEDIATION OF PUBLIC AND PRIVATE PROPERTY RIGHTS

Hobson envisaged no insoluble problems with regard to the mediation of individual and social claims to property. Both could be incorporated within the organic framework. Thus, along with other New Liberals, he insisted that 'it must be plainly understood that there is no question of individual *versus* society':

There are no conflicting claims; such notion of conflict only arises so long as we conceive the individual as he is not – viz. a *mere* isolated unit; when we conceive him as he is, it is only a question of harmonising the different sides of his nature. ... [F]or when the individual is seen with his social bonds of feelings and interests, to ignore these would be to inflict injury upon the fulness of his individuality by ignoring one important aspect of it.[86]

In establishing how this harmony might be conceived, Hobson provided, in the words of one scholar, what was 'probably the most adequate theoretical expression of the change of perspective that had emerged within liberalism.'[87] Hobson articulated this change in perspective in terms of a 'federation of interests' between individuals and society:

84 Ibid., 152
85 Ibid.
86 Ibid., 223
87 Freeden, *The New Liberalism*, 111

The unity of ... social-industrial life is ... a federal unity in which the rights and interests of the individual shall be conserved for him by the federation. The federal government, however, conserves these individual rights, not, as the individualist maintains, because it exists for no other purpose than to do so. It conserves them because it ... recognizes that an area of individual liberty is conducive to the health of the collective life. Its federal nature rests on a recognition alike of individual and social ends, or speaking more accurately, of social ends that are directly attained by social action and of those that are realised in individuals.[88]

This general formulation of the relationship between individualism and collectivism attempted to avoid the old antagonisms by making both ideals mutually dependent. It seemed an ingenious third option – a veritable 'mixed economy' of ideals – whereby traditional liberal tenets were preserved at the same time a new priority was given to the collective life.

Unfortunately, upon closer inspection, Hobson's formulation is not as pleasingly symbiotic as it first appears. According to Hobson, certain liberties should be handed over by society to individuals, because this would ultimately serve the common good. But this argument is not very different from the utilitarian argument proposed by J.S. Mill. Hobson had rejected the latter's qualification that the exercise of these personal liberties could be based on the distinction of being 'self-regarding.' As has been shown, Hobson thought Mill's categories of self- and other-regarding actions unrealistic. By the same token, however, on what basis could it be decided when individual liberty was serving social ends and when it was not? Hobson in fact provided two answers to this question. His answers seem contradictory and, moreover, in the one case appears to jeopardize the traditional tenets of liberalism.

Hobson's first answer was, in effect, to beat a path back to Mill, but to do so on the grounds of biology:

The real wrong of sumptuary laws ... prescribing how the individual citizen shall spend the money and time at his disposal, and forcing the natural instincts into certain grooves, consists in the neglect of the teachings of evolution regarding the mode of progress. The great majority of eccentricities ... of conduct are considered in themselves wasteful and even socially injurious: but from the standpoint of race progress they must be regarded as experiments in life. Every variation in individual conduct which has ini-

88 *Work and Wealth*, 304. See also *Wealth and Life*, 165-6.

tiated a new step in social progress starts as an individual aberration. ...
Modern biology ... enforce[s] most powerfully the plea of J.S. Mill.[89]

Hobson did not develop this biological defence of individualism and therefore failed to indicate whether it provided a means of advancing beyond
those difficulties he had detected in Mill's approach. However, his statement
would suggest that, as a general rule, the onus was on the state to minimize
its claims so as to promote individuality and social progress.

In Hobson's second, and more characteristic, answer, this priority is
reversed and a concern for social efficiency seems to militate against granting
much leeway to 'individual experiments in life':

'The history of progress is the record of the gradual diminution of waste.'
From this standpoint the Social Question will find its essential unity. ...
  Little trouble is yet taken to discover the special aptitudes of citizens in
relation to the special needs of society, ... and of furnishing not a negative
and empty 'freedom' to undertake this work, but the *positive freedom* of
opportunity. A whole cluster of education problems ... demanding, not a
separate empirical solution, but a related organic solution, with direct
regard to full economy of social work, appears as part of the Social Question. *Every failure to put the right man in the right place, with the best faculty
of filling that place, involves social waste.*[90]

It would be easy to conclude from this statement that Hobson is a Plato
redivivus. At the very least it would seem to transform Mill's noble heretics
into social wastrels, and it is not difficult to imagine other ways in which this
preoccupation with social efficiency could run afoul of liberalism's traditional
regard for individualism. Hobson, for example, sometimes endorsed the
recommendations of eugenicists – whose studies were receiving renewed
interest around the turn of the century – with an enthusiasm quite unwarranted, given the nascent state of eugenics, and quite untypical of other liberals in his circle.[91] This was especially so in his early works. Later, he

---

89 'Character and Society,' in P. Parker, ed., *Character and Life* (1912), 94-5
90 *The Social Problem*, 7, 10 (emphasis added)
91 In ibid. (pp. 214-15), for example, Hobson argued that 'to abandon the production of
   children to unrestricted private enterprises is the most dangerous abnegation of its
   functions which any government can practice.' Hobson suggested that, as a last resort,
   government should be empowered to enforce family planning so as to prevent 'unfit
   propagation.' However, in part, this policy was advocated on the dubious assumption

modified his advocacy and concentrated on environmental change as the primary means of improving the human stock. However, Hobson never rescinded his opinion that problems of heredity could not be left exclusively to private regulation and individual choice.[92]

Hobson's own way of resolving these difficulties (in so far as he recognized them) was to admit that a good deal of expediency was unavoidable in such matters. M. Freeden has suggested that Hobson's pragmatism in this regard should be viewed as 'more of a strength than a weakness.' For in a time of 'changing concepts, ideas and social facts,' flexibility in interpretation was 'more applicable and more vital than the Millian dogmas.'[93] While this is a plausible defence of Hobson's vacillation, it is also important to recall that Hobson's concession to expediency was made within a framework of analysis which insisted that there were natural laws of property guarding the division between social and individual property rights and liberties. Although Hobson believed that natural law was too 'slow working' to be entirely satisfactory as a safeguard,[94] he was convinced it at least ensured that the demarcation between public and private rights could not be obliterated altogether (as J.S. Mill had feared). Hobson's concession to social expediency did have a bottom line:

Society exists, not, as is sometimes maintained, in order consciously to secure the separate welfare of its individual members, but to secure the health and progress of society always realized as a spiritual organism; but this end, interpreted at any given time in terms of 'social utility,' has been seen to involve the care and promotion of individual health and progress. It can never be in the interest of society to attempt to dominate or enslave the individual, sucking his energies for the supposed nutriment of the State; any such endeavour would be futile for ... an attempt to exploit those energies, or to take away that 'property' which nature has set aside

that criminality was hereditary and that the 'causal relations' between mental, moral, and physical weakness were 'sufficiently close and constant to make it certain that the survival and growth of physical unfitness' meant a 'fairly correspondent growth of mental and moral unfitness.'

Contrast this, for example, with L.T. Hobhouse's much more guarded assessment of eugenics in *Social Evolution and Political Theory* (1911), chap. 3, 'The Value and Limitations of Eugenics.' It is noteworthy, however, that on this issue of population control, J.S. Mill's thinking was closer to Hobson's than it was to the mainstream of liberalism. See *On Liberty*, 132.

92 See *Confessions*, chap. XII, 'The Welfare Economics of Population.'
93 Freeden, *The New Liberalism*, 111
94 *The Social Problem*, 115

for individual support and progress, would defeat its end by drying up the sources of such energy and 'property'.[95]

To rob a person of his natural right to private property was to deprive him of his developmental powers and society of a vital source of productive energy. Such action inevitably was counter-productive.

Hobson was later to appeal to the experience of history to bear out this conclusion. 'History,' he claimed, even the recent history of Russia under the Bolsheviks, or Italy under Mussolini, showed 'no instance of durable success' in evoking in the individual 'a spurious consent to work which is not the expression of his own free will.' Modern industry demanded a 'real consent to work,' and this required a 'personal interest on the workers' part, interpreted in *narrower* terms than public service, or the welfare of the community.'[96] By setting a minimum or natural condition for the expression of individuality, Hobson kept within the classical liberal tradition.

95 Ibid., 224. This also would seem to be the basis of Hobson's objection to D.G. Ritchie's use of the argument for the social origin of rights to deny the existence of individual rights. See ibid., 94.
96 *Wealth and Life*, 236 (emphasis added)

7

Democracy and the General Will

1 THE GENERAL WILL AS SPECIES CONSCIOUSNESS

Philosophers and statesmen often speak contemptuously of what they call 'the
herd-mind,' denying it any rational or moral quality. But it is not possible to
explain how any of those social institutions which make a civilised society have
arisen without imputing some common urge based on the recognition that all the
members of the human herd are very much alike, want the same things and can
best attain them by peaceful regular cooperation. The herd-mind has within it the
nucleus of what philosophers call a 'general will.' *The Recording Angel*, 109-10

Hobson's organic theory of society inevitably raised the question of the existence of a collective mind or general will: organic co-operation in the economic
realm provided a distinct 'commonwealth,' but was there a 'common-will' to
utilize this wealth for community purposes?

Hobson believed that a collective mind in society was a reality: indeed, he
argued that its existence was coterminous with human history. It was part of
the instinctual make-up of mankind, graven, as Rousseau had said, as much
upon the heart of man as upon his reason. The following statement, taken
from *Work and Wealth*, expresses this first key element in Hobson's theory
of the general will:

The animal organism ... is endowed with energy of body and mind, operating through an equipment of instinctive channels towards its own survival
and development and the survival and development of the species. Where
there is a danger lest too much energy should be consumed on individual
ends, too little on specific [i.e. species] ends, the social or self-sacrificing
instincts are strengthened in the individual and reinforced by the herd ...

as where plunders of the common stock or shirkers in common tasks are
destroyed by the ... herd. The instinct for the survival and development of
the ... species cannot be satisfactorily explained as belonging only to the
psycho-physical equipment of the individual members. On this basis, viz.
that of attributing a social nature only to the individual members of a society, the acts of devotion and self-sacrifice, and still more the acts of pre-
paratory skill, the elaborate performance of deeds that are means to the
survival and well-being of a future generation become mere haphazard
miracles ... Such conduct is not made intelligible by any other hypothesis
than that of a collective life of a species.[1]

The general will, then, had its roots in man's species instincts; it was one of
the 'hard facts of life,' not 'vague theory' as some so-called realists were apt
to contend. Consequently, the 'validity of the general will' did 'not depend
upon the degree of conscious rational purpose' it had 'attained.'[2]
 Hobson, however, was not content to leave the good of the whole in the
care of this 'blind faculty of organic self-protection.' By itself, this instinct
was too weak to withstand the process of individuation, which had been,
according to Hobson, a major characteristic of the evolutionary movement
from an 'instinctive' to a 'rational' economy:

The instinctive economy allows little scope for individuality of life, the
dominant drive of its 'implicit' purpose is specific, i.e. subserving the
maintenance and evolution of the species. ... It might almost be said that
the dawn of reason is the dawn of selfishness. For rational economy involves a conscious realisation of the individual self, with ends of its own
to be secured. ... Thus the displacement of the instinctive by the rational
economy is evidently a critical era, attended with grave risks due to the
tendency towards an over-assertion of the individual self and a consequent
weakening of the forces making for specific life. Man, the newly conscious
individual, may perversely choose to squander organic resources 'intended' by nature for the race upon his own personal pleasure and needs.
He may refuse to make as a matter of rational choice those personal
efforts and sacrifices ... which no animal, subject to the drive of instinct, is
able to 'think' of refusing.[3]

1 *Work and Wealth* (1914), 351-2
2 Ibid., 303, 353
3 Ibid., 22

From this flowed the second key element in Hobson's theory of the general will, namely, that if 'reason' were to come to the aid of the species it had to be 'socialised.'[4] Thus far 'reason' had functioned primarily as an instrument for furthering individual utility. But Hobson discerned an important distinction between man's short-term interests as an individual and his long-term interests as a member of a community, race, and species. It was necessary for reason to encompass this wider synthesis of interests. Ultimately, rationality would become synonymous with species-consciousness and this would comprise the general will, in *excelsus*.

This expansive vision of the general will marked the essential difference between Hobson's analysis and that of Bernard Bosanquet, the major exponent of this doctrine in Britain during the first quarter of the century. Hobson criticized Bosanquet for limiting the actualization of the general will to the boundaries of the nation-state. In his opinion Bosanquet's philosophy was a prescription for international anarchy, carrying with it the threat of militarism and domestic oppression. Thus, citing a passage from Bosanquet's master-work, *The Philosophical Theory of the State* (1899), where it is argued that the nation-state is the 'widest organisation which has the common experience necessary to found a common life,' Hobson objected stating that this view of the 'ethical self-sufficiency of a nation' could be pressed to the point 'as virtually to repudiate the ethical fact and utility of the conception of humanity.' The upshot of Bosanquet's argument, in practical terms, was to 'deny the validity' of 'any standard of the conduct of nations towards one another.'[5]

To this extent Hobson shared the opinion of his friend Hobhouse that the doctrine had played its part in leading nations down the rapids to war.[6] But unlike Hobhouse, whose position is noted shortly, Hobson did not reject the doctrine of the general will. Indeed, instead of backing away from the idea, he insisted on a more grandiose conception in order to expose those occasions when the doctrine was misused by narrower interests. The converse of this, of course, is the possibility that Hobson rendered his doctrine so vacuous as to be unhelpful.

The prime instruments in this process of socialization, according to Hobson, were not enlightened individuals but associations, for it was in association that individuals tended to develop a distinct 'collective consciousness.' It is important to understand that by this Hobson did not mean merely that

4 Ibid., 23
5 *Imperialism* (1902; 3rd ed., 1938), 166
6 *Democracy after the War* (1917; 4th ed., 1919), 111-14

an individual's range of social sympathies was extended, but that the individual took on a new 'persona – a social identity – which meant that he worked 'not for his separate self,' but for the whole, and attained his separate well-being in the proper functioning of that whole.[7] There was not, he contended, 'a school, a church, a club' which did not 'impress a common character on its members ... by some direct assimilation of the separate minds.' Indeed, 'even the most fortuitous concourse of a mob in the streets of Paris or London' exhibited a character that was uniform, 'dominated for the time being by a single feeling or idea' and which differed 'widely from the known character ... of its component parts.'[8] This sense of 'wholeness' was the special *organic* 'product' of associations, and was not to be 'found as such in the individual.'[9] Put in Rousseauean terms, Hobson was arguing that the general will of any association was not the 'Will of All,' i.e., the aggregate of the individual wills, but was the will of a distinct 'group mind' with values of its own. Any lesser conception was unlikely to 'suffice to support the commonweal.'[10]

In the school, the club, and the church the group mind was 'writ small,' but Hobson believed that there also could be found in the evolution of society at least the germ of a rationalized general will, less vigorous, perhaps, than the instrumental reasoning that had been developed by the individual will, but none the less strong enough to warrant the hypothesis that a society had a psycho-physical identity separate from that of its members:

The earliest beginnings of animal gregariousness, sexual feelings, and other primary instincts of association, with the mutual aid they give rise to, are a first testimony to the existence ... of a real though rudimentary society, physical and psychical in nature. Civilisation has its chief meaning ... in this unity of Society. ... Thus through [the] ... instruments of common social life, language, art, science, industry, politics, religion, society gathers a larger, more solid and various life. Race, nationality, Church ... often present intense examples of a genuinely common life and purpose. *These are not mere social contracts of free individuals, seeking by coöperation to forward their own ends. Such a conception of mutual aid is ... false. ... The statement that 'man is a social animal' cannot merely signify that among man's equipment of feeling and ideas there exists a feeling and idea of sympathy with*

---

7 *Work and Wealth*, 16
8 *The Crisis of Liberalism* (1909), 74-5
9 *Wealth and Life* (1929), 32
10 *Work and Wealth*, 302

other men. That is only how it looks from the standpoint of the cell. *It means that humanity in all its various aggregations is a social stuff*, and that whatever form of coalescence it assumes ... there will exist a genuinely organic unity, a central or general life, strong or weak, but, so far as it goes, to be considered as distinct from and dominant over the life and aim of its members. ... May not, then, the whole process of the rationalisation of man be regarded as a bringing of the individual man into vital communion of thought and feeling with the thoughts and feelings of the race, of humanity.[11]

Hobson realized that his positing of a distinct collective consciousness and feeling of mankind was bound to sound mysterious to liberals who learned their individualism from Hobbes or Bentham, but he saw this simply as a reflection of their false premises. Individualist philosophers failed to appreciate man's innate capacity to care for 'the whole,' because their starting point was man regarded as a self-centred private individual – an individual, Hobson delighted in pointing out, who was described by the ancient Greek philosophers as an 'idiotes.'[12] Thus he acutely observed that it was very difficult for orthodox liberals 'to recognise any possibility of disinterested motive' since 'all such motives were ruled out *ex hypothesi*.' On the other hand, if monadic man was recognized as being 'subject to the dominant control of some wider life than his' (i.e., the life of the species), then the mystery of 'public service' disappeared: man became capable of self-sacrifice or disinterested conduct because he was 'a centre of wider interests than those of his own particular self.'[13]

Much more perplexing to Hobson than the orthodox liberal position was the refusal of certain progressive liberals, like L.T. Hobhouse and R.M. MacIver, to give credence to the existence of a distinct 'social mind,' even though they agreed that the purely self-regarding individual was a fiction. For these thinkers, the 'group mind' spelled tyranny, and they sought, in Hobson's words, to repudiate 'all values not directly translatable into personal ends.'[14] The issue essentially turned on the question of the use of force in achieving the social good. All were agreed that it was utopian to expect the growth of a social will in an environment that permitted certain selfish interests to take unfair advantage of the efforts of others who were attempting to

11 Ibid., 307-8, 355-6 (emphasis added). See also 'The Political Basis of a World State,' in
    F.S. Marvin, ed., *The Unity of Western Civilisation* (1915).
12 *Le Sens de la responsibilité* (1938), 6
13 *Work and Wealth*, 356
14 *Wealth and Life*, 35

will the common good. They disagreed, however, as to the value (and as a consequence also as to the amount) of force to be exercised in checking this selfishness. Much depended on whether this dissent was viewed as an act of conscience or obduracy. Hobhouse, for example, in several of his works, bitterly attacked the kind of position advocated by Hobson as pernicious, since the contention that self-sacrifice should be seen as self-expression, that is, the expression of a distinct social self, in his opinion led straight to Rousseau's justification for 'forcing men to be free,' and this he found abhorrent. Like his mentor T.H. Green, Hobhouse believed that to call force by any other name was to anaesthetize the moral sense, and therefore was in breach of hallowed liberal principles. It followed that, although Hobhouse was convinced that the state must be used to provide individuals with the opportunity for self-improvement, he was no less convinced that no individual should be forced to improve himself: 'If we refrain from coercing a man for his own good, it is not because his good is indifferent to us, but because it cannot be furthered by coercion. ... It is not possible to compel morality because morality is the act of a free agent.' Consequently, even though Hobhouse allowed that in a conflict between individual conscience and the common good, the latter 'must have its way,' he also insisted that such action be undertaken only as a last resort, reluctantly, and on the clear understanding that force was being used. The 'right to protest' was also to remain with the individual.[15]

Hobson, on the other hand, seemed keener to excuse the use of force, not only because he saw it as a necessary instrument for maintaining 'external order,' as Hobhouse had argued, but also because he was confident that the general will, properly arrived at, embodied a *higher* standard of morality than did the individual will. On this basis, force used by the community could be viewed as an instrument for the good. This presumption in favour of the general will, however, would seem just as inappropriate as Mill's presumption in favour of the individual will, which Hobson had earlier criticized. It too readily suggests that dissent is the result of ignorance, or worse, conceit.

Hobhouse's comments, then, have definite applicability to Hobson's conceptualization of the general will. For example, in several of his works Hobson maintained that in a democratically planned society it would be necessary to curtail the liberty of employers to impose lock-outs and the liberty of employees to go on strike, in favour of a system of compulsory arbitration.[16]

15 Hobhouse, *Liberalism* (1911), 143, 149. An interesting discussion of possible inconsistencies in Hobhouse's argument in this regard is given in Stefan Collini, *Liberalism and Socialism* (1979), 123-4.
16 See 'Democracy, Liberty, and Force,' *Hibbert Journal* (1935), vol. 34; *Democracy and a Changing Civilisation* (1934), 115-17; and *The Conditions of Industrial Peace* (1927), 120f.

He further argued that a democratic state would be entitled to use force against any employer or employee who attempted to assert his particular interest above those of the community. Hobson's explanation of the fate of these dissidents is very Rousseauean. They are 'put down' according to the

true function of coercion, or force in the economy of freedom. Narrower liberties may be suppressed in favour of broader liberties, lower liberties in favour of higher, i.e. of such liberties as are essential to the achievement of finer personal and social values. ... At every step in the march of man toward a wider, closer social and political coöperation, some element of physical as well as moral force has been required to secure and maintain the new achievement. More liberty and opportunity upon a higher level are only thus attained.[17]

The right to settle disputes before equitable arbitration tribunals was viewed by Hobson as a higher level of freedom than the right to strike or lock-out because the latter suffered from two serious defects: first, it failed to recognize that 'no man can be a just judge in his own cause'; and second, it involved 'risks or injuries to others' who were not parties to the quarrel.[18] Thus, in insisting upon the method of compulsory arbitration, Hobson appears to disarm the recalcitrant before the higher morality of the general will, thereby 'forcing men to be free.'

Interestingly, Hobson did not share the view of most liberals that the use of force necessarily eliminated genuine choice, and thus negated the moral worth of a recalcitrant's subsequent decision to adhere to the general will. On the contrary, he argued that force, if properly used, could actually enhance the conditions of a genuine moral struggle. Much depended on the economy of time involved in mobilizing the different facets of personality:

Why does what we call our 'higher nature' so often succumb to the temptations of our 'lower nature,' why do our bodily desires, or our short range impulses, so frequently triumph over our rational self? It is not because, when fairly pitted against one another in a 'moral struggle,' the lower motives prove themselves stronger than the higher. It is because they employ a rush tactics that carries us away before the moral forces of our personality are fully mobilised. The 'irrational' instincts get their work

17 'Democracy, Liberty and Force,' 40
18 *The Conditions of Industrial Peace*, 120

done quicker: the process of reflection and self-realisation involves delay, and this delay is often fatal.[19]

In this light Hobson maintained that the use of force to prevent a recalcitrant from pursuing a selfish course would also provide a breathing space in which the rational self could be mobilized. Once this delay had been gained, Hobson was confident that 'this reasonable self will *itself* enforce a claim for an ... impartial settlement.'[20] Thus Hobson retained the element of choice – albeit a choice made during a period of enforced 'cooling-off' – as the mark of a moral decision. Without the exercise of force, an individual would have difficulty in liberating himself from the desires of his 'lower nature.'

However, what was to be done if the recalcitrant continued to refuse to adhere to the general will was a question left unanswered by Hobson. The fact that the dissenting opinion is seen as being prompted by 'lower motives' would seem logically to lead to a devaluing of the importance of social criticism. Why respect that which is merely irrational or capricious? Yet Hobson is a strong advocate of the right of free speech. 'The right to think wrongly, and to freely express such error,' he insists, 'is justly held to be essential to the process of selection and rejection by which truth is evolved.' Indeed, unorthodox opinions were to be encouraged as a 'necessary safeguard for the vitality of all accepted truths.'[21] Hobson's assumption, then, that the reasonable self would ultimately triumph within the psyche of the dissident, leading him to accept the withdrawal of his 'narrower liberties' by the democratic community, turns out to be a way of avoiding some very awkward problems associated with the idea of forcing men to be free. Was the dissident to be led to a 'higher freedom,' even while his 'earthly body and foolish mind,' to repeat Isaiah Berlin's famous formulation, 'bitterly reject it, and struggle against those who seek however benevolently to impose it'?[22]

Hobson did appreciate that there was some merit in his opponents' case. 'The attribution of values to institutions' rather than just to individuals did involve 'risks.' The general will, no doubt, could become ossified and bureaucratized, and consequently exercise a crippling authority over its constituents. But Hobson was not convinced that 'bureaucracy and conservatism' were 'inherent in associations.'[23] And he suggested that at least part of

19 *Problems of a New World* (1921), 134. See also *Imperialism*, 229.
20 *Problems of a New World*, 135 (emphasis added)
21 Ibid., 71, 72
22 *Four Essays on Liberty*, 134
23 *Wealth and Life*, 35

the explanation for Hobhouse's and MacIver's excessive dread of the group mind was attributable to personal biases in their study of associations:

Two predispositions incline most 'intellectuals' either to reject or to disparage the existence or worth of community sentiment and to regard the feelings, tastes, conscience of individuals as the sole source and arbiter of value. One is the dread of a 'herd-mind' identified with mob rule, disorder and ochlocracy. 'Intellectuals' are essentially introverts, cultivating their separate minds, jealous of spiritual autonomy, and hostile to such coöperation as will expose their minds to mass-suggestion. ... The other is the apprehension of a God-state ... under which either dominant personalities or dogmas exercise a devastating discipline over the private mind. ... [This makes] suspect among free minds, any other values or loyalties, than those of conscious personal choice. Among thinkers there is always a fear of the ruder, more emotional urge of community life. ... These feelings ... colour the view taken by many ... [philosophers] about the nature of community.[24]

The cure for these ills was not the disparagement of community but the greater participation of the masses in politics. A 'crowd' was capable of 'nobler judgments and greater heroism than its average member,'[25] but in order to realize this capacity it was necessary that such groups be democratized. Hobson put great faith in the educative effect of participation. Politics, he insisted, 'is not only a branch of knowledge but of conduct' and in all conduct the 'possession of power and the responsibility attaching to it is of the essence of the educative process. Paradoxical as it seems, you must do a thing before you can know it.' To argue, as some critics did (Hobson mentions no one by name) that the participation of the masses in politics should be delayed until they become more knowledgeable was to fail to appreciate the educative effects of participation. Only by participating could the ordinary citizen 'gain a full incentive to acquire the special information and capacity of judgment' necessary to rationalize the group mind.[26]

---

24 Ibid., 28-9. See also *Confessions*, 71, where Hobson takes advantage of his close friendship with L.T. Hobhouse to suggest that, in large part, it was Hobhouse's personality that made him stress individuation 'as the end and object of all social processes.' Hobhouse apparently was fastidious about exercising personal control 'in all affairs down to the smallest home detail.'

25 *A Modern Outlook* (1910), 313

26 *Towards International Government* (1915), 207

Conversely, Hobson blamed the sham of democracy in his time for the 'disordered sociality of the common man' and his 'craving to think in swarms.'[27] An electorate would remain 'little better than a mob, so long as it is treated like a mob, deprived of all opportunity of sober reflection and judgment upon intelligible issues, and goaded at intervals to orgies of electoral excitement, in which passion, prejudice and sporting instincts are set to determine the representation of the people.'[28]

Hobson thought it necessary to make a number of reforms in the institutions of liberal democracy if these were to provide the heuristic service he had outlined. Among the most notable of these proposals was his advocacy of the referendum. Hobson's interest in the referendum was kindled in the debate that emerged during Asquith's Liberal administration over the reform of the House of Lords. Hobson feared that removing the veto powers of the House of Lords would merely advance the autocracy of the cabinet and its domination over the House of Commons. He therefore proposed that the House of Lords, suitably reformed, and a designated minority in the House of Commons, should have the concurrent power to procure a referendum on important issues. He exempted finance bills on grounds of their complexity, and also certain matters affecting foreign relations, but otherwise considered all issues worthy subjects for direct popular control.[29] Hobson's proposals were also derived from his interesting observation that by the turn of the century elections were increasingly conveying mandates of specific kinds rather than simply endorsing the representative's right to exercise an unfettered judgement. 'By formal pledges, deputations, petitions, the electorate [had] considerably qualified the representative system.' In this light, he argued that the referendum was essentially a way of democratizing this process and thereby helping to protect the public from 'the present illicit or informal operation of the mandate,' which enabled 'small minorities to exert an excessive influence upon the structure of Bills.'[30]

Hobson's advocacy, however, went beyond this classic 'shoe-pinching' argument for democracy as a protective device against 'misfits,' i.e., class legislation.[31] The referendum was intended not only to protect but also to improve the quality of public opinion, by making citizens more responsible for the formulation of key policies.

27 'Character and Society,' in P. Parker, ed., *Character and Life* (1912), 82
28 *The Crisis of Liberalism*, 26
29 Ibid., 38-9
30 Ibid., 35
31 One of the earliest examples of this argument is found in Aristotle's *Politics* (Penguin ed., 1962), 125. Hobson also made use of this metaphor in *The Crisis of Liberalism*, 83.

[The] Referendum is based upon a recognition that no form of representation is perfect, and that certain particular defects ... can best be met by special and direct appeal to the fount of government. ... There is in every people a half-conscious recognition of the fact that the will of the people is not really operative unless it is able to perform concrete acts of government. The instinctive craving for self-realization through responsible conduct is a collective as well as individual feeling. This feeling is not satisfied by the act of choosing a representative once in five or six years. ... As an individual needs the responsibility for concrete acts of conduct in order to maintain and educate his personality, so it is with the collective personality of a nation.[32]

Perhaps equally revealing as to the steadfastness of Hobson's faith in the educative powers of democratic participation was the fact that his own observations on the actual workings of the Swiss referendum indicated numerous examples where the people had voted in an 'ignorant' and 'prejudiced' manner. None the less, he remained convinced that abiding by the popular will was preferable to the alternative of '"faking" ... progress by pushing legislation ahead of the popular will.' Making mistakes was a 'necessary incident in the education of democracy.' For if the public were 'not afforded the opportunity of making mistakes and learning from them, what sort of education,' he asked, 'are they getting, and what sort of progress can they make?' Here was to be found the 'very kernel' of the case for democratic participation, rather than in some 'mystic assumption' that 'the people's will is always wise and just.' It was, then, 'far more profitable for reformers to be compelled to educate the people to a genuine acceptance of their reform than to "work it" by some "pull" or "deal" inside a party machine.'[33]

This argument was initially directed at the Fabians and especially at the élitist schemes of H.G. Wells, but later Hobson was also to use it to good effect in criticizing the vanguard role that the Bolshevik party had claimed for itself by distinguishing, in Hobson's words, the supposed 'real will' of the proletariat, which it intuits, from the 'dumb or biased expression of that will contained in a popular response to an electoral appeal.' This distinction, in Hobson's view, represented 'the curious penetration of Hegelian doctrine into the Marxist philosophy' and was vitiated, as were all élitist doctrines,

---

32 *The Crisis of Liberalism*, 15-16
33 Ibid., 41, 46. Here it is worth repeating that this 'mystic assumption' was not one that Hobson himself always successfully resisted, as the immediately preceding discussion regarding his conception of the 'higher morality' of the general will indicates.

by its assumption that 'the common man has nothing of value to contribute.'[34] It followed that Hobson was willing to support mass involvement in politics even though this might, in the short term, make the pace of reform slower than he would have personally wished.

In addition to calling for the introduction of the referendum, Hobson also sympathized with the much more radical proposal, put forward by Guild Socialists and Syndicalists, to substitute 'industrial' for geographic or residential criteria as the basis of democratic representation. Although he feared syndicalist sectarianism, Hobson saw merit in its forging of stronger ties between industrial groups. He believed that to some extent this would foster the emergence of a general will, though the danger of extremism, as will be made clear later, was never far from his mind:

The real contribution made by [the] ... ferment of Syndicalism and Guild Socialism is towards a radical reformation of the democratic state, by insisting upon a proper representation in it of the productive, or functional, grouping of the people. The failure of democracy is justly attributed in large measure to the fact that residential areas are not in themselves adequate units for the electoral expression of the general will. Neighbourhood is too feeble a bond of interest or of spiritual community. It needs ... to be ... reinforced by the closer community of the workshop, the craft, the profession.[35]

A second major advantage of functional representation, according to Hobson, was that it made clear that political democracy could not be achieved, as earlier reformers like the Chartists had once hoped, without the entanglement of economics: 'industrial servitude' was 'inimical to political liberty.'[36] Hobson pointed to the reaction of the western nations to the Russian revolution and its early experiments in industrial representation as a great object lesson in the significance of this reform:

There [is] one indispensable condition for the harmony between democracy and capitalism. Democracy must be kept political. ... The abolition of all property qualifications, adult suffrage, secret ballot, proportional representation, even the referendum and initiative, the extreme forms of democracy, are easily compatible with the maintenance of a capitalist order in

34 *Democracy and a Changing Civilisation*, 63-4, 76
35 *Democracy after the War*, 176
36 *Work and Wealth*, 220

Society. Property can always make good its defences, provided that the
ultimate basis of representation is locality – that is to say, a basis which
excludes close and effective community of economic interests. ... The
danger of the spread of Bolshevism ... [and] the reason why the Soviet
must be discredited is ... lest our working-class movement should take
from that experiment a certain element of proletarian strength which ...
would be a direct and important challenge to the rights of property. ... That
element ... [is] the admission of functional representation into the processes of government.[37]

In other words, the principle of functional representation drew attention to the
fact that politics alone could not solve the problems of economic inequality.

Of course, this refusal by Hobson to separate politics and economics was
basic to his organic approach; it forced him to define democracy as a 'kind of
society'[38] rather than as a separate set of political institutions and methods, as
later contemporaries of his were wont to do.[39]

Possibly the term and concept 'democracy' by common usage give an
undue prominence to the distinctively political aspect of the movement. ...
But I choose democracy as the expression of ... wider aims, because it
makes the appeal to the power of a self-directing people, operative in industry, in government, and in all other institutions and activities of social life,
as the goal of co-operative endeavour and the instrument for the attainment or support of all the special forms through which the common life
finds expression.[40]

Hobson's remarks on the heuristic merits of democracy, if taken to their
logical conclusion, might be construed as implying the rejection of a system
of representative democracy in favour of direct democracy: for was not the
effect of any lowering of the scope of participation to lessen the opportunities
for ordinary men to learn the arts of collective self-government?

This conclusion, however, seems to be inconsistent with other statements
where Hobson stressed the importance of expert leadership as a logical corollary of his organic theory of society:

37 *Problems of a New World*, 164-5, 170-1
38 On democracy as a kind of society, see C.B. Macpherson, *The Real World of Democracy*
(1965).
39 See, for example, R. Bassett, *The Essentials of Parliamentary Democracy* (1935), and Evan
Durbin, *The Politics of Democratic Socialism* (1940). Both these works criticize specifically
Hobson's conception of democracy.
40 *Democracy after the War*, 153

The popular doctrine, 'One man one vote,' is as a theoretical principle pure undiluted individualism. It rests upon a curious twist in the logic of Equality. Every man's life is worth as much to him as every other man's life. Society consists of all men, therefore every man's life is worth as much to society as every other man's, and every man ought to have the same voice in directing social conduct as every other man.

Now ... that every man's life is of equal value to society, in the sense that it can yield equal social service, is not only false but absurd. ... There is, of course, a sense in which the equal value of life for all is admitted, and is embodied in the equality of all men before the law. But this equality of men as objects of social conduct does not imply a corresponding equality as agents in social conduct. ... The organic view of society entirely repudiates any such equality as a theoretical principle. ... [P]olitical power ought to be distributed in proportion to ability to use it for the public good. ... The true formula of political justice ... [is] 'From each according to his powers.'[41]

Hobson's preferred rule of political justice, then, was founded upon the ancient principle of proportionate rather than absolute equality. Along these lines Hobson suggested that the introduction of a system of proportional representation would be useful in helping to prevent 'the loss to the State of her ablest and most honourable legislators who cannot hope or desire to obtain election under the existing system of polling'; and he further speculated that a 'developed organic Democracy' would have a 'trained body of political specialists,' to 'take over' much of the technical legislative work 'so badly done or so badly left undone by our elective assemblies of legislative amateurs.'[42]

But if some were more competent than others and consequently should be accorded a greater role in politics, then this seemed to raise a certain tension between the principle of participation and the principle of competence. Which was more important for good government? Faced with this dilemma, Hobson tended to give priority to the principle of participation. Not that participation would ever succeed in turning all men into experts, but he trusted that its educative effect would raise the level of understanding sufficiently to enable those who had less to contribute to defer to the rest solely on *rational* grounds:

41 *The Crisis of Liberalism*, 78-80
42 Ibid., 13, 85

The reverence of one who understands, though he may not possess, the superior qualities of one set in authority over him ... is the moral support of [democracy]. ... The education of rational democracy is vital and effective just in so far as it is calculated to evoke and sustain this sentiment.[43]

Underlying Hobson's argument here is the contention that the principle of participation incorporates the principle of competence – it improves *both* the experts and their popular judges – whereas the latter principle has no necessary connection with spreading the level of political awareness or with strengthening the general will. On the contrary, giving too much priority to expertise only enhanced the likelihood of those experts substituting 'the good of their class or calling' for the public good, or, on the off-chance that they remained disinterested, their wisdom none the less would be merely 'the vaporising of theorists unfamiliar with the human stuff whose vital interests they are handling.' Hobson considered this to be the essential wisdom of Lincoln's paradox that 'self government is better than good government.'[44] Ultimately the two were the same, but in the meantime it had to be realized that only the former was genuinely progressive. Lack of competence was an argument for more participation not a reason for postponing it: this was the essential element, according to Hobson, of the democrat's faith.[45]

2 THE ASSAULT ON THE GENERAL WILL: THE FORCES OF IMPROPERTY

The seizure of a large portion of the fruits of ... social productive energies, required for the full support and further stimulation of these energies and for the wider human life they are designed to serve, and their assignment to persons who have not helped to make them, do not need them, and cannot use them ... [stamps] the badge of irrationality [on the system] ... and impairs that spirit of human confidence and that consciousness of human solidarity ... which are the best stimuli of individual and social progress. *Work and Wealth*, 187-8

When Hobson attempted to link his analysis of the general will more closely to contemporary society, he found that capitalism was a very contradictory

43 *John Ruskin* (1898), 205
44 *The Crisis of Liberalism*, 84; *Democracy and a Changing Civilisation*, 77
45 Hobson, of course, was not the first liberal to discover this tension between participation and competence, although it was not usual to resolve it in favour of participation. An interesting discussion of these two principles, based on an examination of J.S. Mill's writings on politics, is found in Dennis F. Thompson, *John Stuart Mill and Representative Government* (1976). See also Carole Pateman, *Participation and Democratic Theory* (1970).

force with regard to the strengthening of democracy. At its most auspicious, capitalism had helped promote the growth of democracy by forging the objective conditions of a socialized life:

> Where masses of men are ... associated for work and life, there exist the best conditions for the emergence and the operation of that sane collective will and judgment which, in the sphere of politics, constitutes the spirit of a progressive democracy. ... There is ... a half-instinctive, half-conscious drive of collective wisdom, set up by associated working class life which the needs of modern capitalistic production have established, a genuine spirit of the people, however incomplete in its expression, which makes for political righteousness ... [and the] learning [of] the art called democracy.[46]

By pulling people into factories, dividing their labour so as to make each dependent on the other, capitalism had provided the groundwork for the growth of the democratic spirit. Ironically, this meant that even the failings of capitalism could be viewed as a positive force for collective action and co-operation. How long, for example, could the 'ideology of self-blame' be imposed upon the unemployed individual, when he witnessed hundreds, even thousands, of his fellows being thrown out of work daily as a result of the vagaries of the trade cycle? Economic crises would provide the masses with a practical lesson in collectivist logic: 'social evils require social remedies.'[47] Similarly, Hobson argued that the concentration of capital, 'while it breeds and aggravates the diseases of trade depression,' also facilitated the work of 'social control,' since it would be easier 'to inspect a few large factories than many small ones.'[48]

But countervailing tendencies were at work within capitalism frustrating this potential for joint action under a common will. Thus Hobson observed that 'this socialisation [was] far more advanced in objective fact than in thought and feeling.'[49] While capitalism had socialized society, it had failed to socialize man.

The reasons for this were various. In large part Hobson saw the dilemma as being endemic to the competitive market system. First, production for exchange rather than for use, that is, production for the general market, presented a powerful obstacle to the 'realisation of the social meaning of industry':

---

46 'The General Election: A Sociological Interpretation,' *Sociological Review* (1910), 116-17
47 *John Ruskin*, 199
48 *The Evolution of Modern Capitalism* (1894), 359
49 *Work and Wealth*, 26

When a man made a watch or a pair of shoes and sold them to his neighbour, or known customer, his work had for him a distinct human significance. For, making the whole of a thing, he realised its nature and utility, while, seeing the man who wore his watch or shoes, he realised the human value of his work. Now [with the growing sub-division of labour and related expansion of markets] ... he performs one of some ninety processes which go to make many watches, or he trims the heels of innumerable shoes. The other processes he cannot do, and does not accurately know how they are done. His separate contribution has no clear utility, and yet it solely occupies his attention. Not only does he thus lose grasp of the meaning of his work, but he has no opportunity of realising its consumptive utility. For he cannot know or care anything about the unknown person in some distant part of the world who shall wear the boots or the watch he helped make. The social sympathy of coöperative industry is thus atrophied by the conditions of his work.[50]

Second, the fact that this production for the market was done under the whip of competition only enhanced the process of fragmentation and derationalization. Competition resulted in 'moral waste,' because it undid the bonds of fraternity.

The real gravamen of the charge [against competition] rests on a distinctively moral assumption. If, as the defenders of the competitive trade system assert, the system is in essence and in result co-operative, and designed to serve the industrial system as a whole, can that end be satisfactorily attained by a procedure which concentrates the will of each human unit not upon that end, not even upon a clearly recognised means to that end, but upon a purely selfish consideration which entirely eliminates the social service?

The moral economy of the business consists in the more or less conscious co-operation of all the wills engaged in it towards a common end; the moral economy of the trade is supposed to consist in the conscious opposition of the wills engaged in it. Surely there must here be involved a huge waste of moral force ...?[51]

50 Ibid., 250
51 *The Industrial System* (1909; 2nd ed., 1910), 317. See also *Work and Wealth*, 251, where he views the capitalist system as it is represented in the thought of the classical economists and asserts that 'No graver injury has been inflicted on the mind of man, in the name of science, than the pre-potence which the early science of Political Economy assigned to the competitive and combative aspects of industrial life.'

The capitalist mode of production with its round-about, even anarchic, method of delivering the goods and its stimulation of selfish and combative instincts resulted in the atrophy of a more conscious sense of community. Nor did cartels or their like improve this moral situation. Although monopoly displaced competition within certain trades, the 'dominant motive' in all such combinations was still the consideration of private profit; consequently there was still 'no security that any public utility in the wider sense [was] served.'[52] Hobson would have no truck with theories of what has come to be termed the 'soulful corporation,' the notion of corporations becoming less selfish and more socially responsible.[53]

On the contrary, from a slightly different perspective, Hobson argued that the trend within capitalism was for the firm to become increasingly soul-less as the cash nexus in the big corporations replaced the more personal ties of the small family business:

'Compagnie Anonyme' is the significant French name for a Jointstock Company with its unknown shareholders. But this depersonalising process is everywhere inseparable from the magnitude and intricacy of modern business. ... The capital belonging to a crowd of persons, who are strangers to one another, is massed into an effective productive aggregate, and is set to coöperate with masses of labour power whose owners are divorced from all direct contact, either with the owners of the tools and material, or with the purchasers of the product. ... A great modern business is in its structure less effectively human than was the small workshop which it displaced.[54]

Both capitalists and workers, then, were becoming the 'mere functionaries of economic categories,' the outcome of which was the generation of feelings of impotence and dejection.

But if competition weakened the spirit of fraternity, it also did great damage to that other principle of the 'democratic trinity' – equality.[55] And this likewise forestalled the growth of a general will under capitalism:

52 *The Industrial System*, 319
53 *Rationalisation and Unemployment* (1930), 89-90. One of the earliest exponents of this
   view was the American economist Simon Patten, with whose work Hobson was familiar.
   For a brief outline of Patten's views, see E.K. Hunt, *Property and Prophets* (1972), 111-13.
54 *Work and Wealth*, 252
55 With reference to the third member of this trinity – liberty   – it has already been shown
   that Hobson believed that competition had advanced liberty in its negative aspect but not
   positively.

The chief argument for economic and political democracy, for equality of opportunity, is that it is essential to enable every man and woman to attain ... [self-respect]. For self-respect and all that it implies ... is not consistent with the existence of castes of over-men and under-men; the pride generated from the one condition is as remote from true self-respect as the servility which marks the other. ... [It] is only the self-respecting man who respects his fellows; it is only he who feels he gets his due that is solicitous and exact in seeing that others get their due. Such a man alone has educated in him a sense of social justice unembittered by personal grievance and extended by sympathy towards others ... A man living with self-respect in the society of his equals, husband and wife equal within the home, equal opportunities in industry and education, his social instincts no longer maimed by the selfish struggle between individual and individual, nation and nation, would for the first time be free to express his social sympathies. ... Until such conditions are ripe for such a life the ideal personality cannot be born.[56]

When an individual is denied the opportunity for self-development, this is not only a personal tragedy but also a social tragedy, for it is unlikely that a frustrated, embittered individual will commit himself to the common good. He is too swayed by what Rousseau termed *amour-propre*, a sense of envy born of a lack of self-respect. To Hobson, therefore, it seemed evident that political democracy was 'almost empty of value without economic democracy in the sense of equal access to the use of all the factors of production.'[57] Without this opportunity, an individual cannot fully develop his potential, know himself, and thereby gain that self-respect which Hobson saw as the prerequisite of him respecting others.

Hobson's final and perhaps weightiest indictment of capitalism was its irrationality. Irrationality was inimical to the emergence of a general will. This did not mean that the general will was a pure intellectual construct. As has been shown, Hobson thought that the basis of the general will was located in man's organic instincts. However, it did mean that some correlation, a *quid pro quo*, had to exist between the effort of willing the social good and the effect, if this social instinct were to be properly nurtured. Capitalism destroyed that link. It did so primarily by making property a matter of plunder or power, rather than a reward for work:

56 'Character and Society,' 65-6, 102
57 *Confessions* (1938), 176

The rational basis of the acquisition of property is the 'natural' relation of effort to satisfaction. ... So a society where force or fraud habitually or frequently displaces this sane process of acquiring property, where some persons eat bread *sudore vittus alieni* and others consequently sweat without eating, is not only economically enfeebled, but is irrationally constituted. And this unreason in the social organism corrupts and derationalises the individual members.[58]

The capitalist system of apportionment was but one remove from gambling, and it was to be expected, therefore, that like gambling it too would operate in an atmosphere riddled with omens, taboos, and prejudices. The social will could not breathe in an atmosphere so permeated by chance:

Distributive justice appeals not only to good feeling, but also to reason. When a man gets wealth by some lucky turn of the wheel of fortune, or by some sudden *coup*, some brave display of advertisement, or even by gift or inheritance, our reason is not satisfied, *we are affected by a sense of insufficient causation*. Similarly when a hard-working man is unable to earn enough to keep his family in decency ... we feel that the economic system is out of joint and operates irrationally. ... A sound conception of Ethical Democracy requires that the vague feeling of unfairness ... shall become a definite sense of injustice.[59]

The irrationality of capitalism was attested to in other ways. 'Chance and fraud,' 'bulling and bearing,' 'rings and corners,' and manipulation of all kinds assisted in defeating 'the reasonable uses of a money market.'[60] The insecurity of the trade cycle generated among many a feeling of 'harassing and impotent anxiety,' as they awaited their fate at the hands of forces apparently beyond their control: 'the chance and hazards of modern business' were the 'negation of rational free choice.'[61] Modern advertising was a 'liberal education in unreason,' inflicting upon the public the 'derationalising and humiliating process of being made a victim to a lie.' In sum, capitalism meant that the citizen's life was subject to a myriad of 'utterly incalculable

58 'The Ethics of Gambling,' *International Journal of Ethics*, vol. 15 (1905), 136-7
59 'The Ethics of Industrialism,' in S. Coit, ed., *Ethical Democracy* (1900), 94, 101 (emphasis added)
60 Ibid., 95
61 *Democracy and a Changing Civilisation*, 86

blows of fortune' and this alienating condition undermined 'all directly educative forces to rationalise' the general will.[62]

3 CUI BONO?

Sixty years ago 'they' were foolishly afraid of popular franchise. They know better
now. Experience has taught them that the working-class movement in politics is
innocuous, so long as the mind it expresses is the mind of a mob. 'Their' party
machinery, their press, their handling of political and social events have, therefore, been continually directed to making and preserving a mob-mind, sensational,
fluid, indeterminate, short-sighted, credulous, disunited. In such a mentality there
is no will of the people, no effective common sense. *Democracy and a Changing
Civilisation*, 105

Hobson's list of those groups who benefited from the denigration of the
community spirit was fairly typical of that of left-oriented radicals of his time.
At the centre of what he termed 'the circle of reaction' were the capitalists,
landlords, and the military. These were the major forces of 'improperty.' In
the outer circle stood a motley collection of imperialists, protectionists,
bureaucrats, authoritarians (mainly located in the 'ideological apparatus' of
society, i.e., the schools, the church, and the press), the judiciary, and the
purveyors of various 'opiates' – brewers and the organizers of charity and
sports.[63]
    The structural support of the two most prominent elements in this circle of
reaction – the capitalists and the landlords – has already been described in
earlier chapters of this study. The third element, the military, came to play a
significant part in Hobson's analysis as a result of his reflections on the origins of the First World War. In Hobson's opinion the war exposed a close
identity of interest between capitalism and militarism. Capitalism made militarism both possible and necessary.
    Historically, capitalism had been a boon to the military:

Though armed forces ... have always been part of the equipment of government, the poverty of nations until recent times made it impossible to
keep any large proportion of a nation in expensive idleness for work of
destruction, still less to train the whole manhood of a nation for armed
national service. ... It is significant that the practice of maintaining great

---

62 'The Ethics of Industrialism,' 95-6
63 *Democracy after the War*, 146-9

standing armies spread throughout the European system at the very time when 'the industrial revolution' was beginning to make ... [its] way.[64]

The military, then was dependent upon the surpluses that capitalism generated; it was these that made modern militarism possible. On the other hand, the mode in which these surpluses were created generated sufficient domestic and international conflict to make military might a necessity to capitalism. It was a relationship of mutual interdependence. In this light Hobson thought it necessary to reject the assumption of 'Cobdenism and ... the liberalism to which it appertained,' namely that 'war and militarism were doomed to disappear with the advance of industry and commerce.' Instead, Hobson placed the armed forces alongside the forces of impropery at the centre of the reactionary movement.[65]

In 1910 Hobson supplemented this structural analysis of the central forces of 'impropery' by providing a psephological account of their strengths. The general election of 1910 gave him the opportunity to search out the men of property so as to determine their numbers, where they lived, what kinds of occupation they pursued, and which political issues excited their anger or approbation. The results of this study were read by Hobson in a paper before the Sociological Society in February 1910.[66] According to one historian of the discipline of sociology, Hobson's paper marked 'a new departure in British social analysis.' It was the first time that a systematic attempt had been made to 'interpret gross turn-out and party preference data in terms of class and regional variations.[67] To use an over-worked piece of Victorianism, Hobson may be considered the 'Father of modern voting-studies.'

The metaphor of a circle of reaction was carefully chosen by Hobson. It was meant to convey the idea that each of these 'interests' was in 'direct community' or 'sympathy' with every other member of the circle, and that eventually all roads led back to the economic taproot of the system: exploitation. Hobson was careful, however, not to lapse into a simplistic conspiracy theory of politics. Capitalist rule was not that transparent. Even financiers and industrialists, who were in the best position, according to Hobson, to manipulate affairs according to their wishes, were 'neither clever enough nor unscrupulous enough to invent and arrange all the elaborate political, moral

---

64 Ibid., 28-9
65 Ibid., 29
66 This paper was later published in the *Sociological Review* (1910) entitled 'The General Election: A Sociological Interpretation.'
67 Philip Abrams, *The Origins of British Sociology* (1968), 228

and intellectual apparatus of the reactionary alliance.'[68] To an important
extent, the overlapping of these other interests was an unintended coinci-
dence. From this Hobson drew what was in effect a distinction between the
manifest and the latent aspects of class rule:

The absence of conscious solidarity and continuity of purpose in these
principles of reaction ... [may be] attributed in part to the fact that *each has
a special outlook and interest of its own and conceives itself as using the others
for its own ends*. The simplest instance is the interplay between the political party leader and the financial and industrial magnate, in which the
former blackmails the latter to fill the party purse which is his instrument
of political and personal importance, while the latter views the same trans-
action as one which gives him a hold upon the party policy. ... This difference in the *direct* purpose of the co-operative forces conceals the meaning
and obscures the actual facts of cooperation.
    Still more is this the case when we are dealing with the auxiliary and
secondary forces of reaction. ... [For example] the great and highly elaborated machinery of sport and amusements ... is organised in order to
stimulate and exploit the tastes of the people, it is not concerned with the
reactions upon the cause of democracy produced by the sedatives and dis-
tractions it supplies.[69]

This was, in effect, a 'hidden-hand' theory of conspiracy. At one level the
competition and conflict in interests between various political, economic,
and social élites was genuine, while at another level it was spurious, for its
ultimate result was altogether different: it effected 'a subtle and powerful
conspiracy ... to defend class power and to defeat democracy.'[70]
    It is regrettable that Hobson did not examine the workings of this hidden
hand in politics as closely as he had examined Adam Smith's version of it in
classical economics. To speak of an 'unintended' conspiracy is probably a
misnomer, but more important Hobson did not explain why he assumed
that, for the most part, the unforeseen consequences of this competition
between élites would be always beneficial to the long-term interests of the
forces of reaction as a whole. Hobson did suggest, however, that the conspiracy was strengthened precisely because some of its members were not aware
of the wider ramifications of their actions and hence not conscious of their
complicity:

68 *Democracy after the War*, 101
69 Ibid., 131-3 (emphasis added)
70 Ibid., 133

The vulgar imputations of hypocrisy sometimes brought against the
Church, the universities, the 'capitalist' Press, as conscious willing tools of
property and class rule ... [are] false. ... A Tory or sham Liberal politician
might have a notion that he was in politics to protect property and privi-
lege and might do his work none the worse. But it is essential to the reactionary role of the Church that its clergy should be blind to the play of the
reactionary influences, as it is to the reactionary role of the universities
that their teachers should feel themselves to be genuine and single-
minded devotees of disinterested culture. *Open-eyed hypocrisy would spoil
them for the reactionary service.*[71]

The fact that the circle of reaction was to some degree built upon ignorance rather than clear-sighted collusion was part of its strength, but this
advantage could also be turned against it. As the next section will show,
Hobson believed that those groups who were genuinely deceived as to the
larger role they played, if properly approached, could help social reformers
break the circle of reaction.

4 THE CHALLENGE TO IMPROPERTY: A COMMON FRONT OF PROGRESSIVE FORCES

Industrial war seems to follow the same law of change as military war. As the
incessant bickering of private guerilla war has given way in modern times to occasional large, organised, brief and terribly destructive campaigns, so it is in trade. ...
The dread of these dramatic lessons is growing ever greater, and the tendency to
postponement and conciliation grows apace. *Problems of Poverty*, 221

For Hobson the 'general will' originated in the mass of the people, not in any
particular group, class, or other section of it. There were no special cadres of
the common will, no particular interest that could be considered the embry-
onic form of the universal interest. As will become evident, however, Hobson did believe that under certain circumstances the 'more mobile elements'
in society could play a crucial role in mediating between the sectional view-
points of the major social classes. In this regard Hobson's position is not
unlike that of Karl Mannheim's, as presented in his well-known work, *Ideology and Utopia*; indeed, Hobson is sometimes mentioned as a precursor of
Mannheim.[72]

71 Ibid., 134 (emphasis added)
72 See Louis Wirth, 'Preface' to Karl Mannheim, *Ideology and Utopia* (1936), xvi.

For a brief moment around the turn of the century, Hobson foresaw the possibility of a significant section of the Liberal party severing its connection with the wealthy bourgeoisie and taking its remaining lower-middle-class supporters into a fruitful alliance with the trade unions, then freshly politicized under the impact of the Taff Vale judgement. In the *Echo* of October 1901, Hobson argued that this 'new party' would rally members around the issues of anti-imperialism and social reform. The new party was to be less sectional than the established parties. Hobson pitched his appeal at the ILP rather than the newly formed Labour Representation Committee, which was probably a tactical mistake. The ILP's initial response was cool but not hostile. However, with the ending of the Boer War the consensus among radicals weakened and Hobson's proposals came to nothing.[73] Indeed, not only was the old *ad hoc* co-operation between the ILP and the Liberals not solidified in the manner Hobson had hoped, but in 1906 the Labour party declared itself fully independent of the Liberal party, although for several years thereafter it continued to seek electoral accommodations with the latter.

Even though Hobson himself was later to leave the Liberals in 1916, subsequently to join the Labour party in 1924, he was never convinced that the Labour party was the proper instrument of social reform. In his autobiography Hobson wrote that he had 'never felt quite at home in a body governed by trade union members and their finances and intellectually led by full-blooded Socialists.'[74] What Hobson disliked about the Labour movement was its sectarianism. As he stated as early as 1899:

Even were the recurrent dream of a federation of all trade-unions in a nation, or even in the industrial world, so realised as to secure the most powerful solidarity of labour, *we should still be confronted by a 'class' situation of this social problem*. It is sometimes urged that, since society ought to demand and to receive labour from all according to their capacity, such a solidarity in the labour movement would be genuine socialism. But, taking labour movements and labour parties as present economic and political factors, that ideal identification is not realised. As a present fact, the labour movement, even in its widest significance, is distinctively a class movement, though comprising the largest and perhaps the most deserving class, and, as such, *must simply be regarded as the largest form of individualism*. Neither the workshop, nor the trade, nor the working class as a whole can be considered to have a claim upon the 'whole product of labour.'[75]

73 Cf. Philip Poirier, *The Advent of the Labour Party* (1958), 177-8
74 *Confessions*, 126
75 'Of Labour,' in J. Hand, ed., *Good Citizenship* (1899), 104-5 (emphasis added)

Hobson consistently held to this position for the next forty years.[76] Thus, while Hobson was active within the Labour party, he was not devoted to it. He was constantly looking to see how its policies would react upon other 'progressive forces,' and in particular the lower middle class and professional groups. As late as 1938 Hobson was seriously contemplating the likelihood of a Lib-Lab coalition, on the grounds that such a coalition would be closer 'to the average electoral mind than any full-blown Socialism.'[77]

Nor did these so-called 'full-blooded' socialists and trade unionists, it must be added, always feel comfortable with Hobson. Ernest Bevin, for example, publicly criticized Hobson for an article published in the *New Leader*, in 1924, in which Hobson charged that the recent strike activity of the unions – undertaken during Ramsay MacDonald's first Labour government – was evidence of their pursuing a 'separatist policy' hostile to socialism. Bevin replied, in effect, that Hobson and other like-minded liberals were the hostile element for preaching a community interest where there was none, and for asking trade unionists to overlook present injustices in the hope that sometime in the future a more perfected scheme of industrial relations could be evolved. 'Were we to sit and theorise,' said Bevin, 'as to the action we will take someday when our machinery is perfected we should never get the machinery, nor would there exist the spirit to utilize such machinery were it available.'[78]

Imperfectly aligned with the Labour party, Hobson was even further out of jar with the two other important radical movements of his time, syndicalism and guild socialism. Both of these movements rejected 'parliamentary socialism' in favour of 'industrial socialism,' using the factory as their basic unit of organization and direct action through strikes, industrial sabotage, and so on, as their primary means of protest. Both movements manifested a strong distaste for the state, portraying it as an oppressive Leviathan in the service of the capitalist class, and argued either for its complete abolition or at least for a severe curtailment of its authority. In its place they favoured a markedly decentralized association of producers' guilds or syndicates.

Hobson viewed this rejection of the state in favour of the factory as a stride towards an even greater sectarianism than he had found within the Labour party. He detected among the writings of the syndicalists and guild socialists many of the same fallacies that had earlier led liberals to discredit the state in

76 See, for example, 'Thoughts on our Present Discontents,' *Political Quarterly* (1938), 53, where he wrote that 'the formal Socialism' of the Labour party served as a 'mere screen' for the 'group separatism' of the trade unions.
77 *Confessions*, 125
78 Ernest Bevin, *The Record* (April 1924). Quoted in Alan Bullock, *The Life and Times of Ernest Bevin:* I, *Trade Union Leader 1881-1940* (1960), 243

favour of a policy of *laissez-faire* or self-help. They seemed to assume, for example, that the general interest could be arrived at simply by aggregating the separate interests of all the individual trades:

But the ordering of industry upon a basis of perfect trade-unionism, each trade being independent and exercising full control over the profits of industry, is subject to precisely similar criticism to that which condemned co-partnership upon the scale of the single competing business. A trade taken by itself has interests distinct from, and discordant with, the interests of other trades and of society, and trade individualism is not to be recognised as an ultimate social order. ... Industry is not a mere aggregate of separate trades, and a solution based upon the supposition that it is remains basically unsound.[79]

Hobson thus saw a striking parallel between 'anarcho-syndicalism' and the ideology of liberal capitalism. Both agreed that the common good would emerge spontaneously from the striving of separately organized trades. In this sense, syndicalism was less a negation of capitalism than its inverted reflection.[80]

Hobson also asserted that the narrowness of syndicalist ideology was evident in its failure to represent the worker in any regard other than his interest as a producer. Syndicalism thus ignored the more general and varied interests a person has as a consumer:

The producer's tendency to restrict output and raise prices ... so injuring the consumer, is not adequately met by the consideration that in such a society as we are contemplating [i.e., where non-productive classes have been eliminated] all producers would also be consumers. The trouble is that the proletariat will continue to realise its interests more clearly as producers than as consumers, and it will be far more strongly organised [under syndicalism] to enforce them.[81]

This criticism had less applicability to the guild socialists since they did plan to set up a consumers' council to safeguard these interests. However,

79 'Of Labour,' 104
80 It is noteworthy a recent assessment of workers' control in Yugoslavia by Svetozar Stojanovic has many similarities with Hobson's earlier critique of syndicalism. See Stojanovic, *Between Ideals and Reality* (1973), esp. chap. VI, 'Self-Government in a Socialist Community.'
81 *Democracy after the War*, 174-5

Hobson discerned within these schemes for a consumers council a bias towards the continuous enlargement of self-government in industry, preventing guild socialists from granting sufficient powers to the council so as to enable it to exercise a genuine suzerainty over the economic realm. The guild socialists preferred to speak in terms of 'coordinate powers' between the guild's council and the consumers' council,[82] but for Hobson this merely conjured up the ominous image of an 'intra-national Balance of Power fraught with the same defects and dangers as the international Balance of Power.'[83]

It has been shown already that Hobson did not reject outright the concept of functional representation embodied in guild socialist and syndicalist schemes. Indeed, even after the enthusiasm of radicals for functional representation began to ebb, Hobson still advocated the idea. Thus in 1934 he continued to insist, as against the Webbs (who, as prototypical parliamentary socialists, once characterized guild socialism as meaning railways for the railwaymen and sewers for the sewermen) that a functional assembly was essential if liberal democracy was to be properly equipped for the new economic role demanded of it.[84]

Hobson's own proposals for a 'national industrial council' included the provision that it be 'invested with certain regulative and administrative powers for the realisation of the common good of industry.[85] It was not to be a merely consultative body. Hobson did not detail the division of functions to be undertaken by this council and by Parliament, and in this regard his blue print was perhaps even less clear than those of the guild socialists and syndicalists, but as to the division of powers he was adamant: final determinative power, even in 'strictly' economic matters, had to reside in Parliament:

The term 'general will' may be difficult of definition and of application, but it must in some form stand at the back of all government which deserves the name social. In other words, *a new industrial order cannot dispense with the ultimate sovereignty of the State.* Society cannot live on separate functions which are not functions of any organism but run 'upon their own.' There must be some body competent to compare the respective claims of the several industries, and this body must represent the

82 See, for example, G.D.H. Cole, *Guild Socialism Re-Stated* (1920).
83 *Democracy after the War*, 175-6
84 *Democracy and a Changing Civilisation*, 95
85 *Incentives in the New Industrial Order* (1922), 156

citizen-consumers, for only in their lives and welfare do the claims under consideration find an organic contact. ... As a producer, a man performs one single economic function; as consumer, he brings into personal unity and harmony the ends of all the economic functions. That is why in the new Social Order a consumers' State is entitled to direct the flow of new productive power into the several industrial channels and to form a final court of appeal. ...[86]

Hobson buttressed this argument by pointing to the 'recent Communist experiment in Russia,' where it had been found necessary for the Communist party to 'wield [the] full powers of the political state' in order to co-ordinate and direct economic tasks. Hobson considered it significant that the Bolsheviks, who in the early days of the Revolution supported the workers' control movement, had 'not sought to displace [the political] State by a distinctively economic organisation.[87] And, indeed, as Margaret Cole has pointed out, it was the realization that workers' control had failed in the USSR that ultimately 'spelt the end of guild socialism as an organised movement.[88]

Hobson did not deny that the guild socialists and the syndicalists had good reason to be disappointed with the experiment in parliamentary socialism. Thus in a spate of harsh indictments he concurred that Labour MPs were often 'drugged or outwitted in the game of politics,' and were largely impotent before 'a Cabinet absolute in its control of legislation.' Perhaps more significant, Hobson accepted the syndicalist and guild socialist argument that capitalist rule had always been to a large extent 'extra-Parliamentary.' In this light he contended that the selection of a 'few labour leaders' for positions in the Board of Trade, or the appointment of a handful of workmen to the magisterial (sic) bench did not constitute a 'real check on class government.'[89] But the answer to these problems, in Hobson's opinion, was not to be found in 'negating' the state: 'Whatever may be the vices of a capitalist state, there was only one remedy,' and that was 'to convert it into a democratic state.'[90]

Again, the guild socialists and syndicalists showed a 'sectional bias' that was inappropriate for this task. Interestingly, Hobson did not find fault in their advocacy of 'direct action' tactics as such. A certain initiative of this kind from below was essential. Moreover, if this pressure was militant, even

---

86 Ibid., 149-51
87 *Wealth and Life*, 379
88 *The Story of Fabian Socialism*, 185
89 *Problems of a New World*, 169, 170
90 *Democracy after the War*, 173

violent, Hobson was none the less willing to condone it, at least to an extent quite untypical of liberal thinkers. One explanation for this is that Hobson had never found much cause for assuming that power-holders could be convinced to leave their positions of power solely on the basis of reasoned argument and moral suasion. Thus, as early as 1898, Hobson had criticized Ruskin's plea that the 'captains of industry' become more chivalrous in their relations with the workers, on the grounds that there were 'two formidable barriers' to such voluntary conversion:

In the first place ... these captains [must be convinced] that their present conduct is 'dishonest.' At present the vast majority of them are satisfied that, in taking all the ... emoluments they can get, and in spending them for their private purposes, they are strictly 'within their rights.' ... Any one who has ever tried to persuade another of the wrongfulness of any conduct consecrated by long use and concealed within a vast network of complex action, will be convinced of the impracticability of this method of reform. ... In the next place, even were it possible to put the injustice of their present conduct plainly before our 'captains,' the generation of 'honest' motives out of mere intellectual conviction is by general admission extremely difficult: it is all the difference between seeing the right and doing it, when the doing implies a complete abandonment of a customary and agreeable line of conduct. ... Such a reversal of the whole spirit of ... [rule] cannot be effected by arguments or moral appeals.[91]

Physical pressure, therefore, had its legitimate place in any movement for reform. Hobson refused to put himself alongside 'the moral absolutionists who would cast away all carnal weapons, trusting to the sword of the spirit.'[92]
   Nevertheless, Hobson concluded that the tactics of the syndicalists and guild socialists were badly misdirected. They placed too much emphasis on the role of force or direct action. Such hopes, in Hobson's opinion, were dashed against the simple fact that the superior wealth and arms of the propertied classes, operating through the 'class-state,' made them 'impregnable ... against assault from without.'[93] Militant socialists, therefore, could not go it alone; they required additional help. Here Hobson reverted to his discussion of the role of reason in the process of social change:

There is no ground for believing that an effective transformation of our social economic system can be achieved by any available muster of prole-

91   *John Ruskin*, 197-8
92   *Problems of a New World*, 206
93   Ibid., 203

tarian force, unaccompanied by some such organised endeavour to convert, detach and win over a considerable number of the present allies of reaction. *Proletarian force unaccompanied by an appeal to reason, will consolidate resistance.* ... The threat of physical coercion, either by armed violence or by the direct action of a general strike, paralyses all the *latent liberalism* in the classes and welds them into a stiff, unyielding body, using for their successful defence the better equipped forces which wealth, prestige and superior generalship place at their disposal.[94]

This was written close on the heels of the Russian revolution. Hobson, however, considered the Russian case to be 'the exception that proves the rule';[95] it was an incredible product of the Great War and therefore he did not regard it as contravening his thesis as to the general impregnability of the ruling classes.

It is clear that Hobson put most of the responsibility for avoiding violent confrontations on the working class, that is, he assumed that the ruling class would not resort to authoritarian methods unless attacked by proletariat. However, it is noteworthy that Hobson sometimes proposed a contrary thesis, namely that in times of economic depression, the bourgeoisie was likely to *initiate* an attack on workers' rights, regarding these as concessions they could no longer afford.[96] This would seem to imply that the strategy of the workers in times of economic depression should be different from that pursued during a period of economic prosperity. In the former situation there was less onus on the workers to act moderately. Although Hobson did not develop this point, other thinkers, like Harold Laski, and G.D.H. Cole, who were similarly impressed by the events of the Depression, were to reach the same conclusion, and on this basis argue that a concessions policy was no longer appropriate as a strategy for labour.[97]

These considerations aside, Hobson appeared convinced that, if the working class did moderate their tactics, this could only help advance their cause. In order to do this, however, it was necessary for them to reject the 'vulgar notion,' propagated by narrow-minded sectarians like the syndicalists, that 'the plutocracy and the bourgeoisie were solidly united in a clear determination to keep down and exploit the proletariat.'[98] Such cynicism clouded the

---

94 Ibid., 207-8 (emphasis added)
95 *Democracy after the War* (1st ed.), 58
96 *Democracy and a Changing Civilisation*, 35. See also *Traffic in Treason* (1914), passim.
97 See, for example, Laski's critique of Fabian socialism on this basis in *The Rise of European Liberalism* (1936), 157-61. For Cole, see A.W. Wright, *G.D.H. Cole and Socialist Democracy* (1979), 164-75.
98 *Democracy after the War* (4th ed., 1919), 135

fact that there were elements within the ruling élites who were not conscious of their reactionary role, and given the right circumstances and prodding, these elements could be persuaded to desert their class:

It is necessary to sap the intellectual and moral defences of the enemy.
[But] this can only be done assuming that they are for the most part honest and well-meaning men, genuinely deceived as to the inner meaning
and effects of the services they render to reaction, and by getting them to
see the truths which have been hidden from them in the complicated
folds of modern structures. ... I do not mean that this new Appeal to
Reason among the ... auxiliaries of reaction can at all dispense with the
organisation of democratic forces among subject classes, or even with the
necessity of a bitter struggle which may take the form and substance of a
class war. But success in that struggle will depend not more upon the
organisation of the forces of democracy than upon the disorganisation of
the forces of reaction. And this latter achievement depends upon the
strength and skill of the Appeal to Reason. This is the special service
which the scattering of intellectuals, deserters from the upper class and
bourgeois creeds, is best capable of rendering to the cause of democracy.
For they have liberated themselves and can therefore help liberate
others.[99]

An appeal to reason, then, still had the capability to break through class
barriers and settle conflicts on a basis of justice and humanity. Certainly as
regards to the inner core of the ruling class, the 'captains of industry,' concessions would have to be forcibly wrested from them. But there were also
'more sensitive and mobile minds' among the bourgeoisie, who were susceptible to reason. New Liberals – 'deserters from bourgeois creeds' – could
deliver these potential allies of the proletariat, provided the workers broke
with socialist sectarians preaching a 'superficial psychology' and an 'intransi-
gent' sociology. There were, in Hobson's opinion, 'whole groups' among the
educated classes – teachers, clergy, journalists, artists – who could be 'deeply
touched by the ideal of a juster and better social order.' Perhaps even more
significant, there were many 'managers, inventors, scientific and business
experts' who were beginning to realize the wastes of an economic system
that rewarded ownership rather than productive service.[100] In a common
front with New Liberals, the working class could use 'the sword of the spirit'
to 'wound and weaken the self-confidence of the garrison' by impressing

99   Ibid., 135, 137
100 *Problems of a New World*, 210

upon these groups the reasonableness and justice of their cause.[101] This strategy had to be installed as a primary consideration in the tactics of revolution, for it was the only way to inhibit the bourgeoisie's recourse to force, otherwise undertaken with a conviction born of self-righteousness.

Clearly Hobson believed that he had determined a fruitful middle course between a revolutionary socialism, which tended to be counter-productive, and the truth of the warning he had earlier given orthodox liberals, that 'small remedies for great diseases do not produce small results: they produce no results.'[102]

5 SELECTIVE SOCIALISM:
A REFORM PROGRAM FOR A PROGRESSIVE FRONT

If democracy is to have a chance of winning, it can only be by the union of all those genuinely progressive forces which have hitherto acted apart. ... [Then] we shall for the first time begin to realise that hitherto baffling hope which has deluded several generations of democrats, the power of numbers. Democracy has never yet had this power; its friends as well as its enemies have always succeeded in dividing the mass mind and the mass energy, by canalizing it into innumerable feeble, isolated or conflicting channels. *Democracy after the War*, 153-4

The central aim of Hobson's reform program was to redistribute the 'unproductive surplus.' He saw this surplus as the cause of underconsumption crises and as the source of irrationality in capitalism, which inhibited the growth of a social will and prevented citizens from attending to their social welfare. At the same time, however, Hobson wanted to eliminate this unproductive surplus in a way that was sufficiently discriminatory so as not to push the middle class into a reactionary bloc with the propertied classes. In Hobson's estimation, each of these problems found its solution in an analysis of the 'incentive to produce':

The true [socialist] case lies, not in an insistence that labour is the sole source of wealth, still less in the narrow meaning of labour which excludes and disparages brain work, but in a clear, informed insistence upon the wasteful application of the incentives applied [under capitalism] to evoke all the best physical and intellectual powers of production in their rightful proportions and combinations. The wasteful application of incentives arises

---

101 Ibid., 2
102 *The Crisis of Liberalism*, 134. Hobson attributes this aphorism to J.S. Mill.

from the unsatisfactory condition of the 'markets' in which the various requisites of production are bought and sold, that is to say ... [it] is due to the inequality of bargaining power. ... Those who get more than suffices to evoke the best use of the ... productive instrument they sell, tend to employ that surplus wastefully. ... But this realisation of the true origin and 'waste' in our economic system involves a complicated analysis of many different sorts of bargain. ... It fails to establish a dramatic hero and villain, and so to evoke the emotional excitement of a sporting conflict, with a knock-out blow and spoils of victory.[103]

The major defect of the market system in allocating incentives is that it rewards not only work but also ownership, in so far as the right of an owner to dispose of his factor as he pleases enables him to contrive to make that factor scarce and thereby extract an extra levy. Worse, not only is payment for ownership unproductive, it is invariably diverted from payments to productive workers whose resource is not scarce. Those most likely to be hurt by this confiscation are unskilled workers. At the extreme, then, the market economy produces a class of monopolists taking huge scarcity rents and a group of sweated workers in constant danger of falling below the level of subsistence. In between are the vast majority, whose incomes are a complex mix of earned and unearned increments. To attend to these various problems, Hobson proposed three basic forms of redistribution: (a) the enforcement of a minimum wage standard; (b) the nationalization of monopolies; and (c) a system of graduated taxation. Hobson clearly hoped that by tackling social reform from the perspective of incentives he would be utilizing a principle dear to the middle-class, yet one that was at the same time potent enough to unite the middle class with the working class as 'productive workers' against the propertied classes, who would be exposed as parasites and wastrels.

a / A Minimum Wage
In 1926, as a member of the Independent Labour party's Committee on a Living Wage, Hobson had summed up the struggle for a living wage as an effort 'to compel [the] anarchical market to honour a higher law than scarcity.'[104] By this time the demand for a 'living wage' had figured as an item on Hobson's reform agenda for over a quarter of a century.[105]

---

103 *Free Thought in the Social Sciences* (1926), 149-50
104 *The Living Wage* (1926), 28
105 See, for example, *The Social Problem*, 163

242 New Liberalism

Hobson was not alone in advocating this policy. As one scholar has commented, 'the idea of creating a floor to the market economy was ... an attractive one' to many New Liberals, 'promising as it did to conceive of reform as contributory to the continued efficiency of the market economy, while succouring those unfortunates who fell through the sometimes rotten floor.'[106] Indeed, on these terms, the idea of a minimum wage had met with some practical success.[107] For example, in 1909 the Liberal government had set up 'trade boards' in several 'sweated' industries, like chain-making, box-making, and tailoring, with powers to fix minimum wages. Then, in 1911, the principle of establishing minimum wage rates was extended beyond sweated industries to include the coal mines. Agriculture was to follow in 1916. Finally, at the end of the war, the Whitley Committee, of which Hobson was a member, recommended increasing the number of trade boards to include several other 'distressed industries.'[108]

In Hobson's opinion, these measures indicated that liberals were willing to concede that wage bargains could not 'in all cases safely be left to the freedom of individual contract.' Further, they seemed agreed that trade unionism was not an altogether effective answer to this problem, especially in the low-skilled trades. Here experience showed that 'no substantial, general or reliable advance was possible under these methods,' for the 'low skilled labour markets were always overstocked, and the struggle for bare life precluded such effective organisation as was needed for powerful trade union action.'[109]

None the less, liberals were wary, according to Hobson, of establishing a statutory minimum wage as a general principle. They preferred to regard it as an emergency or eleemosynary measure. As one 'Yorkshire liberal' wrote in a letter to the Nation in reply to Hobson's advocacy of minimum wage legislation, Hobson failed 'to perceive that once a wage is conceded beyond the economic value of the labour ... you cannot stop at any particular figure but give away the whole case against socialism.'[110]

Hobson realized that the setting of a minimum wage standard was a difficult one, depending on whether 'productive efficiency' or a 'good life'

106 H.V. Emy, *Liberals, Radicals and Social Politics, 1892-1914* (1973), 167
107 Hobson gives a brief overview of minimum wages policy in his article 'The State and the Minimum Wage in England,' *The Survey*, vol. 33 (Oct. 1914-March 1915), 503-4.
108 Hobson's friend Hobhouse was appointed chairman to several of these boards. See J.A. Hobson, M. Ginsberg, eds., *L.T. Hobhouse: His Life and Work* (1931), 55f. For details of the Whitley Report, see G.D.H. Cole, *Workshop Organisation* (1923), chap. XIII.
109 'The State and the Minimum Wage,' 503
110 Cited in Emy, *Liberals, Radicals and Social Politics*, 239

was taken as the gauge. The former was the standard preferred by the liberals, the latter by socialists. But this was not, in Hobson's opinion, grounds for socialists and liberals to be at loggerheads. This impasse had arisen because both parties were disposed freely to separate questions of productivity and distribution. This was most clearly the case with those socialists who demanded that income be distributed according to needs, rather than productivity, and then proceeded to describe 'a level of needs far beyond the limits of the existing "pool of wealth," however equitably distributed.'[111] In this regard, there was some merit to the liberals' claim that it was necessary first 'to get higher production before [it was possible] to provide a satisfactory economic life for the bulk of the working class.' But the liberal economist, in turn, was wrong in suggesting that the workers' demand for a higher standard of living imperilled productivity and that the only standard of wages permissible was one that covered 'mere physiological sufficiency.' Such a claim was counter-productive, in the strict sense of the word, for two reasons. First, it failed to recognize that higher wages would raise real productivity by helping to eliminate the wastes of underconsumption. Second, it failed to appreciate that the worker was not a 'mere machine' that converted 'so much fuel into industrial energy,' but that his will to work was in large part motivated by 'moral' considerations, not the least of which was his sense of receiving a fair share of the opportunities provided by a progressive economy.[112] Unless this moral element was appeased, the workers' incentive to work was bound to slacken and productivity fall. It followed that the establishment of a minimum wage would involve several sets of calculations. First, the testimony of 'medical men and women,' 'experts in housing and education,' and 'practical housewifes' would be taken in order to ascertain what scale of expenditure was necessary in order to meet the physical needs of the worker. Further calculations would have to be made, along the same lines, to ascertain the basic requirements of a 'cultural' or 'civilised' life. Finally, in order to relate these needs to the capacity of the economy to yield such an income, 'a careful statistical study of the national income' would have to be undertaken to determine: '(a) what is the present share of the wage-earning class, and (b) what margin exists to which it may advance a claim.'[113]

Hobson did not doubt that such calculations would be complex and controversial. His main point, however, was that, providing it was realized that pro-

---

111 *The Conditions of Industrial Peace*, 50
112 Ibid., 51, 65, 66
113 *The Living Wage*, 31

ductivity and distribution were interrelated, the apparent impasse between liberals and socialists could be circumvented by an intelligent appreciation of the *economy* of high wages.

However, Hobson was not so optimistic as to suppose that the fixing of a minimum wage above subsistence costs would always pay for itself in increased productivity. Thus he argued that, if it was found that a firm was genuinely unable to pay its workers minimum wages (and provided that the business was one that should be kept alive in the public interest), then a public subsidy should be provided from an 'excess profits' tax levied on companies exacting scarcity rents.[114] Hobson cautioned that in granting this subsidy it would be important to distinguish those cases where the inability to pay minimum wages arose from 'political or economic causes outside the trade,' from those attributable to 'internal inefficiencies.' This was a technical matter to be determined by an 'expert body of impartial arbitrators.'[115] The essential point to realize, in Hobson's opinion, was that the principle of a 'fair wage' was grounded in the notion of the 'social determination of values':

So long as the basic principle of industry is that every business is dependent for its finance upon the quantity of goods it can sell and the price it can get for them, and that this income is the only source out of which wages, ... and other costs can be met, the attempt of any outside body to regulate wages by some general principle of equity or humanity cannot be successful. ... For, as this social determination of value means that the particular business cannot in reality control the income at its disposal, it, therefore, cannot safely undertake fixed payments out of this income. ... Its financial prosperity or adversity ... is mainly due to the general productivity of the system as a whole.[116]

This proposal to redistribute the social surplus so as to maintain at least a minimum fair wage throughout the economy was one that confounded the old divisions between socialists and liberals. This, in Hobson's opinion, provided a new rallying point for progressive social reformers. Essentially, their task was to redress the balance not only between strong and weak trades, but also between well-organized and ill-organized labour. One of the most patent examples of this new alignment of economic forces was to be found in the

114 *The Conditions of Industrial Peace*, 60
115 Ibid., 53
116 *Wealth and Life*, 174-5. See also *The Conditions of Industrial Peace*, 62.

struggle between sheltered and unsheltered trades, that is, between those protected from foreign competition and those subject to it. Here trade unionists were discovering 'to their consternation,' that there was a real divergence of interest between the workers in these two groups and, worse, that the workers in unsheltered trades perhaps had more in common with their bosses than they did with the more privileged workers in the protected businesses.[117] To this extent, the worker-capitalist relationship no longer accurately represented the split between the 'haves' and the 'have-nots':

The capital and labour in sheltered or protected trades are under strong incentives to cease their wasteful and inconclusive quarrels over the surpluses which their privileged positions enable them to extract, and to seek some provisionally satisfactory apportionment of these between dividends and wages. When capital and labour in such trades are both well-organised, trusts ... may, by judicious concessions to employees, make a new alignment of economic forces, *substituting a struggle between groups of stronger and weaker trades for the cruder conflict between capital and labour in the units of production.* Even when no such pacific arrangements are made ... the greater ability of organised labour in these trades to extract by collective bargaining some share of [the] ... surplus, serves to reduce their sense of solidarity with labour in the unsheltered trades, and to feed some feeling of their identity of interests with capital in the trade of whose prosperity they are joint beneficiaries. With the growing tendencies of cartelisation ... in staple industries and the tariffs and other subsidies for favoured trades, this division between sheltered and exposed industries plays an ever greater part in determining the distribution of the aggregate product.[118]

Hobson alluded to numerous other examples where this combination in capital and labour seemed to bring new conflicts into the economic world, unaccounted for in earlier analyses of class conflict. In these earlier analyses, the emergence of monopolies seemed to foretell only the proletarianization of the *petit bourgeoisie*, not the raising of a new labour aristocracy. Given this new configuration of economic forces, Hobson was fairly optimistic that the large majority of middle and working classes, not in the fortunate position of being 'strong bargainers,' eventually would agree, as already noted, to the establishment of a system of compulsory arbitration, with powers to prohibit

117 *Wealth and Life*, 179
118 Ibid., 179-80 (emphasis added). See also *Incentives in the New Industrial Order*, 18-19.

any strike or lock-out which threatened to jeopardize the chances of the members of some other trade receiving their fair wage. Despite the perceptiveness of these remarks, however, there was a certain naiveté in Hobson's suggestion that these new economic developments provided an auspicious opportunity for social reformers; after all, these reformers now would be pitted against the best organized elements of *both* capital and labour.

b / The Nationalization of Monopolies
The common enemy of progressive liberals and socialists were the monopolists. Nationalization was one obvious means of ridding the economy of monopolies. Although Hobson recognized that his proposition that 'all property in modern life is socially made and valued,' if taken to its logical conclusion, seemed to imply that 'all private ownership and private enterprise in production should be liquidated,'[119] he, in fact, stopped well short of this conclusion. None the less, as Brailsford has commented, Hobson did sketch 'a surprisingly bold programme of nationalisation. His long list of industries and services suited for nationalisation [included] ... steel, coal, transport, electricity and banking.'[120]

Hobson's policy of nationalization was founded upon what he termed the 'organic interplay' of routine and innovation, mechanization, and art. Hobson urged that routine, mechanized industries be nationalised. He did this on several grounds. First, he argued that any industry tended to become routinized if it was supplying 'the common needs of the masses of the people,' because this provided it with a large, steady market.[121] And to leave the supply of necessities in the control of one or two private corporations was an invitation to monopoly. The state, therefore, had a duty to undertake the supply of necessities in the control of one or two private corporations was an large corporations could be disassembled into small competitive units,[122] and, as previously mentioned, the notion that such corporations were in the process of socializing themselves 'in spirit', thus becoming less profit-oriented and more socially responsible.

The second reason for nationalizing routine industries was the fact that mechanized and standardized processes of production made them suitable for administration by state officials. This did not mean, however, that nationalized industries should be run by civil servants subject to no control other

119 *Property and Impropery* (1937), 178
120 *The Life-Work of J.A. Hobson* (1948), 20
121 *The Social Problem* (1901), 175
122 *The Conditions of Industrial Peace*, 99

than that exercised through parliamentary representatives. Hobson believed – perhaps somewhat prematurely – that this form of state socialism was 'no longer acceptable in any quarter';[123] it was likely to be inefficient and might even result in state bureaucrats substituting their will for the 'general will.' In this regard it is only necessary to reiterate a point made earlier, namely that to Hobson it was vitally important that the demand for public ownership be fortified by a demand for the functional representation of producers and consumers in any scheme of industrial government. Not only was this necessary in order to make state officials aware of these interests, but it would also serve to educate the employees and consumers in the wider concerns and responsibilities of industrial self-government, thereby providing a basis upon which to build a sense of 'public service.' Hobson was also confident that, in the case of the producers, this 'social will' would serve as a new economic force helping to advance productivity in the nationalized industries, although he remained unconvinced by what he termed the 'soft psychology' of the Left, who contended that this 'new consciousness' would be sufficient to make boring jobs attractive to the workers.[124] For the most part, workers in routine industries would seek fulfilment in their leisure time, and Hobson viewed it as a prime goal of the 'new industrial order' to maximize free-labour time.

There were, however, limits to the policy of nationalization. The centralization of capital was not an all-encompassing process of industrial evolution (as Hobson supposed had been claimed by the adherents of 'scientific socialism')[125] It could not be expected, therefore, that all business would eventually pass under direct public administration. Hobson suggested two reasons for this. First, in some cases, standardization of the productive process was obstructed by the nature of the materials used. Agriculture was a case in point. Differences in soil and climate made it very difficult to put farming on a collective basis. This was especially so in Britain, but even in the Soviet Union, Hobson noted, the 'private plot' played a significant part in agricultural production.[126] The state might supervise the use to which agricultural lands are put and the marketing of agricultural products, but the complete nationalization and central planning of agriculture was inappropriate. Similarly, there were many other trades and crafts where the refractory nature of the materials used precluded the full use of routine methods. Here, small-scale production and private enterprise were likely to survive.[127]

123 *Problems of a New World*, 241
124 *Incentives in the New Industrial Order*, chap. v
125 *The Social Problem*, 179
126 *Property and Impropery*, 194
127 See *The Evolution of Modern Capitalism* (1894; 2nd ed., 1906), 412.

Secondly, the individuality of the consumer and his demand for goods that satisfy his special tastes militated against the routinization of industry. Ultimately this was a much more significant factor because it pointed to the correct organic relationship between individualism and socialism:

All progress, from primitive savagedom to modern civilisation ... appear[s] as consisting in the progressive socialisation of the lower functions, the stoppage of lower forms of competition, and of the education of the more brutal qualities, in order that a larger and larger proportion of individual activity may be engaged in the exercise of higher functions, the practice of competition on higher planes and the education of higher forms of fitness. ... This is, in fact, the philosophic defence of progressive socialism. ... To suppose that the reduction of all machine-industry to public routine services ... will imply a net diminution in the scope of individual self-expression, rests upon the patent fallacy of assigning certain fixed and finite limits to human interest and activity, so that any encroachment from the side of routine lessens the absolute scope of human spontaneity and interest. ... [But] experience does not teach the decay but the metamorphosis of individuality. Under socialised industry progress in the industrial arts would be slower and would absorb a smaller proportion of individual interest, in order that progress in the finer intellectual and moral arts might be faster and might engage in a larger share of life. ... In a progressive society thus conceived ... socialisation and individuation grow inseparably related.[128]

The nationalization of routine industries which expressed man's common needs simultaneously released fresh energies for the pursuit of higher crafts and arts expressing the more individualistic aspects of the consumer's personality and calling forth more conscious skills in the producer. For Hobson, this was an on-going process of social individuation.

Once again Hobson determined that there was much to unite progressive liberals and socialists in a common cause against monopolists. The public ownership of monopolies could be viewed as a prerequisite to the flowering of that 'true individualism' desired by liberals, provided that socialists similarly recognized their past error in assuming too 'lightly' that a 'well planned socialism can itself maintain the due liberty of research, personal freedom of creative expression and experimentalism, required for skilled satisfaction of non-routine consumption.' In hard material terms this meant that social-

128 Ibid., 420-1, 427

ists had to appreciate that in non-routine industries 'prizes, profits and other rewards' may be needed to 'call forth the necessary productive qualities of the craftsman, artist or skilled risk-taker.'[129]

In his *Confessions* Hobson seems well pleased with this 'serviceable balance' between socialism and individualism, yet the inconsistency between this and his analysis, noted earlier, of the job satisfaction that comes with doing skilled and adventurous work is obvious. Moreover, as Brailsford points out, it is none too clear where Hobson would stand with regard to industries which supply basic human needs, yet are continuously engaged in new research and exploration, and hence are not routine industries in Hobson's sense of the word. Brailsford cited the Imperial Chemical Industry as an example.[130]

c / A System of Graduated Taxation

The redistribution of income through a system of graduated taxation was Hobson's preferred means of social reform. Indeed, so keen was his preference that T. Kemp has claimed that Hobson supposed that taxation provided a means of eliminating unearned incomes without disturbing 'existing property relations.' In other words, Hobson failed to see that 'the distribution of income flows from the capitalist process [of production]' and therefore was blind to the superficiality of his reliance on taxation.[131] The logic of this argument, which has its origins in Marx's comment on the 'high absurdity' of J.S. Mill's attempt to promote social reform by separating the laws of production and distribution, is unassailable.[132] What is doubtful, however, is whether this criticism can be fairly applied to Hobson. To begin with, unlike Mill, Hobson nowhere claims that the distribution of wealth can be changed without incurring repercussions in the realm of production. Quite the contrary. There are several passages in his works where he expressly links the two: 'We do not produce a lot of wealth,' he writes in *The Industrial*

---

129 *Confessions*, 199
130 *The Life-Work of J.A. Hobson*, 21. But see *The Conditions of Industrial Peace*, 100.
131 *Theories of Imperialism*, 35
132 See Marx, *Grundrisse*, reprinted in R. Tucker, ed., *The Marx-Engels Reader* (2nd ed., 1978), 293. Interestingly, Hobson attempted to defend Mill from this charge of economic naiveté by pointing to passages in the *Principles of Political Economy* and Mill's *Autobiography* where Mill speculates that the *dominant* economic association of the future would be the producers co-operative. Hobson suggests that these speculations indicate that Mill was aware that his proposals for improving the living conditions of the labouring classes would necessarily involve changes in the organization of production, and that the laws governing the latter therefore could not be regarded as 'belonging to the order of Nature.' See *Confessions*, 24.

System, 'and then afterwards distribute it.' Rather 'production and distribution ... take place simultaneously' and are 'in a sense identical processes.'[133]

Not surprisingly, given his awareness of this inter-connection, Hobson was also aware that his proposals to redistribute income in favour of wage-earners, involved a challenge to what he termed 'the autocratic government of industry by the owners.'[134] In *Work and Wealth* he went so far as to claim that the touchstone of all proposed schemes of industrial reconstruction should be their 'ability to divert into wages a portion of the unproductive surplus.'[135] In order to meet this challenge Hobson supported various measures designed to encourage workers' participation in industry. These measures, as already noted, ranged from the support of Whitley trade-boards and workers committees,[136] to the establishment of a national industrial council, run on functional lines, and the nationalization of monopolies and essential industries, where control would be given to boards representing the employees, among others, and not simply vested in the central bureaucracy.

These recommendations no doubt do not come close to satisfying Marxist criteria regarding the kinds of changes required in order to achieve an egalitarian society. But this is simply to re-enter the debate between reformists and radicals, and strictly speaking this is not the intent of Kemp's critique. What Kemp attempts to do, in effect, is to short-circuit that debate by arguing that Hobson is so economically naive that he commits a *logical* error in calling for a redistribution of income without recognizing that this is also a call to change capitalist property relations. However, it now should be evident that Hobson is aware of the interdependence of production and distribution, and hence commits no logical error; and further, he pursues that logic by attempting to combine his proposals to reallocate the unearned incomes of capitalists, with measures designed to reallocate their powers within the realm of production.

This said, it remains true that Hobson was willing to mount such a challenge only as a last resort. He preferred to use the instrument of taxation because it seemed a more discriminatory instrument of redistribution.

The Industrial System, 56-7
134 *Problems of a New World*, 242
135 *Work and Wealth*, 254-5
136 Appendix E in Cole's *Workshop Organisation* contains an interesting supplementary report of the Whitley Council, signed by Hobson, among others, requesting government action on the setting up of works committees designed to increase workers participation in decision-making in various industries.

It was Adam Smith who first established the principle that state taxation should be based on the principle of 'ability to pay.' But not surprisingly disputes had quickly arisen over what constituted 'ability to pay.' At one time or another, landlords, capitalists, and proletariat had each been singled out as the group best able to bear taxation. Now, while Hobson agreed that 'the really taxable elements of income, those which have a true "ability to pay," must be those that are unnecessary to maintain or promote socially serviceable processes of production and consumption,' he rejected the proposition that any one group was the residual claimant of surplus income and thus possessed an exclusive 'ability to pay.'[137] The reasons for Hobson's rejection of this proposition have already been given. Here it is only necessary to emphasize that he attributed the source of much of this surplus income to 'work' done by the state. Hence in taxing surplus incomes the state was merely reclaiming public property: it was not infringing private property rights. Hobson thus ventured to suggest that his theory of the 'social surplus' provided a 'new moral' basis for the finance of the state.[138] Further, Hobson clearly believed that his 'non-sectarian' approach to the question of sources of taxable income would provide a common ground for progressive reformers.

Hobson found, however, that in envisaging the application of his principle of taxation problems arose, robbing it of some of the elements of discrimination which, at first, had seemed to constitute one of its chief merits. Basic among these problems was Hobson's inability to determine the margin at which it could be confidently claimed that no surplus income was being received by the agent of production.

The use of marginal analysis to determine the point at which surplus income began had been introduced by Ricardo in his study of land rent. Ricardo claimed that the worst land in use – land at the margin of cultivation – paid no rent and consequently that all rents taken on other lands being used for the same purpose were purely 'differential,' i.e., they measured the superior productivity of these lands above the margin.[139] Later, this analysis of marginal productivity was developed in two opposite ways. Economists like J.B. Clark and Stanley Jevons argued that under conditions of perfect competition all factors would be paid at the marginal *rate*, in amounts corresponding to their individual productivity, and hence there would be no surplus incomes. As has been noted, Hobson rejected this doc-

137 *Taxation in the New State* (1919), vii, 10
138 Ibid., 76
139 Ibid., 25-6

trine primarily because it ignored the organic character of production. The other adaptation of marginalism was made by the Fabians, in particular G.B. Shaw, Sidney Webb, and Sydney Olivier.[140] The Fabians agreed with Clark and Jevons that the price of factors was determined by the least efficient or marginal producer, but denied that this destroyed the notion of surplus value. Instead, they pointed to the increasing imperfections of the market economy which enabled the holders of 'scarce' resources to retain for themselves the extra value created by those agents who were more than marginally productive: 'the whole differential advantage of all but the worst industrial capital,' wrote Webb, 'like the whole differential advantage of all but the worst land, necessarily goes to him who legally owns it. The mere worker can have none of them.[141]

Although the Fabian interpretation of marginalism was much more to Hobson's liking than that of Clark and Jevons, he none the less rejected their position. Hobson contended that it was the strong bargainer – the agent best able to dictate the terms of access to his factor of production – who determined the marginal price per unit, not the marginal or 'no rent' producer. Hobson thereby turned marginal economics on its head: it was price that determined the margin, not the other way around:

The only sense in which the worst acres of land, or the worst workers, or the worst machines can be said to determine the price per unit ... is that this price is, and must be, just enough to evoke their use. ... But this does not imply that the marginal factors exercise any special determinant influence as 'causes' of the price. The price per unit ... is caused by a variety of forces of demand and supply in which the marginal factors play no appreciable part. ... Of course an acre that gives out twice as much productive power as another gets twice as much payment in rent. ... [However] this obvious consideration can throw no light on any principle [of distribution]. ... The real issue is concerned to discover and define what shall be the respective payment per unit for ... productive power.[142]

140 See G.B. Shaw, 'Economic,' in *Fabian Essays* (1889); Sidney Webb, 'The National Dividend and its Distribution,' in Sidney and Beatrice Webb, *Problems of Modern Industry* (1902); and Sydney Olivier, *Capital and Land* (1888). The best overview of the Fabian theory of surplus value or rent is found in A.M. McBriar, *Fabian Socialism and English Politics* (1962), 29-47.

141 S. Webb, 'The Difficulties of Individualism,' in *Problems of Modern Industry*, 238-9

142 *The Industrial System*, 103-4. It should be clear from this statement and the foregoing analysis that although the Fabian concept of rent may be considered an extension of the Ricardian analysis of land rent, based on productivity differentials, this is not an adequate description of Hobson's theory. Indeed, in *The Economics of Distribution*, 124,

Since it was the strong bargainer who was in the best position to influence market forces so as to establish a price per unit most likely to accrue him a surplus payment, Hobson considered it probable that this marginal price itself would include an element of 'surplus,' or taxable income:

The rent of different qualities of land [capital and labour] appears to be directly determined by the fact that some of the land has an alternative use, and that it may refuse to contribute to the supply unless a certain price is paid. But though the alternative price that can be got for some other use determines a lower limit of marginal rent, there is nothing to prevent the marginal rent rising higher than this. If the 30s. land has an alternative use, it is possible that use might yield only 25s.; now though the owner of the land would consent to take 26s. rent, he may be able to get 30s., because there is, for the time, an absolute scarcity of land available for this supply. In a word, he may be able ... to take a forced gain of 5s. ... *For many, if not most, purposes land at ther margin of cultivation will pay a positive rent.*[143]

Hobson had thus uncovered a possible source of surplus income which the Fabians were prone to let slip by, untaxed. But this left him with a very perplexing problem: if the margin no longer provided security of measurement, on which objective basis could a clear distinction between costs and surplus be made? Hobson, although aware of this dilemma, was unable to provide an answer, and eventually admitted, as will be shown shortly, that his system of taxation would be much less refined in practice than it was in theory.

This problem of measurement was further compounded when Hobson attempted to evaluate costs and surpluses in subjective terms. Consider the following illustration given by Hobson:

John Smith of Oldham will not save and apply his savings unless 3 per cent is secured to him; the Duke of Westminster, who gets the same price for saving, would save for 1 per cent, or even zero. ... It follows that ... the 3 per cent investments ... of the Duke of Westminster will [bear a tax] and a system of direct discriminative income tax could secure a contribution to the revenue from the so-called 'minimum interest' paid to the Duke. ...

he explicitly rejects the association. P.T. Homan, *Contemporary Economic Thought* (1928), 308, is in error in this regard.

143 *The Economics of Distribution* (1900), 129-30 (emphasis added)

[The] objectively conceived surplus is [thus] supplemented by a 'subjective' surplus consisting of the differential surpluses of certain owners ... who do not require the payment of the normal minimum price ... to evoke the industrial use of the particular power which they own.[144]

This seems plausible; yet it is by no means clear by what standard these various motivations could be measured and compared. The sacrifice involved in saving might be quite reasonably linked to size of income, but to what degree? and where to draw the line? Along the same lines, would it make sense to tax two people doing the same job, at different rates, because one enjoyed the work while the other hated it? How would it be possible to prove to a middle-class white-collar worker that he should be taxed more than a blue-collar worker because mental exertion was less costly than physical exertion, or vice versa?

These questions are so obvious, of course, that Hobson could not help but be aware of them and the danger they represented to the consensus he wished to build between the working class and middle class. It is interesting that in his earlier works Hobson seemed fairly confident that such problems would take care of themselves, in that he supposed that any tax improperly imposed on a piece of income representing a real cost of production would be quickly shifted until it came to rest upon some element of surplus income. In his later works, by contrast, he became convinced that this process of 'shifting taxes' could do a great deal of damage before the final settlement was accomplished.[145] Yet, recognizing this problem, Hobson was still unable to provide the yardsticks necessary if his system of taxation were to operate in the discriminating fashion he proposed. Ultimately he was obliged to compromise and plead that:

the difficulty in measuring these surpluses in all cases, or of distinguishing them from legitimate rewards or incentives of initiative, enterprise and personal efficiency, does not impair either the theoretical validity of the distinction, or its practical importance in all thoughtful proposals for making the economic system more equitable and more productive of human values.[146]

Even though a compromise, this was still a powerful legacy to leave progressive reformers.

144 *The Industrial System*, 238-9
145 Compare, for example, *The Economics of Distribution*, chap. x, with *Taxation in the New State*, chap. 3, or *The Industrial System*, chap. xiv, sec. ii.
146 *Wealth and Life*, 212

8

Conclusion: Hobson's Place
in the Liberal Tradition

It has been argued in this study that behind Hobson's better-known (though sometimes misunderstood) theories of underconsumption and imperialism is to be found a much less credited doctrine, the theory of organic surplus. Further, it has been maintained that, unless this idea of an organic surplus is appreciated, the coherence of Hobson's thought is lost, for it alone provides the bridge between Hobson's economic and political thought. For this reason, emphasis has been placed upon Hobson's contention that the organic surplus marks the point at which the 'co-operative whole' is no longer represented by the sum of its separate, individual parts. Hobson's concern for the 'parts' kept him allied with traditional liberalism, but it was his awareness of the distinctiveness of the 'whole' – in both political and economic activity – which provided the basis for his New Liberal approach to political economy.

In examining this contention more closely, first with regard to Hobson's economics, it was shown in chapter 3 that the starting point for Hobson's critique of classical economics was his rejection of the 'individualist notion of production.' Production was an intrinsically social activity, creating a surplus product in excess of the aggregate of individual contributions. If the attempt was made to distribute this surplus on an individualistic basis, the result was the creation of a mass of unproductive wealth.

Chapters 4 and 5 examined the economic ramifications of the existence of this fund of unproductive wealth. Either that wealth was reinvested, thus creating a stock of capital goods capable of producing a supply of commodities in excess of market demand, or it was invested abroad. The first option resulted in underconsumption crises, the second in imperialism. Both of these features have been examined in detail. The point to stress, however, is that underconsumption and imperialism are essentially derivatives of Hobson's theory of organic surplus. The creation of an unproductive surplus is not, as some scholars have suggested, solely the consequence of imperfections in a market economy, but a defect even of a perfectly competitive market. Unless the organic nature of the surplus is recognized, the depth of Hobson's critique of liberal economics cannot be properly appreciated. Further, it has been shown that Hobson's starting point for criticizing the classical economists' equilibrium theory (Say's Law) is his rejection of Adam Smith's dictum that 'what is prudence in the conduct of a private family can scarce be folly in that of a great nation.' Again, the import of Hobson's critique of liberal economics is not fully comprehensible unless it is recognized that Smith's dictum was essentially a denial of Hobson's organic perspective.

An appreciation of Hobson's organic theory also makes it clear that any study of Hobson's thought is incomplete without an examination of his political analysis. Since production is a collective activity and the industrial surplus is organic, it follows that this product cannot be legitimately distributed through the market, for this mode of exchange is individualistic. The social product has to be publicly appropriated and this required political action – state intervention. An understanding of Hobson's organic approach, therefore, makes it clear that it is not possible to leave politics aside when discussing his economics; the two are integrally linked. This point notwithstanding, the fact remains that for the most part scholars have subjected Hobson's economics to a separatist treatment.

Hobson's political analysis does more than round out his economics by providing a fitting instrument of appropriation – the welfare state; it also supplements his economics. Thus, as has been shown in chapters 6 and 7, Hobson, though utilizing T.H. Green's theory of objectification, advances beyond Green and his followers to claim that public property is the prerequisite for the growth of a social or general will in society. Conversely, Hobson's critique of capitalism is more severe than that of most contemporary liberals because he saw capitalism not only as crippling the life-chances of many individuals, thus despoiling traditional liberal ideals, but also as a tumour derationalizing the 'social mind.' Hobson's political philosophy thus stretches liberal tenets to their limits by linking social property with social personality.

Once it has been shown that the major elements of Hobson's contribution to liberalism can be integrated on the basis of his theory of the organic surplus, a final question remains: does not this new appreciation of the essence of Hobson's thought, by its own accord, raise serious doubts as to Hobson's affinity with the liberal tradition?

It is a common-place that liberals generally have been wary of the organic metaphor. This wariness results from a concern that the organic metaphor tends to lose the parts in the whole: an arm severed from the body is no longer an arm but a piece of flesh, but an individual separated from his fellows remains an individual, less noble, perhaps, but still an individual. For example, C.E.M. Joad, a contemporary of Hobson's who was not adverse to viewing the state as a living organism, none the less claimed that on balance the analogy did more harm than good to political theory: 'For between the human body and the body politic there are highly important differences. ... The organs of the human body have admittedly no rights of their own and no ends of their own. The individual members of the State have both individual rights and individual ends.' Moreover, society only came into being 'through the association of its members'; therefore, 'the existence of its individual members is ... logically prior to that of society, even if they do not precede it in point of time.' On the other hand, 'there is no sense in saying that the organs of the human body precede the body.' Joad concluded that society had 'no purpose save such as is realized in the lives of its members.'[1]

This was not Hobson's conclusion. As has been shown Hobson insisted that there were distinctively social goals – species goals – to be valued for their own sake and not just as a means to the fulfilment of separate, individual ends; and that it was difficult to conceive of an individual existing apart from society, let alone improving himself, without the positive assistance of his fellows. Such opinions did not entail Hobson denying altogether the right of individuals to some personal autonomy in their activities for, as has been shown, he hoped to harmonize 'parts' and 'wholes' in a federal unity.

The nature of this unity, however, is not without problems. First, although Hobson did not confuse the ideal and the actual when examining capitalist society, since he was well aware that the capitalist state did not represent the ideal organ of rationalization to which his theory pointed, but was an instrument of the forces of 'improperty,' there is little doubt that he envisaged the state in its final democratic form as having a higher purpose than any of its members or parts. The state becomes the guardian of men's best interest and is obliged to bring the ideal and the actual into harmony. Now, to what extent Hobson's ideal of a federal unity of 'parts' and 'wholes' relies upon that strong moral imperative which liberals believe invariably accompanies such a conception of state superiority, namely 'forcing men to be free,' is not

1 'The State as 'Living Organism' and as 'Society,'' in W. Browne, ed., *The Leviathan in Crisis* (1946), 164, 165

clear. Hobson does not give this matter the attention it deserves. The nugatory effects of his assumption that the general will embodies the highest morality, on the individual right of dissent, would seem obvious. It is, therefore, both surprising and disappointing, given his close association with Hobhouse, to find Hobson at times asserting as 'truth' that 'force applied selfishly and by individuals or sections is bad. Force applied socially by organised society is good.'[2] What is clear, however, is that Hobson thought it necessary to grant his organic state something more than the contingent status traditionally ascribed to the state by liberals.

This requirement of 'forcing men to be free' also helps explain the moral earnestness that pervades Hobson's works. In part the austere tone of his books merely betrays the origin of his thought in the period of late Victorian decline. The 'social problem' pressed too closely on him to allow much room for the kind of liberal romanticism that figured more prominently in the works, say, of Wilhelm von Humboldt and J.S. Mill. But such earnestness also sprang from his sombre recognition that the ideal of a federal unity of social and individual interests required the sacrifice of at least part of the liberal heritage, namely, those rights judged to be intrinsically anti-social. Hobson's New Liberalism, though it sought to marry socialism and liberalism, nevertheless could not promise the best of both worlds.

Now that the guiding idea of Hobson's work has been pinpointed, it is possible to indicate his place in the liberal tradition. One immediate difficulty that arises, however, is that this tradition is very heterodox, and therefore does not provide a clear backdrop against which Hobson's contribution can be assessed. As Professors Bullock and Shock have argued:

At first sight, the most striking thing about the Liberal tradition is its intellectual incoherence. ... It owes much to the Dissenters with their strong belief in individualism, the place of conscience in politics and their democratic tradition of self-government, but something also to the Whigs with their aristocratic tradition of civil rights and religious liberty and their dislike of arbitrary government. It inherits a belief in natural law and natural rights only to see these scornfully repudiated by Bentham and the Philosophical Radicals in favour of the principle of utility. From the Classical Economists ... it derives the orthodoxy of free trade and *laissez-faire*, yet at the end of the 19th century embraces the heretical view of working-class radicalism that something ought to be done for the poor.[3]

2 *Notes on Law and Order* (1926), 25
3 Bullock and M. Shock, eds., *The Liberal Tradition* (1967), xix

Although Hobson's thought touches almost all of these themes of liberalism, either directly or by construction, it would be a hopeless task to attempt to assess his work with regard to such a diverse discourse.

A more fruitful approach is to follow Bullock's and Shock's suggestion that the catholicity of liberalism 'is the strongest argument in favour of treating liberalism historically,' and examine Hobson's contribution in the light of those elements of liberal doctrine that were pre-eminent during the nineteenth century.

The response of liberals to the growth of trade and industry during the early period of the industrial revolution was to emphasize the benefits of self-interest, competition, and self-help. These were the characteristic themes of the classical economists and the philosophical radicals. As Bentham put it: 'The request which agriculture, manufactures and commerce present to governments, is as modest and reasonable as that which Diogenes made to Alexander: "stand out of my sunshine." '[4]

Classical political economy and the classical theory of political liberalism both began as a protest, the former rejecting mercantilism, the latter the rule of the landed aristocracy. In both cases the state was identified with the activities of sinister interests and a corrupt and inefficient bureaucracy. It was this identification to which the New Liberals objected. Liberty meant something more than the absence of restraint or civil liberty; it meant the positive opportunity to realize human capacities. Liberty, therefore, had to be translated from political into social and economic terms: 'Liberty without equality is a name of noble sound and squalid result.'[5] To provide equality of opportunity, however, necessitated the use of the state as an agency of reform. Consequently, New Liberals sought to undermine the doctrine of *laissez-faire* and thereby disabuse old liberals of their distrust of the state. In this task Hobson took on the main responsibility for attacking the premises of classical economics, while Hobhouse, Samuel, Ritchie, and others concentrated on the political philosophy of old liberalism.

Basically, what Hobson did was to show that the classical conception of free enterprise was based on the false assumption that in the long run economic resources tended to be fully employed. Instead uncontrolled capitalism generated cycles of underconsumption and mass unemployment. The irony of this situation was that, if Say's Law about markets was to function effectively, it could do so only in an economic environment where the state

---

4 *Manual of Political Economy* (1843), cited in Bullock and Shock, eds., *The Liberal Tradition*, xxiv

5 L.T. Hobhouse, *Liberalism* (1911), 86

continuously intervened in order to prevent the economic surplus from being over-invested. Hobson thus showed that state intervention was essential if capitalism were to be saved from its excesses. He further attempted to show that not only did this state action enhance the long-run efficiency of capitalism, but it was also just, since the surplus belonged to the public not the capitalist.

Hobson's contribution to the cause of New Liberalism deserves more attention than it has received in the past. This is not only because, as has been the burden of this study to show, he was a seminal thinker in the realm of economics, but also because he tackled the *laissez-faire* doctrine in the area where its grip was the strongest and therefore most difficult to dislodge. This general point is made clear by considering the following assessment of Bullock and Shock.

An inveterate distrust of the power of the State was characteristic of 19th century Liberalism up to the last decades of the century, from Bentham to Acton. But there was a difference between the liberal attitude towards the State in economics and in politics. The principle of a *natural* identity of interests which, in the economic sphere, meant *laissez-faire*, did not extend to the political sphere. ... Thus, in economics ... the principle of utility pointed to *laissez-faire* and trust in the natural play of forces to produce the greatest happiness of the greatest number. In politics, however, ... the principle of utility pointed in the opposite direction. ... In an iconoclastic frame of mind ... the Philosophical Radicals demanded the submission of all institutions – legal, constitutional, ecclesiastical – to the rationalist criteria of utility. ... 'I asked myself,' Bentham records, '*how* this or that institution contributed to the greatest happiness? – *Did* it contribute? – If not, what institution *would* contribute to it?' It was this frame of mind which made Benthamite ideas the impetus behind the greater part of the reforming activity for which the years from 1815-1870 are remarkable.[6]

This contention that there is a conflict in classical liberalism between the principle of the natural harmony of interests which governs its economics and the principle of the artificial identification of interests which governs its politics was first proposed by E. Halevy in the 1920s and has met with some criticism.[7] However, even those critical of this position do not deny that it

6 Bullock and Shock, eds., *The Liberal Tradition*, xxv-xxvi
7 See E. Halévy, *The Growth of Philosophic Radicalism* (1928); Lord Robbins, *Political Economy Past and Present* (1976), chap. I and *passim*; Harold Schultz, ed., *English Liberalism and the State* (1972), part IV: and Shirley Letwin, *The Pursuit of Certainty* (1965), 146-7.

was in economics that laissez-faire doctrine had its greatest influence. Thus by breaking that hold, Hobson can be said to have had a pre-eminent role in preparing the way for the emergence of the welfare state.

Finally, Hobson's thought deserves resuscitation because the liberal-socialist synthesis which his work attempts continues to have relevance. Perhaps the simplest way to indicate this is to see whether Hobson has anything to contribute to Keynesian economics, which is invariably assumed to have eclipsed Hobson's economic theory. Like Hobson, Keynes refused to accept the conventional antithesis between socialism and liberalism, but his synthesis tipped the balance more in favour of the latter than did Hobson's. It was this fact that prompted Hobson to ask, upon the publication of the *General Theory*, 'how far Mr. Keynes ... fully realises the amount of interference which society would have to make with private initiative and enterprise in order to attain his desideratum of an individualism purged of its defects and abuses.'[8] Here Hobson was referring to the fact that, compared with his own analysis, Keynes' approach seemed to place less stress on the disruptive effects produced by monopoly elements in the economy. As has been shown, 'forced gains' were the *bête noir* of Hobson's economics, and he advocated a number of 'socialistic' measures designed to redistribute these unearned incomes.

Several recent studies on applied Keynesian economics would seem to confirm Hobson's prognosis by calling attention to the problems monopolies create for governments attempting to fine-tune the economy.'[9] Much of the dilemma of 'stagflation,' that is, high unemployment combined with large state budgetary deficits and inflation, has been attributed to an overly confident application of the Keynesian maxim: 'If demand is right supply will look after itself.' Monopolies can impede the operation of the fiscal and monetary tools Keynes designed to achieve balanced economic growth. Government attempts to boost aggregate demand in times of recession by increasing expenditures tend to be defeated by monopoly elements who respond to that demand by setting higher prices rather than by increasing productive output and hence employment; conversely, government schemes to curb inflation by decreasing expenditure are likely to be offset by monopoly elements who prefer to maintain their prices in the face of falling demand by cutting back on production instead.

8 *Property and Improperty* (1937), 56. The statement continues: 'the question remains open whether this delicate task can be performed, so long as "the ownership of the means of production" remain in private hands.'
9 See, for example, the papers by Geoffrey Barraclough, Robert Skidelsky, Aubrey Jones, Robert Lekachman, and Stuart Holland, in Robert Skidelsky, ed., *The End of the Keynesian Era* (1977).

In these circumstances, doubts have arisen as to whether the Keynesian focus on the management of aggregate demand provides a satisfactory alternative to the socialist case for public ownership as a means of regulating the conditions of supply. By the same token, it is arguable that Hobson's attempt to incorporate both the demand and allocative aspects of the problem into his theory of economic crises continues to have contemporary relevance, set in terms of a left Keynesianism.

From the other side of the political spectrum, even the 'most savage' critics of liberalism, as John Dunn has commented, are seldom decided as to whether they have 'come to destroy liberalism or to fulfil it,' and concomitantly, whether 'liberals are morally vicious' or 'simply sociologically naive.'[10]

For those critics who take the former view, arguing that socialism constitutes a radical departure sufficient to render all that went before merely pernicious and suited for the scrap heap of history, Hobson has little that is positive to offer. But for those critics[11] who believe that socialism actually completes liberalism by freeing what is best in its ideals from a crippling class integument, Hobson's problematic remains pertinent, and his works continue to have something to contribute to this on-going debate. Hobson was the least sociologically naive of liberals.

10 *Western Political Theory in the Face of the Future* (1979), 28-9
11 In this connection see Michael Harrington, *Socialism* (1977); Steven Lukes, *Individualism* (1973), 157. C.B. Macpherson, *The Life and Times of Liberal Democracy* (1977), 2. Harrington's work is especially interesting in this regard, for he presents a strong case that the welfare state – Hobson's ideal – has likewise become a captive of this class integument, functioning to a considerable extent to socialize the losses of capitalism, whilst leaving private the gains. None the less, Harrington insists that his analysis of the 'severe limits' capitalism imposes on the welfare state, is 'not designed to prove that liberals ... are foolish and deluded, but rather that their liberal values can only really be completely achieved on the basis of a socialist program.' *Socialism*, 334

Bibliography of Hobson's Writings

The bibliography contains books, pamphlets (shown by an asterisk), and articles cited in the text.

1889   *The Physiology of Industry* (with A.F. Mummery) London: Murray

1891   *Problems of Poverty*
London: Methuen (2nd ed., 1894; 3rd ed., 1896; 4th ed., 1899; 5th ed., 1905; 6th ed., 1906; 7th ed., 1910; 8th ed., 1913)
'The Law of Three Rents,' *Quarterly Journal of Economics*, vol. v (April), 263-88

1893   'Subjective and Objective Views of Distribution,' *Annals of the American Academy of Political and Social Science*, vol. 4, 378-403
'The Academic spirit in Education,' *Contemporary Review*, vol. 63 (Feb.), 236-47

1894   *The Evolution of Modern Capitalism*
London: Walter Scott (rev. eds., 1906, 1916, 1926)

1895   'Mr. Kidd's "Social Evolution,"' *American Journal of Sociology*, vol. 1, 299-312

1896   *The Problem of the Unemployed*
London: Methuen (rev. eds., 1904, 1906)

1897   'The Influence of Henry George in England,' *Fortnightly Review*, vol. 62 (Dec.), 835-44

1898   *John Ruskin, Social Reformer*
        London: Nisbet
        'Free Trade and Foreign Policy,' *Contemporary Review*, vol. 74
        (Aug.), 167-80

1899   'Of Labour,' in J. Hand, ed., *Good Citizenship*,
        London: G. Allen, 95-110

1900   *The Economics of Distribution*
        New York: Macmillan
        The War in South Africa: Its Causes and Effects
        London: Nisbet
        'Capitalism and Imperialism in South Africa,' *Contemporary Review*,
        vol. 77 (Jan.), 1-17
        'The Ethics of Industrialism,' in S. Coit, ed., *Ethical Democracy:
        Essays in Social Dynamics*
        London: Grant Richards, 81-107

1901   *The Psychology of Jingoism*
        London: Grant Richards
        The Social Problem
        London: Nisbet
        'Before and After the Jameson Raid,' in H.J. Ogden, ed., *The War
        against the Dutch Republics*
        London: National Reform Union, 16-24
        'Socialistic Imperialism,' *International Journal of Ethics*, vol. 12, 44-58

1902   *Imperialism: A Study*
        London: Nisbet (rev. eds., 1905, 1938, with a new introduction by
        Hobson)
        Ann Arbor, Michigan, (1965 reprint, with an introduction by Philip
        Sigelman)
        'Ruskin and Democracy,' *Contemporary Review*, vol. 81 (Jan.), 103-11

1903   'Protection as a Working-Class Policy,' in H.W. Massingham, ed.,
        Labour and Protection
        London: T. Fisher Unwin, 38-92

1904   *International Trade*
        London: Methuen

'Marginal Units in the Theory of Distribution,' *The Journal of Political Economy* (Sept.), 449-72

1905   'The Ethics of Gambling,' *International Journal of Ethics*, vol. 15 (Jan.), 136-48

1906   *Canada To-day*
London: T. Fisher Unwin
'J.S. Mill,' *The Speaker*, 26 May, 177-8
'Science and Industry,' in J. Hand, ed., *Science in Public Affairs*
London: Allen and Unwin, 172-206

1908   'An Appreciation,' in A.F. Mummery, *My Climbs in the Alps and Caucasus*
London: Thomas Nelson, 9-15
'Old Age Pensions: The Responsibility of the State to the Aged Poor,'
Sociological Review (July), 295-9

1909   *The Crisis of Liberalism*
London: P.S. King (repr. 1974 by Harvester Press, Brighton, with an introduction by P.F. Clarke)
The Industrial System
London: Longmans (rev. ed., 1910)
New York: Augustus M. Kelley (repr. 1969, with an introduction by A.L. Bekenstein)

1910   *A Modern Outlook*
London: Herbert and Daniel
'The General Election: A Sociological Interpretation,' *Sociological Review* (April), 105-17

1911   *The Science of Wealth*
London: Williams and Norgate (rev. eds., 1914, 1934, 1950). The 4th edition has a preface and epilogue by R.F. Harrod.
An Economic Interpretation of Investment
London: Financial Review of Reviews

1912   *Industrial Unrest**
London: National Liberal Club
'Character and Society,' in P. Parker, ed., *Character and Life,*'
London: Williams and Norgate, 53-107

1913   *The German Panic**
London: Cobden Club
Gold, Prices and Wages
London: Methuen

1914   *Work and Wealth, A Human Valuation*
London: Macmillan
Traffic in Treason, A Study in Political Parties*
London: T. Fisher Unwin
'The State and the Minimum Wage in England,' *The Survey*, vol. 33, 503-4

1915   *Towards International Government*
London: Macmillan
'The Open Door,' in C.R. Buxton, ed., *Towards a Lasting Settlement*
London: Allen and Unwin, 85-110
'The Political Basis of a World-State,' in F.S. Marvin, *The Unity of Western Civilisation*
London: Oxford University Press, 260-80

1916   *The New Protectionism*
London: T. Fisher Unwin
Labour and the Costs of War*
London: Union of Democratic Control

1917   *Democracy after the War*
London: Allen and Unwin (2nd ed., April 1918; 3rd ed., Nov. 1918; 4th ed., rev., July 1919)
Forced Labour*
London: National Council for Civil Liberties

1918   *1920: Dips into the Near Future* (pseud. Lucian)
London: Hedley Bros.

1919   *Taxation in the New State*
London: Methuen
Richard Cobden: The International Man
London: J. Dent

1920   *The Obstacles to Economic Recovery in Europe**
London: Fight the Famine Council

'Ruskin as a Political Economist' in J. Whitehouse, ed., *Ruskin the Prophet*
London: E.P. Dutton, 81-98

1921   *The Economics of Reparation**
London: Allen and Unwin
Problems of a New World
London: Allen and Unwin
'The Ethical Movement and Natural Man,' *Hibbert Journal*, vol. 20, 667-79

1922   *Incentives in the New Industrial Order*
New York: Thomas Seltzer
The Economics of Unemployment
London: Macmillan (rev. ed., 1931)
'The Douglas Theory,' *Socialist Review*, vol. 19, 70-7; and 'A Rejoinder to Major Douglas,' 194-9

1926   *Notes on Law and Order**
London: Hogarth Press
Free Thought in the Social Sciences
London: Allen and Unwin
The Living Wage (with H.N. Brailsford, A. Creech Jones, E.F. Wise)
London: Independent Labour Party

1927   *The Conditions of Industrial Peace*
London: Allen and Unwin

1929   *Wealth and Life*
London: Macmillan

1930   *Rationalisation and Unemployment*
London: Allen and Unwin
'Social Thinkers in Nineteenth Century England,' *Contemporary Review*, vol. 137 (April), 453-61
'The Social Control of Credit,' in Kirby Page, ed., *A New Economic Order*
New York: Harcourt Brace, 287-300

1931   *God and Mammon*
London: Watts

Poverty in Plenty
London: Allen and Unwin
L.T. Hobhouse: His Life and Work (with Morris Ginsberg)
London: Allen and Unwin
'The State as an Organ of Rationalisation,' *Political Quarterly*, vol. 2,
30-45

1932   *The Recording Angel*
London: Allen and Unwin
Saving and Spending: Why Production Is Clogged*
London: 'New Leader Reprint,' Independent Labour Party
From Capitalism to Socialism
London: Hogarth

1933   *Rationalism and Humanism**
London: Watts
'Underconsumption: An Exposition and a Reply,' *Economica*, vol. 13
(Nov.), 402-17, 425-7

1934   *Democracy and a Changing Civilisation*
London: Bodley Head
'Under-Production and Under-Consumption,' *New Statesman* (24
March), 442-3
'Book Review: *What Marx Really Meant*, by G.D.H. Cole, *Political
Quarterly*, vol. 5 (July-Sept.), 452-4
'Force Necessary to Government,' *Hibbert Journal*, vol. 33, 331-42

1935   'Democracy, Liberty and Force,' *Hibbert Journal*, vol. 34 (Oct.),
35-44
'Under-Consumption and its Remedies,' in G. Hutton, ed., *The
Burden of Plenty?*
London: Allen and Unwin, 47-61

1936   *Veblen*
London: Chapman and Hall
'Roosevelt's Triumph,' *Contemporary Review*, vol. 150 (Dec.), 649-55
'Is Democracy an Empty Word?' *Hibbert Journal*, vol. 34 (Jan.),
529-38

1937   *Property and Improperty*
London: Gollancz

1938   'Thoughts on Our Present Discontents,' *Political Quarterly* (Jan.), 47-57
Le Sens de la responsabilité dans la vie sociale (with Herman Finer and Hannah Mentor)
Brussels: Institut de Sociologie Solvay
Confessions of an Economic Heretic
London: Allen and Unwin (repr. 1976, Harvester Press, Brighton, with an introduction by Michael Freeden)

UNPUBLISHED SOURCES
Hobson Papers, (R) Z 6621 H9C1, The Brynmor Jones Library, Hull University, England
Samuel Papers, House of Lords Record Office, File nos. A/10, A/155

Index

www.ingramcontent.com/pod-product-compliance
Lightning Source LLC
Chambersburg PA
CBHW021854020426
42334CB00013B/332

9 781442 651401